THE SECOND
I SAW YOU

THE SECOND
I SAW YOU

*The True Love Story
of Rupert Brooke
and Phyllis Gardner*

LORNA C. BECKETT

THE BRITISH LIBRARY

Dedicated with much love to my Mum,
whose unwavering love, support and belief
made writing this book possible.

First published in 2015 by
The British Library
96 Euston Road
London NW1 2DB

British Library Cataloguing-in-Publication Data
A catalogue record for this book is available from the British Library

ISBN 978 0 7123 5792 0

Designed and typeset by illuminati, Grosmont
Printed in Malta by Gutenberg Press.

PUBLISHER'S NOTE
Numbers in square brackets in the text refer to images in the plate section.

CONTENTS

ACKNOWLEDGEMENTS

I must start by thanking my family, especially Mum and brother Jason, for their encouragement and support, and Annie and Chloe for always being there for me.

I'm indebted to the late Professor Jon Stallworthy and Sir Andrew Motion, the Rupert Brooke Trustees, for choosing me to be the editor of this book. For one who has been passionate about the life and work of Brooke since the age of 11, there is no greater honour. I am grateful to them both for their help, but a special mention must go to Jon, who was always so kind, patient and generous in spirit and encouraged and advised me throughout.

It has been a privilege and pleasure to have had this unique opportunity posthumously to come to know Phyllis Gardner, for whom I shall always feel great affection.

During my lengthy research I have been helped by so many. Some I fear I will forget to add here, but special mention must be made of the following key individuals:

Katharine Beal, who as a girl knew Phyllis Gardner, and therefore has shared with me wonderful memories and insights, most generously giving to me one of my most treasured possessions: an exquisite illuminated book of Scottish ballads by Phyllis; the late Ann MacEwen, Maitland Radford's daughter, with whom I had the pleasure of spending two highly memorable days in her beautiful Exmoor home, reading my way through the correspondence between Phyllis and her father; Jessica Schroder, who kindly gave me a bed for the night and complete access to her late father-in-law's amazing Brooke collection and permission to quote from it, and more recently her son Freddie, who has inherited the collection. I am most grateful to Philippa Young, a distant relative of Phyllis Gardner who thankfully found her way to me; she has generously shared photographs and research she has done into her family history and kindly given me her blessing to publish the Gardner material.

Others who have helped and encouraged me in my research include: Dame Mary Archer, Juliet Barker, John Bayley, John Briggs, Jean and Kenneth Clew, Steve Crook, Paul Delany, Peter Denyer, I D Edrich, Nicolas Furlong, Ted Gibbons, Dr David W J Gill FSA, Linda Hart, Robina Hattersly, Dominic Hibberd, Steffan Hill, Bridget Hole, Theo Honohan, Willy Jacobs, Ruth Jenkins, Griff Rhys Jones, Hilary Jupp, Anne Kirwan, Emer Lawlor, Rosie Lewis, Dr Jane Lucy Lightfoot, Lady Jennifer MacLellan, Diane Marston, Howard Moseley, Elizabeth Murphy, Elizabeth Murray, Daniel Nieciecki, Dr Bruce Osborne, Hugh Pelly, Ianthe Pratt, Wenda Roe, Shaune Shearer, Kate Sleight, Stephen Rhys, Karen Smith, Andrew Sim, Dick and Maryam Spiers, Jenny Taylor (St Mary's Church, Maidenhead), Peter Thronemann, Peter Ward, Julian Watson, Sheila Webb and Lewis Wood.

Along the way I encountered a great deal of colourful and inaccurate information regarding Phyllis Gardner and her family – which had been published, and related to me, by a well-known Irish wolfhound breeder who claimed he had known Delphis and Christopher Gardner. This sent me on many a wild goose chase, but ultimately ensured that thorough research was done so that the true facts could be established and published here.

My sincere thanks must also go to my agent Barbara Levy for all her hard work and guidance, and to David Way and the British Library for wanting to publish my book. It has been a pleasure to work with editors Robert Davies and Catherine Bradley; for a novice such as myself, their enthusiasm and kind guidance has been much appreciated.

The following archives have been invaluable for my research:

The British Library (Jamie Andrews and Helen Melody); King's College, Cambridge; Modern Archive (Patricia Maguire); Newnham College, Cambridge, Archive (Anne Thomson); Dartmouth University, Rauner Special Collection (Sarah); University of Sussex, Special Collections (Karen Watson); British School at Athens (Amalia G Kakissis); University of London Library; Van Gogh Museum, Amsterdam (Monique Hageman); St Felix School (Fran Dalcorn); Special Collections, University of Virginia; Library of The London School of Economics and Political Science; Kennel Club Library; Society of Women Artists; Maidenhead Library; Surrey History Centre; Slade School of Art (Gill Furlong).

A last word of thanks must go to my son Thomas and daughter Kate, who came into my life after I had finished writing this book – and in doing so gave me a new and far greater passion to pursue.

PICTURE CREDITS

The author and publishers are grateful to the following for permission to reproduce illustrations:

1 © King's College Library, Cambridge. RCB/Ph/262; 2 © King's College Library, Cambridge. RCB/Ph/164; 3 © King's College Library, Cambridge. RCB/Ph/74; 4 © National Portrait Gallery, London. x13124; 5 Private Collection; 6 The Private Collection of Philippa Young; 7 Private Collection; 8 British School at Athens; 9 Private Collection; 10 © British Library. Add MS 89076/4; 11 By permission of the Provost and Fellows of King's College, Cambridge, and the Rupert Brooke Society; 12 Private Collection; 13 Private Collection; 14 © British Museum. 1924,1021.6; 15 Private Collection; 16 Private Collection; 17 Private Collection; 18 Private Collection; 19 Private Collection; 20 Private Collection; 21 Private Collection; 22 Private Collection; 23 © St Felix School, Southwold; 24 © Rupert Brooke Society; 25 © Rupert Brooke Society; 26 © Rupert Brooke Society; 27 © Rupert Brooke Society; 28 From the Rudyard Kipling Papers at the University of Sussex; 29 Private Collection; 30 Private Collection; 31 The Schroder Family; 32 © British Library. Add MS 74741A.

PREFACE

The discovery of the letters and memoir documenting the previously unknown love affair between Rupert Brooke and Phyllis Gardner was both remarkable and exciting; their story of love, conflict and loss, expressed with spirited vibrancy against a backdrop of impending war, makes these writings poignant, timeless and accessible. There can be no better or truer way of gaining insight into the lives and personalities of Brooke and Gardner, and the rapidly changing times in which they lived, than through their own words.

In 1917, two years after Brooke's untimely death from septicaemia on his voyage out to fight in the Gallipoli campaign, Virginia Woolf reflected:

> anyone who helps us to remember that volatile, irreverent, and extremely vivacious spirit before the romantic public took possession of his fame has the right to our gratitude. If the legend of Rupert Brooke is not to pass altogether beyond recognition, we must hope that some of those who knew him when scholarship or public life seemed even more his bent than poetry will put their view on record and relieve his ghost of an unmerited and undesired burden of adulation.[1]

Unlike Phyllis Gardner's, Rupert Brooke's life has been documented in great detail from birth to death, owing to his poetical talent, ensuing fame and a number of friends, the most notable among them being

Sir Edward Marsh and Sir Geoffrey Keynes, who were dedicated to keeping his memory alive.

Marsh's memoir, published in 1918, was initially combined with *The Collected Poems of Rupert Brooke* and then later published on its own. It was the first form of biographical literature on Brooke to be made available to a very eager public, but Brooke's friends and mother – and even Marsh himself – were not happy with it. When he had initially showed Mrs Brooke the manuscript of his memoir in August 1915, she had strongly objected, both to Marsh's appointing himself for the task without her permission and to the way in which he had portrayed her son. Their relationship rapidly deteriorated, but eventually both reluctantly agreed upon an amended version. On publication, Virginia Woolf described the result as 'a disgraceful sloppy sentimental rhapsody, leaving Rupert rather tarnished'.[2] The sentiment was shared by most of Brooke's closest friends.

Critical reception of March's memoir was generally positive in the press, however. *The New Statesman* called it an 'able and sympathetic sketch', and the *Westminster Gazette* was similar in tone: 'The picture is incomplete. It is not a full-length portrait by a master, but a delightful sketch by a friend … Mr Marsh has fitted with loving skill … a mosaic both rich and illuminating. A delightful picture.' *Punch*, through its generous praise, underlined why Woolf and others hated it: 'Those of us who remember Rupert Brooke differently will perhaps best appreciate how well Mr Edward Marsh … has carried out his task of friendship. The result is an admirable picture of one whom the gods loved and gifted generously.'

Marsh was also responsible for the publication of *1914 and Other Poems*, *Letters from America* and *John Webster and the Elizabethan Drama*. When Mrs Brooke died in 1930, she excluded Marsh from her choice of literary executors,[3] so he handed the mantle to Geoffrey Keynes, who went on to produce a number of books. Perhaps most notable of these was *The Letters of Rupert Brooke* which, due to opposition from Brooke's friends, took him over 20 years to publish, at great personal expense.[4] Keynes made it his lifelong duty to create an impressive archive of Brooke's manuscripts at King's College, Cambridge, heavily drawn upon by numerous biographers over the years.

Marsh and Keynes thus largely controlled the public perception of Brooke after his death – yet both were prone to holding back, or editing out, information which would have tarnished the golden, romanticised Rupert Brooke they, and others, had inadvertently created. To be fair, it should be noted that their editorial choices were not unusual for that time. Brooke's blunt sexual references and explicit language would have been considered taboo, and because most of his friends were still alive while Marsh and Keynes were active, indiscreet or potentially upsetting references made by Brooke in his correspondence regarding friends and family had to be edited out. Such modifications, combined with the general tidying-up of his image, inevitably resulted in a blunted, blander depiction of the real man.

During his lifetime Brooke had, not always knowingly, sown the first seeds of this unrealistic adulation. Not only strikingly handsome, he also exuded great animal magnetism, charisma and openness which frequently dazzled those who met him, both male and female, and led to his having an almost celebrity status at Rugby and Cambridge. This in turn meant that Brooke felt the need to play up to the image others held of him, something he admitted to his friend and fellow poet Frances Cornford when describing his meeting with Henry James: 'Of course I did the fresh, boyish stunt, and it was a great success'.[5] But in reality it must have been a strain to feel the need to keep up such a façade, especially when it often conflicted with very real feelings of self-doubt and bouts of depression. 'My subconsciousness is angry with every dreary young woman I meet, if she doesn't fall in love with me: and my consciousness is furious with her if she does,' he once confessed.[6]

Despite the astute young Siegfried Sassoon half wishing he could find fault with Brooke ('Eddie's adoring enthusiasm had put me somehow on the defensive'), he recalled how he soon fell under Brooke's spell on their first meeting at Edward Marsh's flat:

> It was his kindness, I think, which impressed me, and the almost meditative deliberation of his voice. His movements, too, so restful, so controlled, and so unaffected. But beyond that was my assured perception that I was in the presence of one on whom had been conferred all the invisible attributes of a poet. To this his radiant good looks seemed subsidiary. Here, I might well have thought – had my divinations been expressible – was a being singled out for some transplendent

performance, some enshrined achievement. That, I believe, was the effect he made on many of those who met him as I did, and on all who fully understood the strength and sweetness of his nature.[7]

Gwen Raverat, a close friend since Brooke's student days and always known for being admirably forthright and frank in her manner, knew Brooke well. After his death she was keen to quash any overly romanticised accounts of him, yet she too inadvertently added to them:

> Perhaps the most obvious thing about him was his beauty. He was not so beautiful as many another man has been, and yet there was something in his appearance which was impossible to forget … there was a nobility about the carriage of his head and the shape of it, a radiance in his fair hair and shining face, a sweetness and a secrecy in his deepset eyes, a straight strength in his limbs, which remained for ever in the minds of those who once had seen him, which penetrated and coloured every thought of him.[8]

It would seem that few were immune to Brooke's charms. Among those able to see him with clearer eyes, however, was Virginia Woolf. In 1918, following a discussion with Brooke's long-standing friend James Strachey, in preparation for writing her review of *The Collected Poems* which contained Marsh's memoir, she noted in her diary: 'We couldn't say much about Rupert, save that he was jealous, moody, ill-balanced'.[9] Even so, she acknowledged a more favourable impression a few years later, admitting in a letter to Gwen Raverat:

> Leonard, I think, rather disliked him; in fact Bloomsbury was against him, and he against them. Meanwhile, I had a private version of him which I stuck to when they all cried him down … – based on my week at Grantchester, when he was all that could be kind and interesting and substantial and downhearted … He was, I thought, the ablest of all the young men; I did not then think much of his poetry, which he read aloud on the lawn; but I thought he would be Prime Minister, because he had such a gift with people, and such sanity, and force … My idea was that he was to be a member of Parliament, and edit the classics: a very powerful, ambitious man, but not a poet.[10]

E M Forster, an acquaintance of Brooke's, fellow King's man and Cambridge Apostle, probably got closest to the truth, however, writing to a friend in August 1915:

You ask about Rupert Brooke. Considering we were on Christian name terms, I did not know him well, though enough to contradict the legends that the press are weaving round him. He was serene, humorous, intelligent and beautiful – as charming an acquaintance as one could desire – and latterly most friendly. But he was essentially hard: his hatred of slosh went rather too deep and affected the eternal water-springs, and I don't envy anyone who applied to him for sympathy... I don't know whether the above conveys anything to you. If it errs on the side of unkindness he himself wouldn't like it the less, for he was extraordinarily free of conceit and sincerely desired to be done by as he did.[11]

It is hard for us now, imbued with preconceived ideas, to see Brooke as his contemporaries did. During his lifetime he was perceived as very modern, an image he enjoyed and worked at – in the casual way he dressed, in the socialist politics he followed and in his style of poetry, which was often seen as shocking, daring and new. To write about a woman's 'smell'[12] as he did was considered indecent, and to link thoughts of a lover with being seasick[13] disgusted the literary critics. Sentimental or patriotic poems such as 'The Old Vicarage, Grantchester' and his final War Sonnets, which included 'The Soldier', were very much in a minority among the bulk of his works, which were frequently turbulent, controversial and dark in content.

Immediately after his death Brooke was styled by the likes of Winston Churchill for the propaganda machine. Churchill was at this time First Lord of the Admiralty and responsible for forming Brooke's Royal Naval Division, as well as being one of the masterminds of the soon-to-be-considered disastrous Gallipoli campaign. He was consequently eager to portray Brooke as a symbol of all that was golden and good, pure and noble, the embodiment of an England and its heroic youth that would never be defeated, even by the horror of the brutal conflict – when in truth Brooke would come to represent an England and its youth lost forever in the midst of the First World War. Then came the backlash – Brooke glorified war and was shallow, weak and affected; more recently he has been described as a womanising, sadistic, self-indulgent cad. It could be argued that there is some truth in both these views, but equally he was capable of displaying great sensitivity, passion, kindness, generosity and dedication. When only the negative aspects of his personality are focused upon, as has so often been the case in recent years, a distorted picture is given of the real man who, like all of us, had both good and bad qualities. Brooke was a complex, intense and frequently confused young man who in many ways was trying to construct an individual lifestyle, liberated from the conventions of the Edwardian era, and in doing so was often in conflict with himself. Although his life was short, he lived it at full speed and with great vividness; one can only be amazed at how many projects he was running simultaneously. It is no wonder that Brooke exhausted himself at regular intervals, both mentally and physically, with the volume of work required for his fellowship, writing articles, poems and letters, wooing women (sometimes several at a time), making regular trips abroad and maintaining a very busy social life.

An ongoing theme that runs through both Brooke's poetry and prose is his fear of old age, powerfully depicted in his poem 'Jealousy':

> And you, that loved young life and clean, must tend
> A foul sick fumbling dribbling body and old,
> When his rare lips hang flabby and can't hold
> Slobber, and you're enduring that worst thing,
> Senility's queasy furtive love-making.[14]

It was not surprising that J M Barrie's *Peter Pan* appealed greatly to him, and he went to see it repeatedly when it was first staged in London. The idea of marriage and settling down seemed an alarming prospect to Brooke, partly because of his desire to hold on to a youthful, carefree existence, but perhaps also through a greater fear: that he would be dominated and controlled by a wife, as his father was. Mrs Brooke was well known for her forceful personality, which had led Rupert to give her the nickname of 'the Ranee'. Rugby town lore had it that Mrs Brooke would send her diffident husband out into the street with a spade to gather horse manure for her rose bushes, and Hassall in his biography referred to an account of Mrs Brooke arguing with her husband on the stairs at School Field after he had tried to offer unwanted advice regarding her role in looking after the boys in his House at Rugby; apparently Brooke was overheard murmuring to himself as he walked away 'It is *so*, all the same'.[15] Ironically Rupert had a close relationship with his mother and was always drawn to strong, educated women who had a will of their own. However, he became incensed by the Suffrage movement and clearly felt deeply threatened by the possibility of women holding equal rights.

Phyllis Gardner represented this new generation of females, emerging on to the cusp of emancipation for women. The opportunities and freedoms afforded to girls who had finally received a good education, with the sense of their own worth that this instilled, conflicted with the still prevalent ideas of how a lady should behave and her place within society. Gardner's passionate and adventurous nature made her want to push the social and moral boundaries of the time, whether it be through her socialist beliefs, unchaperoned independence or by exploring her own sexuality, yet the strong religious code that had been instilled in her and her own inborn sense of what was right and decent often conflicted with this – never more so than when Brooke entered her life.

Unfortunately, little is known of Phyllis Gardner's life overall. However, one period documented in sharp and intimate detail is those few, intense years recorded in her memoir, beginning on that fateful day in November 1911. For her this was always to be remembered as a defining moment, a landmark in her life – before she saw Rupert Brooke ... and after.

NOTE ON THE TEXT

The correspondence between Rupert Brooke and Phyllis Gardner has been reproduced here in its entirety, as has Phyllis Gardner's memoir. On occasion it has been necessary to move a section of text in the memoir so that it is in the correct chronological order; when this has been done an end note draws attention to the fact.

Both Brooke and Gardner had their own eccentricities in their style of writing and use of punctuation. I have standardised his frequent and varying-in-length dashes and the spaces he left between words and sentences, and regularised the position of addresses and dates in the letters. To ease identification of people mentioned in Gardner's memoir, described in the original only by their initials, I have supplied the full name. Such amendments are shown by square brackets, which have also been used to show when I have joined quotes, so as to avoid confusion with the use of ellipses within other text. All inaccuracies in spelling, punctuation and, particularly in Gardner's case, abbreviation, have been left unaltered, so the particular characters of the writers are not lost.

At intervals my own commentary is added, often drawing upon quotations from letters and poems beyond the correspondence between Brooke and Gardner. It is hoped this helps to illuminate other aspects of their lives, or to illustrate their thoughts at the time.

The British Library holds this entire correspondence as well as Gardner's memoir.

Other notable sources used are the letters written by Gardner to Maitland Radford in which she makes references to Brooke. She writes in a relaxed, frank manner as one does to an old friend, often revealing true thoughts and emotions regarding Rupert and using quite a different tone from letters written to Rupert at the same time. These letters belonged to the late Ann MacEwen, daughter of Maitland Radford, and now reside at the British Library. The final letters and accompanying poem between Edward Marsh and Mary and Phyllis Gardner were discovered by myself among the late John Schroder's collection while researching this book.

INTRODUCTION

On 10 March 2000 the head curator of the British Library Manuscripts Department unwrapped a brown paper parcel secured with sealing wax and string to discover what she described as: 'without doubt, the most exciting documents I have ever de-reserved'.[1] With this was broken a silence kept for over 85 years. For recorded within their pages was the unknown, or more accurately the hidden, love affair between the handsome young poet Rupert Brooke and a young art student with flaming red hair called Phyllis Gardner.

Owing to the very intimate nature of Phyllis's memoir, a 50-year time seal was placed upon it.[2] So the parcel lay quietly waiting for the years to pass, deep in the bowels of the old Library in Great Russell Street. When its embargo had finally passed the package was overlooked, due to the library's move to new premises in Euston Road. Not until over a year later was it allowed at last to reveal its secrets: a correspondence of over a hundred letters between Brooke and Gardner, dating from 1912 to 1915, and her memoir, laying bare with moving honesty the details of their affair from beginning to end.

The importance of this discovery was further intensified because barely anything was known about Phyllis Gardner, let alone her relationship with Rupert Brooke. Until 2000 only a handful of people had been aware of this secret love affair: those surrounding the couple at the time they were together and, in later years, close friends in whom she had confided. Only one of Brooke's more platonic letters, written to her from the South Seas, had been published in Sir Geoffrey Keynes's much-edited edition of his letters,[3] and a single, incorrect reference to her being 'a friend of the Fabian days' was mentioned in Christopher Hassall's biography.[4]

It must have been in 1948, nine years after Phyllis's death, that Delphis, her younger sister, made the discovery while clearing 'Recess', the Gardner's family home in Maidenhead prior to a move to Ireland. She found a handmade maroon leather wallet, lovingly decorated with white flower motifs bearing heart-shaped petals, protecting within its covers the bundle of treasured letters. There was also a memoir: 91 carefully typed foolscap pages held together at the top corner by a treasury tag, the front page blank apart from the words 'A TRUE STORY' typed across the centre and beneath, in Gardner's small, well-formed hand, 'Written during 1918'. A collage of fingerprints dappled the page edges, left by the countless times she had returned to read this memoir over the years and remember. Had Delphis ever been allowed to read these papers during her sister's lifetime, or was this the first time she saw them? In answer, Phyllis's own words come to mind. She was once asked by Rupert: 'will you, I mean, destroy or lock up in the ironest of unopenable boxes, my letters?' to which she replied: 'I have a system of my own of keeping private papers, no one else would possibly see them'.

What thoughts came to Delphis as she sat and read these most intimate pages? Certainly they must have cast her mind back to when she was ten years of age and Rupert Brooke first came into the Gardners' lives, in those last years before the horrors of the First World War changed forever the life they had known. Phyllis was 21 then, having been born on 6 October 1890, at 1 Pemberton Terrace, Cambridge. She was the second of Professor Ernest Arthur Gardner and his wife Mary's four children, but her elder brother died soon after birth on 25 May 1888. Phyllis's birth certificate gives her father's occupation as 'Fellow of Caius College', but her birth was registered by her mother who, it seems, had returned from Greece to have Phyllis while her husband stayed on in Athens, where he was Director of the British

School of Archaeology. Professor Ernest Arthur Gardner was a notable archaeologist and author on ancient Greece. Born in London, where his father worked on the Stock Exchange, he was one of six children, three of whom became distinguished academics; they were brought up as devout Christians by parents who believed 'religion was the great interest in life'.[5]

Ernest was educated at the City of London School and went on to take a First in Classics at Gonville and Caius College, Cambridge. He became the first student of the British School of Archaeology, of which he later served as director, before marrying Mary Wilson in 1887.[6] She had been raised in both Ireland and Scotland owing to her father being an officer in the Scots Greys, where he later achieved the rank of Major. After winning a scholarship to George Watson's College in Edinburgh, Mary went on to Newnham College, Cambridge, and was about to take her London degree when she met her future husband.[7] Phyllis was later to write 'my own family tree has leaves of rose and thistle as well as shamrock':[8] her father accounted for the 'rose' and her mother for both the 'thistle' and 'shamrock'.[9]

Phyllis was taken out to Athens while still a baby so the family could remain together. In 1895 they returned to England, however, and were rather unsettled due to Phyllis's poor health, moving from Barton, just outside Cambridge, to London, and then on to Sandgate in Kent. In 1896 Ernest Gardner was given the position of Yates Professor of Archaeology at University College, London [8].

Fortunately Mary Gardner recorded this period of their lives in a fragment of memoir she had started to write just before her death in 1936. It includes some affectionate glimpses of Phyllis's childhood:

> But the time came when we had to move on from Athens, as one of the main ideas in having a School of Archaeology in Athens was for a succession of young scholars to come out from the universities. We were sorry to go, but felt we had been away from England long enough to feel a little out of things. However, Ernest hoped soon to find work at home, and we went to our Cambridge house, which we had let for the winter, as we usually did.
>
> Our leaving Athens coincided with the expiry of Ernest's Fellowship at his college, so it happened rather awkwardly from a financial point of view for us. We had therefore to think of some way of economising, and

decided to give up the Cambridge house, and take a cottage in a village some miles away.

…The post of Professor of Archaeology in the University of London falling vacant, Ernest applied for it, and was appointed, and held it for nearly forty years. On his retirement a few years ago he was honoured with the title of Emeritus Professor.

This meant giving up the cottage and moving to London and Ernest's mother missed us when we went away. We were visited in our Barton Cottage by many of the scholars in Cambridge, and by many of the friends we had made in Athens.

But Cambridge had not agreed with Phyllis, and she developed a tubercular growth on her neck, which had to be operated on.

On the way home from the hospital, I turned along in the direction of her grandmother's house, but she cried out, "Oh, don't let grandma see me all bandaged up like this".

So the pony was turned round again.

One day I went to the kindergarten for Phyllis, the lady who instructed her came out looking very hot and cross, and said while I was getting in to the cart, "I cannot think how you've taught this child so much without her having the least sense of discipline".

Poor dear, she did not have much chance of being disciplined for some time, as a few months in London were too much for her, and we had to up camp again.

At Sandgate, where we decided to go on leaving London, I took some rooms to see how the place suited Phyllis. On the journey, she had not been dressed, but simply rolled up in a blanket, and for the first few weeks lived exclusively on cream. But the sea air did her so much good that we bought a little house near the sea, and settled down for three years. Phyllis got well enough to attend a school near, where I don't think she was much bothered with discipline, but got on all right. The motto of the school was the name the ladies found on the door when they came, Conamur, from the motto of a regiment once stationed at Shorncliffe.

… Phyllis learnt to swim here, her father taking her on his back in to the deep water. She said to him one day, "Daddy, when you take me in to the water, don't pay any attention if I scream. I don't mean it".

… Phyllis was very fond of going to the circus, so when one came to Folkestone, we went, and I found it usually took a dozen or more grown ups to escort one small child. She was taken to see pantomime, in which a pirate figured. On describing afterwards what the pirate did, she said, "He smoked two cigars at once, and did a great many other things I didn't approve of".[10]

When Phyllis was eight she sent a 'Get Well Soon' letter to Rudyard Kipling, her earliest known surviving letter [28]. Kipling had gone on a family holiday to New York where he and his two young daughters became gravely ill with pneumonia. This was widely reported in both the American and English newspapers, as Kipling had become something of a literary celebrity by this time. Five days after Phyllis wrote this letter, Kipling's eldest and dearly loved daughter Josephine died, aged six; it had been for her that he had written and dedicated *The Jungle Book* in 1894.

There is no known connection between the Gardners and Kipling, so we can only assume that Phyllis was prompted to send the letter because of her love of *The Jungle Book*. The book clearly greatly appealed to her love both of animals and of drawing them, as she illustrates her letter with pictures of 'Bagheera on a tree' and 'Some drawings to amuse you', showing in animated scenes a cat meeting a pack of dogs and the ensuing scuffle. It must have been a loved Gardner family book as later, in 1914, Phyllis wrote to Brooke about Delphis making and selling Jungle Book toys at The Toy Shop in New Bond Street.

> Radnor Cottage,
> Sandgate, Kent.
>
> March 1st, 1899
>
> Dear Mr Kipling,
>   I am very sorry you are ill, and hope you will soon get better, as it is uncomfortable being ill.
>   your loving
>   Phyllis Gardner[1]

It is not known if Kipling ever replied to Phyllis. Twelve years later she would once again be sending similarly illustrated letters to a literary man she much admired.

Soon after this the Gardner family moved into a newly built home in the Surrey village of Tadworth, as Phyllis's health was still not considered good enough to live in London. Farm Corner was a rather plain, square, surprisingly modern-looking house, with pale taupe-coloured roughcast covering its external walls and brick arch accents over the windows [22]. It was set in a rural, very picturesque, unspoilt part of the county, made newly accessible by the recently constructed train station. Here Phyllis's sister Delphis was born in 1900, followed by Christopher two years later.

Phyllis's aunt, Alice Gardner, also purchased a house in Tadworth which she aptly named 'Studium'.[12] Like her brothers, Ernest and Percy, she was a distinguished academic, being associate, fellow and lecturer in history at Newnham College – positions achieved despite parental opposition, although Percy gave her his full backing. Alice was among the early women 'pioneers', such as Ella Armitage and Jane Harrison, who pursued a college education at Cambridge.

During her lifetime Alice Gardner wrote a number of books, her key subjects being Byzantine history and religion. In 1906 she wrote *Letters to a Godchild*, on the catechism and confirmation, which was dedicated 'To Phyllis', who was, one suspects, the godchild in question.[13] It offers religious instruction of a general and wholesome kind on Christian life and duty, revealing the kind of childhood influences by which Phyllis would have been surrounded.

It certainly seems from Phyllis's memoir that Aunt Alice exerted a certain amount of power over the Gardner household. Living only a few roads away and making apparently frequent visits, she seemed to keep Phyllis and her family on their toes, as they never knew when she would drop in. In contrast to the rather tyrannical reign she seemed to have over Phyllis and her family, Alice Gardner is remembered by those who attended Newnham as reserved and diffident with hints of a 'sad nature'. Yet she was also recalled for her sense of humour, illuminating smile and great heart and mind, and was seen as 'one of the outstanding personalities in College'.

While living at Tadworth Phyllis attended two schools, the first being The Lodge in Banstead, near to her home. This was a school for young ladies run by a Miss Mary Ellen Mason, well known for her kindness. It was said that her domestic staff 'were to be envied',[14] both because of their employer and the fact that 'The Children' (as they were always referred to) were 'encouraged to help themselves without imposing on the domestic staff … the whole School was like a united family'.[15] However, strict rules were applied so far as simple dress, make-up and jewellery were concerned. Miss Mason also had a great interest in the arts, and would hold literary evenings at her home. Here poets such as John Drinkwater, Alfred Noyes and John Masefield were invited to read their work.

The second school was a groundbreaking one for girls called St Felix, in Southwold, Suffolk, where Phyllis and later Delphis were boarders [23]. Their aunt, Alice Gardner, was a friend of the founder and headmistress, Miss Margaret Isabella Gardiner, and had supported the school from its conception, encouraging her brother Samuel[16] to enrol his two daughters, Mary[17] and Ruth. In 1900 Samuel became chairman, a role he held until his death in 1931.

St Felix was a school ahead of its time, infused with the ethos that its founder, Miss Gardiner, had announced to a friend: 'I am going to make a school where girls are treated like sensible creatures.'[18] Its houses were named after major contributors to women's emancipation, including Nightingale, Fry and Fawcett,[19] and Miss Gardiner insisted that the school should have no gates; anyone who wished to leave could do so at any time. If the girls wanted to learn, there was no need for them to be ruled over – instead it should be a partnership between teacher and pupil. It all worked impressively well. Not surprisingly St Felix produced many pioneers in women's emancipation and ladies of note, three of whom were later to feature in Rupert Brooke's life.[20] Phyllis only spent 18 months at St Felix, from 1907 to 1908; the school magazine *The Felician* gives some tiny hints of her life there. In the December 1907 edition we learn that her house, Fawcett, had taken part in an event put on for the 'servants' entertainment' in which Phyllis had played a rather interesting role:

> Fawcett ended the evening's entertainment by acting "Dottyville". Dottyville was a small private asylum, the patients being lunatics of various descriptions. The play opened with the admission of another lunatic to the asylum; and, to prove the happiness of the inmates, the lunatic's aunt was shown over the establishment. P. Gardner, who imagined herself to be a bath, and M. Bellhouse, a canary, acted their parts well.[21]

We also discover that Phyllis became secretary of the Library Committee and was a member of the Debating Society, in which she seconded a debate on the motion 'War is not justifiable' – a sentiment about which she would later feel differently. It is apparent that Phyllis had an enduring bond with her old school, as she returned over the years to play cricket or attend Old Felician meetings on a regular basis. She was often accompanied by her younger sister Delphis once she, too, had left the school.

In 1908 Phyllis entered the Slade School of Art where she attended three classes a week, and where Isaac Rosenberg, Stanley Spencer and Dora Carrington were numbered among her fellow students. Gwen Darwin (later Raverat), granddaughter of Charles Darwin and a good friend of Brooke's, almost certainly attended the same classes as Phyllis; they both studied Fine Art and the craft of wood engraving, then little practised.[22] In addition, Phyllis attended classes at the Frank Calderon's School of Animal Painting.[23] She had a great affection for animals and at this time a passion for horses – 'her beloved gees',[24] as her mother once referred to them. This love was doubtless enhanced by the location of Tadworth, only a stone's throw away from Epsom, one of England's great horse-racing venues.

Delphis was also artistic, and had a love of literature. After leaving St Felix School she entered University College, London, gaining a BA in Greek Studies in 1923. Phyllis was always to be a strong role model for her. Christopher, the youngest, appears to have been mentally impaired, quite possibly autistic, although it is hard to say how apparent this was early on in his life.[25]

Throughout her sister's memoir, Delphis encountered numerous references to their friends, identified only by initials or first names. She, of course, would have been able to work out very quickly who they were, but why did Phyllis feel the need to veil these identities, even if somewhat lightly? Did she intend this manuscript to be read by outsiders – or perhaps suspect that one day it might be? This, however, would seem doubtful as Phyllis makes the assumption that the reader knows about certain very personal events in her life, such as her troubled relationship with Brian Rhys.[26] A reference is also made to a poem she wrote which is totally unknown to us.[27]

The fact that Phyllis Gardner wrote down her memories of Rupert Brooke in 1918, the same year that Edward Marsh published his own memoir on Brooke, should not be ignored. Ever since Brooke had first introduced Phyllis to Marsh she had disliked him, so one might imagine that she felt the need to counter Marsh's depiction of Brooke in his memoir; the work may have spurred her on to capture in her own words the man she had known. If this was her objective she, like so many of Brooke's friends who tried to write about him after his death, on occasion undermines herself by lapsing into overly glorified language or ideas of who Rupert was, even at one point likening him to an angel. The contrast between the fresh immediacy of their letters and Phyllis's memoir, written once her grief for his loss and the canonisation of his image had cast a rose-coloured haze across her perception of him, is often noticeable.

Unfortunately we do not have the insight Delphis possessed; we can only try to piece together small details or clues to some events in Phyllis's life. Among the fragments gleaned from Phyllis's correspondence with Rupert are references to what would seem to have been her first love, though no name or date is given. The mere handful of her surviving verse includes a poem she wrote in July 1907, which probably alludes to this episode in her life:

Rondeau
So thou art mine? And yet my heart to-day
Beats with no wilder joy: but far away
I look into the future years, and see
Dim forms of mirage, moving silently,
And in their ranks thyself hast come to stay.

Give me thy hand on life's uneven way:
All is not bright, and every month not May,
But pain and grief discomfited shall flee,
      So thou art mine.

Joy of my heart, come here to me and say
One word to give me courage in the fray,
Or with one look from sorrow set me free:
Sweet Peace thou art, and all in all to me:
I shall not fear stern Fate's most dread array,
      So thou art mine.[28]

Phyllis's unreciprocated feelings in this poem may have been for Maitland Radford.[29] Six years her senior, he had the same blond, boyish appearance as Brooke and later became a doctor. David Garnett, a writer and member of the Bloomsbury Group, had known Maitland since they were boys; in a posthumous tribute to Maitland he recalled how his 'physical precision was paralleled by a precision of mind which made him a stimulating companion and a brilliant talker in any society ... I am convinced that had his ambition lain in that direction he would have easily become a dramatist in the tradition of Congreve, Wilde and Shaw ... But he had also, I am tempted to say unfortunately, a strain of idealism which impelled him to serve humanity directly, as a doctor, rather than to devote his life to literature'.[30] Both Maitland and his cousin Evelyn Radford were also friends of Rupert Brooke prior to Phyllis knowing him.[31]

Throughout her memoir Gardner refers to Maitland with great warmth, and this feeling is echoed in her few surviving letters to him written during the First World War. The only other enduring symbol of her affection towards him is an exquisitely carved section of beef rib, which could pass as ivory. On both its sides are depicted, in relief, two winged horses standing before the sun with its rays of light, set against a gold leaf background [29]. Work of such beauty and fineness must have taken her countless hours to carve.

The Gardner and Radford families were well acquainted and remained in contact for many years; Phyllis was also evidently very fond of Maitland's sister Margaret,[32] who wrote poetry and also features in her memoir. Ernest Radford, Maitland's father, was a poet and member of the Rhymers Club,[33] but perhaps he is most noted for his work as a socialist and follower of William Morris, which led to him becoming one of the organisers for the Arts and Crafts movement. Sadly he deteriorated both mentally and physically in early middle age. His wife Caroline (née Maitland), known to all as Dollie owing to her petite stature, was also very active in the literary and socialist world.

Another family mentioned a number of times in Phyllis's letters and memoir are the Rhyses. They were also friends of the Gardner and Radford families, and moved within the same literary and political circles. We learn from Phyllis that Brian Rhys was in love with her and wanted to take their relationship beyond friendship, but she was unable to reciprocate his feelings. Brian was the son of Ernest Rhys, author, poet and, along with W B Yeats, founder of the Rhymers Club, although he is probably best remembered for his role as founding editor of the Everyman's Library from 1906. His wife Grace also wrote poetry and prose.

The Rhys children, Brian, Megan and Stella, were of similar ages to Phyllis, Delphis and Christopher. Their close association is well illustrated by a small crumbling pocket book, which was found, looking completely out of place, among Professor Ernest Arthur Gardner's academic papers, held in the archives of University College London. Its pages, covered in the large, slightly awkward-looking pencil script of a child, provide a wonderful, informal glimpse into the Gardner family household. This charming volume, written by Delphis and boldly inscribed 'Private', is the rule book of the 'Sausages' club – no doubt founded by Delphis, who tops the list of members as '(head)', followed by, in declining order of rank: Stella Rhys ('Best member'), Phyllis Gardner ('good member'), Christopher Gardner ('good') and Brian Rhys ('member') followed by the warning: 'He that looks into this book that is not a SAUSAGE shall have his reward. Delphis Gardner. Head of the SAUSAGES.'[34]

Among the interests shared with the Rhys family was a mutual affection for, and fascination with, their Celtic heritage. In 1927 Grace Rhys included a poem by Phyllis in *A Celtic Anthology*,[35] and Ernest Rhys spoke of the Gardners with respect and affection in his autobiographical writings. Among these was *Wales England Wed*, in which he comments that 'the two Gardner girls did not belong to the London Bohemia in those days. They came of Greek culture'.[36] Ernest also supplies us with a charming vignette, dating from about the time Rupert would have known Phyllis:

> I remember one very jolly children's party on Stella's birthday, to which some grown-ups came to help in the fun … It rained hard that afternoon, and hurrying home over the Heath[37] I had to seek shelter under a tree, and at its foot saw three very small animals, fairy-size, a tiger, a little brown horse, and a horned stag, hardly believing my eyes. Then, as I stooped, a clear voice from somewhere in the branches called out, and in the tree I spied two girlish figures, Phyllis and Delphis Gardner. They were bringing the three carved animals to Stella as a gift, and had put them at the foot of the tree to keep them from getting wet. The two Gardner girls were rare artists, wood-carvers as well as painters; and carved sets of chessmen too, exquisitely coloured, of delicate design.[38]

When the paths of Phyllis Gardner and Rupert Brooke first crossed, both were at a very similar stage in life, studying the subjects they planned to use in their future careers and generally trying to find their way. They also shared comparable family backgrounds and influences: brought up in Christian families, their fathers both tutors steeped in the Classics, with mothers who took a dominant role in their household. Their mothers had a large impact on the lives of Phyllis and Rupert in both a positive and negative sense, whereas, perhaps typical for the time, their relationship with their fathers was affectionate but rather more distant.

Compared to Phyllis, Mary Gardner seemed more confident and bullish in her approach, with a tendency to overpower. She was always very anxious to be a part of the literary world and associated with its stars, despite having only minor talent in this area herself. The poet Robert Frost fumed in a letter to his friend: 'These Gardiners [*sic*] are the kind that hunt lions and they picked me up cheap as a sort of bargain before I was as yet made ... The Missus Gardiner is the worst.'[39] Yet her journal shows Phyllis to have had a very close and equal relationship with her mother, each feeling able to talk to the other about almost any subject.

Brooke on the other hand, in spite of the fact that he admired and was devoted to his mother, lived in constant fear that she would learn too much about his friends and private life – both of which he knew she would find thoroughly reprehensible. Rupert Chawner Brooke was born on 3 August 1887, within sight of Rugby School where his father, William Parker Brooke, was a master. His mother, Mary Ruth Brooke, née Cotterill, had met her husband while acting as matron at Fettes College, Edinburgh. The name Rupert was chosen by his father, who believed it had a dashing ring to it, and his unusual middle name of Chawner by his mother, after a seventeenth-century scholarly Cotterill ancestor. Apparently Mary Brooke enjoyed the fact that, as it was Queen Victoria's jubilee year, a memorial clock was built in Rugby's marketplace to mark the occasion; in her mind it also marked the arrival of her son.

Mary Brooke had a strong but caring personality [24]. She was very protective towards Rupert, largely due to the frequent bouts of ill health he had suffered from childhood; she loved him deeply, but sometimes tried to dominate. He took very much after her side of the family: the

Cotterills tended to be forceful and opinionated, combining a strong Christian and puritanical streak with an active interest in politics and in the welfare of the underprivileged. Rupert did not share his mother's religious zeal – he was an atheist from an early age – but he had an inborn need to worship something. In place of a deity, he increasingly saw Goodness, Beauty and Purity as ideals to venerate. In his paper 'In Xanadu did Kubla Khan', which Brooke read in 1912 to the Apostles, a secret society for Cambridge (male) undergraduates that met and held discussions, he goes some way to defining his doctrine: 'And I also think, now, that this passion for goodness and loathing of evil is the most valuable and important thing in us. And that it must not in any way be stifled nor compelled to wait upon exact judgement.'[40]

The one characteristic Brooke seemed to inherit from his father was a tendency for depression; he himself described his father as 'a very pessimistic man, given to brooding'.[41] Virginia Woolf later described Brooke as 'moody' and 'ill-balanced',[42] a view echoed by many of his closest friends.

Rupert had two brothers: Richard, affectionately known as Dick, who was six years older, and Alfred, three years younger [26]. A sister, Edith, born two years before Rupert, had died aged only 13 months – a terrible blow to Mrs Brooke, who had longed to have a daughter. She appears to have let this become known to Rupert at some point during his youth, and unfortunately this seemed to haunt him. In some way it gave him an explanation for what he believed was the feminine aspect to his nature. In 1912 he wrote of this to Ka Cox:

> I am here because at Fettes, in the seventies, Willie Brooke and May Cotterill got thrown together. And then they had a son and a daughter, and the daughter died, and while the mother was thinking of the daughter another child was born, and it was a son, but in consequence of all this very female in parts – *sehr dichterisch*[43] – me.[44]

A sense of what Rupert was like as a child can be found in his first recorded words, spoken when he was seven and had just been caught by his mother, fighting his younger brother Alfred. 'You're a coward,' she told him, 'to be hurting someone so much smaller than yourself, and if ever I catch you again I shall have to punish you.' To which the boy replied, 'Then *you'd* be the coward.'

Rupert's first taste of formal education began at a preparatory school called Hillbrow, but he did not really flourish in his studies until he arrived at Rugby School, aged 14. The fact that he was placed in his father's House, School Field, where his mother acted as matron, had its pros and cons. Unlike the other boys he was not separated from his family, which doubtless complicated his relations with both his parents and the other boys. Forever under the watchful eye of his parents, particularly his mother, but wanting to be embraced fully by his fellow pupils and not considered by them to be favoured or a possible informer, his unique position in School Field inevitably lent itself sometimes to practical jokes. Legend has it that there was a lift – or what is sometimes known as a 'dumb waiter' – that ran from the kitchen at School Field up to the Brooke family's private quarters. One day the lift bell rang and Mrs Brooke opened the hatch doors, expecting a cottage pie; in its place she discovered Rupert, sitting cross-legged on the shelf with a notice saying 'Mother, behold thy son' pinned to his chest.

During his time at Rugby Brooke was to form important, lifelong friendships with James Strachey,[45] Geoffrey Keynes[46] and Denis Browne.[47] His literary talents became apparent when his poem 'The Bastille' won the school's poetry prize in 1905, and in 1906 he was awarded their King's Medal for Prose. In addition he was co-founder and editor of a literary supplement to the Rugby School magazine, entitled *The Phoenix*. To fulfil the requirements of a 'good, healthy, all-rounder', Brooke was a member of the school rugby and cricket teams, in which he conducted himself respectably enough; he also worked his way up to the rank of second lieutenant in the school cadets.

Despite such conformity, Brooke also managed to underline his own individuality, not least in the way he dressed and styled his hair. In defiance of school regulations he grew his hair long and wore a black silk 'puff' tie, all to enhance what Geoffrey Keynes later recalled as 'his self-conscious role as poet and intellectual'. Significantly, Keynes was also to add '– though I, knowing him better than most, was aware of his occasional descent into phases of deep depression and self-debasement. He was putting on an act, which we all enjoyed and encouraged'.[48] In many ways Keynes's astute observation summed up Brooke throughout his life.

In October 1906 he went up to King's College, Cambridge to study Classics, for which he had won a scholarship. His father had done this before him in great style, not only going on to gain a First, but also becoming the first non-Etonian to become a Fellow of the College. King's must have seemed rather a family affair for Brooke, as his uncle, the Rev Alan England Brooke, was also Dean there. It appeared to be Brooke's fate that his entire educational life would be spent under the watchful eye of his family – first his parents and now 'Brookie', as he was known among the students.

At first Brooke was not happy in his new college life. At Rugby he had been a big fish in a little pond, but at Cambridge it was the reverse. He kept a low profile and was shy in making new friends, choosing to associate mainly with other Rugby pupils who had come up to Cambridge. One exception to this was Hugh Dalton, whom he met when both went for a dual interview with Brooke's uncle. The young men got talking and discovered that they had a great deal in common. Both were ardent supporters of the Labour Party, verging on socialists, and shared the same tastes in literature: Swinburne, A E Housman and Hilaire Belloc. It was not long before they had founded a society for the purpose of reading poetry and holding discussions, which they named the Carbonari.[49]

Fortunately, during his first term at Cambridge, Brooke wandered into the ADC theatre[50] and sat down in the stalls to watch the ongoing rehearsal. He was spotted, approached and asked if he would be willing to play the small, silent role of a herald in Aeschylus's play, *The Eumenides*. In this ancient Greek tragedy, his striking profile was used to full effect. As he described to his mother, the role required him to 'stand in the middle of the stage and pretend to blow a trumpet, while someone in the wings makes a sudden noise'.[51] At one of the performances of this play he was to make a lasting impression on a member of the audience: Edward Marsh, Private Secretary to the First Lord of the Admiralty, Winston Churchill. Marsh immediately felt the impact of Brooke's charisma, and he later recalled his role in a romantic light: 'His radiant, youthful figure in gold and vivid red and blue, like a Page in the Riccardi Chapel, stood strangely out against the stuffy decorations and dresses … After eleven years, the impression has not faded.'[52] In 1939, when Marsh wrote his autobiography,[53] he dedicated an entire chapter to Brooke. Its opening, written in Marsh's typically overblown manner, declares:

> My friendship with Rupert Brooke was certainly one of the most memorable things in my life. In his combination of gifts, of body, character, mind and spirit, he was nearer completeness and perfection than anyone I have known.[54]

Moving within similar social circles, the men met and corresponded on odd occasions. However, it was not until Marsh read Brooke's *Poems* and wrote a praise-filled letter to him, quickly followed by a glowing review of the book in *Poetry Review*,[55] that their friendship really took off.

Another new acquaintance to become a friend of Brooke's, largely because of his association with the ADC, was Justin Brooke (no relation). Through him Rupert was brought into contact with a whole new set of friends, who were to have an enormous impact on him.

On returning home to Rugby at the end of his first term at Cambridge, he discovered that his mother was dangerously ill with influenza. This Rupert rapidly proceeded to catch, then news came that his elder brother Dick was ill with pneumonia too. Little is known about Dick, who appears to have been the family's 'black sheep' due to his partiality to drink. Mr Brooke rushed off to Southsea, where Dick worked at an engineering company, to be by his son's side, but within a matter of days Dick was dead.[56]

Once back at Cambridge, Brooke sought distraction from his grief by offering himself up as a reviewer for the *Cambridge Review*. He wrote many excellent articles for this magazine, as well as for the *Westminster Gazette* and subsequently a number of other literary periodicals. It was also about this time that he started to approach these publications with examples of his poetry; before long they too were being published.[57]

Soon Brooke was to be part of an exciting new venture, the Marlowe Dramatic Society. Recently founded by his friend Justin Brooke, it had the backing of a handful of others including Francis Cornford, a junior Classics don at Trinity, and Jane Harrison, a notable Classicist and Newnham don. Tired of English theatre, especially the rather tame productions of the ADC, they all felt a shake-up was needed. They believed that the answer lay in the vigour of poetry, in particular the much neglected plays of Christopher Marlowe and other Elizabethan dramatists. Brooke took the part of Mephistopheles in the society's very first production, *Doctor Faustus*, which was performed in November 1907; soon after he became the society's first president.

The Marlowe Society proved a great success, largely because it was a reaction against Victorian theatre and tradition; it also revived the presentation of Shakespeare in Cambridge which had not been performed since 1886. The Society continues to flourish to this very day and has spawned many great actors and directors, including Sir Ian McKellen, Sir Derek Jacobi and Sam Mendes, CBE.

The Christmas holidays brought an exciting, if somewhat alarming new experience for Brooke, who found himself skiing and tobogganing in the Alps with a group of 28 undergraduates of both sexes. He wrote to his cousin, Erica, before leaving for Andermatt, that they were 'Mostly young, heady, strange, Females. I am terrified'.[58] Later, after he had been there a while and got to know his companions, he appeared less concerned. 'They are nearly all Socialist, and "interested" in things … They are all great friends of H. G. Wells. Even the Newnhamites[59] and others of their sex and age are less terrible than they might be. Several are no duller to talk to than males.'[60] Among this group were Katharine Cox, known affectionately to her friends as 'Ka', and Margery Olivier. The latter had brought along her younger sister Brynhild, who always seemed to have an intoxicating effect upon men; Brooke was no exception, but he was sensible enough to realise that it was a passing infatuation, commenting in a letter 'I adore her, for a week'.[61] This was just the beginning of his introduction to the close-knit Olivier sisters, who would later play a key role in his life.

Brooke's newfound enthusiasm for his college life and all the opportunities it offered him seemed boundless; so did his energy [5]. As well as founding the Carbonari Society and taking an active part in the Marlowe Society, he also had his eye on becoming a member of two somewhat older establishments – the brotherhood of the Apostles and the Fabian Society. The former, a secret organisation for Cambridge undergraduates, was believed to have been founded in 1820 by 12 students, hence its name. Brooke's entrance into this elitist, all-male group in 1908 was eased by his long-standing friendship with James Strachey

– by this time very much in love with Brooke, although his feelings were never reciprocated. James's brother Lytton had been elected into the Apostles in 1902, and a year later he was joined by Leonard Woolf and John Maynard Keynes, all three of whom later considered key figures in the Bloomsbury Group. The secrecy and exclusivity of the Apostles appealed to Brooke, who read a number of papers to them on varying subjects.

The Fabian Society, which Brooke was also voted into in 1908, was of even greater importance to him as it represented his socialist ideals. Virginia Woolf was later to highlight this aspect of his personality: 'He was keenly aware of the state of public affairs, and if you chanced to meet him when there was a talk or strike or an industrial dispute he was evidently as well versed in the complications of social questions as in the obscurities of the poetry of Donne.'[62] Brooke's political stance may be viewed with less conviction by modern eyes; certainly his romanticised idea of the working class, and the way in which he perceived and wrote about them, appear patronising today: 'I can watch a dirty middle-aged tradesman in a railway-carriage for hours, and love every dirty greasy sulky wrinkle in his weak chin and every button on his spotted unclean waistcoat. I know their states of mind are bad. But I'm so occupied with their being there at all, that I don't have time to think of that.'[63]

In contrast to the other societies that Brooke had signed up to, the Fabians allowed female members. This, following swiftly on the tail of his holiday in the Alps among female company, must have been a novel experience for Brooke, who up until this time had spent his whole school and early college life entirely in the company of males. Among the Fabian members were the two Newnhamites with whom he had just become acquainted on holiday: Ka Cox, who had just become the Society's treasurer, and Margery Olivier.

The second play to be put on by the Marlowe Society in July 1908 was Milton's *Comus*. It proved a landmark production in Brooke's life because of the people with whom he came into contact. The idea of performing *Comus* was proposed to Justin Brooke by the Master of Christ's College, Milton's old college, as the poet's tercentenary was approaching. It was also suggested that the artistic daughter of one of their Fellows, Sir Francis Darwin, son of Charles Darwin, could put her talents to good use in producing the costumes for the play. So Brooke encountered Frances Darwin (soon to be Cornford), and through her Gwen Darwin (later Raverat), another granddaughter of Charles Darwin, whom Frances said had greater artistic ability than herself and planned to go to the Slade next year.

Jane Harrison, a committee member of the ADC and good friend and mentor of Francis Cornford, then suggested that some of her Newnham girls should be enlisted to act in the play. To have female and male students acting alongside one another was considered most irregular at this time – a convention that Justin Brooke could vouch for, as he often had to perform female roles because of his small waist and fine features. As the production was taking place out of term time, however, this radical idea was permitted. Among the recruits were Ka Cox, later to have an enormous impact on Brooke's life, Evelyn Radford (Maitland Radford's cousin) and Mary Gardner (Phyllis's cousin). All three of them were St Felix girls.

Ka Cox was probably acquainted with Phyllis owing to their both having gone to St Felix. She was just at the point of leaving the school as Phyllis arrived, but she returned frequently after this; Ka held a great affection for the place, which had become a second home for her and her sisters following their mother's premature death. In return, she became a much loved figure there among the girls. Furthermore Ka's father, like Phyllis's uncle, had been involved in establishing the school, and she was now at Newnham, where Phyllis's Aunt Alice taught, so it would seem there were many points of connection between them.

It was while rehearsing *Comus* that Frances Darwin, having only known Brooke for a brief time, wrote the poem 'Youth', originally entitled in manuscript form 'R B'. She was captivated, as was almost everyone on first meeting him, by his physical beauty; the poem was inspired by her sight of Brooke illuminated upon the stage by a shaft of light from a window:

A Young Apollo, golden-haired,
Stands dreaming on the verge of strife,
Magnificently unprepared
For the long littleness of life.[64]

Frances later regretted writing this poem, as it distracted from the reality of the Rupert she came to know so well.

On 10 July 1908 *Comus* was performed before a private audience of college Fellows and important guests, the most notable among them being the Poet Laureate Alfred Austin, Thomas Hardy, Edmund Gosse and Robert Bridges who, it must be said, was not terribly impressed by the play and left before the end. The next day the play was performed once again for the public. Lytton Strachey was there to act as reviewer for the *Spectator*; he wrote in favourable terms about the production overall and gave special mention to Brooke's part as the Attendant Spirit.[65]

In April 1909 Brooke wrote to his Cambridge friend Jacques Raverat that 'My history for the past five months is as uneventful and perfect as a bird's. I went to Switzerland and felt a magnificent creature. I returned to Cambridge and read poetry, laughed, and argued, all day and all night, for a term. I have done no "work" for ages: and my tripos is in a few weeks'.[66] [3] Perhaps not surprisingly, but much to Brooke's dismay in imagining his mother's disappointment, he only managed to scrape a Second in his Classical Tripos, a subject in which he had never shone. There was hope of redemption, however: his sympathetic tutors advised that Brooke should drop Classics and utilise his great strength, English Literature, when working towards a Fellowship. They also suggested that he move from his rooms at King's, away from student life and its temptations.

Another distraction had been a somewhat pubescent romance with Margery Olivier's younger sister Noel. He had first met her in 1908 at a Fabians' meeting at which her father, the Governor of Jamaica, had been invited to speak on socialism. Rupert was 20 and Noel only 15. Over the next two years their main contact was through letters with only the occasional meeting, largely due to her family's vigilant watch over the proceedings – understandably they were anxious that Noel should not get too involved at such a young age. In 1910 Rupert and Noel did manage to steal enough time away together later to become secretly engaged, but Noel's feelings towards him soon began to cool and Brooke was held at arm's length. Equally his feelings had never been truly deeply felt; it was more a matter of being in love with the idea of love or, as he later admitted to her, 'I think it's only calf-love – I know about it, it's what I had for you, *gnädige Fräulein*[67] – Calf-love, that goes wrong only hurts so-so – a remedial and finite business'.[68]

Even so, Brooke did offer to dedicate his book of poems to her. Noel declined, so instead he arranged the chronological order in a rather unusual fashion – those poems written before he met her and those after. From this time on he returned to the idea of being in love with Noel whenever a relationship foundered or failed. In truth this was probably largely due to the fact that she was unattainable, and therefore it was safe for Brooke to imagine himself in love with her. Once, in a bluntly honest and somewhat astute letter to James Strachey, he wrote of Noel, 'I think it's on the whole better to be in love with her than most women … As she's unusually unemotional and stony, and as she's backed up by her adamantine family with that loony-man at the head, she may be fairly safe'.[69]

In the summer of 1909 Brooke took his tutors' advice and moved to a picturesque village called Grantchester, one and a half miles downstream from Cambridge. Not only did this change in location remove him from the centre of college life, so he could try and knuckle down to the business of gaining a Fellowship; it also allowed him to pursue a more rustic lifestyle which appealed to his romantic illusions of rural life.

The hope of staunching the flow of visitors and friends to his door was only partly successful. This 'divine spot'[70] proved a great draw to his friends, who travelled out from Cambridge by bike and boat to visit or stay with him. At first Brooke rented rooms at Orchard House, belonging to a Mr and Mrs Stevenson; the couple ran a Tea Garden among the apple trees at the back of the house during the summer months. People would walk from Cambridge, across the meadows – a route long known as the Grantchester grind – and take tea amid the apple blossom. Brooke painted a picture of his new life in a letter to his cousin:

> It is a lovely village on the river above Cambridge… I work at
> Shakespere, read, write all day, and now and then wander in the woods
> or by the river. I bathe every morning and sometimes by moonlight,
> have all my meals [chiefly fruit] brought to me out of doors, and am as
> happy as the day's long.[71]

Brooke was unconventional in his manner of dress – all part of break-ing the 'rules', something in which he took great pleasure. When Hugh Dalton wrote an article on him for the *Granta*, he touched upon this point: 'He is sometimes credited with having started a new fashion in dress, the chief features of which are the absence of collars and headgear and the continual wearing of slippers.'[72] It was not long before he caused something of a stir among the local residents by taking things even further: they were shocked to see Brooke and his college friends, both male and female, swimming naked together, and by his regular practice of going about barefooted. In a letter to his good friend and fellow Cambridge student Dudley Ward, he warned him of the situa-tion before coming to stay:

> Do what you like. But keep FRIGHTFULLY quiet at The Orchard: I've had dreadful scenes with the Stevensons. The village 'talked' because of bare feet. So they MUST keep their boots on! Otherwise they mayn't stay! This is true.[73]

In a letter to Ka Cox, Brooke outlined his group's creed, explaining 'We don't copulate without marriage, but we do meet in cafes, talk on buses, go on unchaperoned walks, stay with each other, give each other books, without marriage'.[74] One of those who came and partook in this liber-ated lifestyle was Virginia Woolf, who had first met Brooke when they were both children. She dubbed him and his circle the 'Neo-Pagans'.

This newfound lifestyle was obviously suiting Brooke well as he was soon to win two University prizes: the Charles Oldham Shakespeare Scholarship and the Harness Essay Prize. Both supplied him with much needed funds. In January 1910, however, Brooke was sent a telegram by his mother calling him back to Rugby as his father was gravely ill. Within days William Parker Brooke had died and Rupert, now the eldest male in the family, had to stay on at Rugby for the whole Lent term, which was over two months, acting as Housemaster of School Field while a replacement was found.

Politics and the Fabians continued to play a large part in Brooke's life. In July he went on a 12-day caravan tour of the south-west of England with Dudley Ward. He made public speeches at villages along the way in support of socialism and the Poor Law reform, following the 1909 Minority Report headed by Beatrice and Sidney Webb. In

November he delivered a lecture entitled *Democracy and the Arts* to the Cambridge University Fabian Society.[75] In this Brooke argued that all artists from every class should be given financial support.

At the end of 1910, urged on by the appearance of 'horrible people' at the Orchard, Brooke decided to rent rooms next door at the Old Vicarage. Its tenants, the Neeves, were offering three rooms and full board for the bargain price of 30 shillings a week, and this place had appealed to Brooke for a long time due to its romantically shabby appearance. He had previously written to Lytton Strachey describing the Vicarage and its owners:

> The Neeves are 'working people' who have 'taken the house and want lodgers' ... They keep babies and chickens ... The garden is the great glory. There is a soft lawn with a sundial and tangled, antique flowers abundantly; and a sham ruin, quite in a corner.[76]

And, after he had moved in, he reported to his cousin:

> All the Spring I alternated between seeing the Russian Ballet at Covent Garden and writing sonnets on the lawn here. This is a deserted, lonely, dank, ruined, overgrown, gloomy, lovely house: with a garden to match. It is all five hundred years old, and fusty with the ghosts of generations of mouldering clergymen. It is a fit place to write my kind of poetry in...[77]

Not surprisingly, Brooke was to leave a lasting impression on those who lived in Grantchester. Many years later Helen Bailey, daughter of the local schoolmaster at the time, recalled her childhood memories of him:

> One evening when we were dawdling home, we saw Rupert Brooke standing quite still near a clump of elms on a little hill called Tartar's Well. He was gazing into the sunset, his head thrown high and fair hair wisping in the wind. I recall how handsome he looked as though it were yesterday.

Her friend Kitty was staying at the Old Vicarage during this time:

> My sister and I started to go bathing from the Old Vicarage gardens ... We used to call on Kitty in the early morning, throwing stones at her window to awaken her. We called 'Kitty, Kitty' very softly so as not to disturb anyone else, but more often than not Brooke would appear at his window and wave to us. Sometimes, too, he would have beaten us to it and we would meet him returning from our[78] early dip in the

river ... he talked to us of swimming, gardens, the weather ... He was always friendly, if a little withdrawn. His head was often in the clouds of composition, however. He would wear flannel bags and an open necked shirt – clothes regarded as rather eccentric, but he did not mind one iota.[79]

The year 1911 started quietly enough for Brooke, but ended in disastrous torment. For the first few months of the year he stayed in Munich, writing poetry and meeting new people, including the painter Clara Ewald[80] and, more importantly, Elisabeth van Rysselberghe,[81] who rapidly fell in love with him. He was later to confess that his feelings towards Elisabeth were only ever those of lust; he saw an opportunity to have an affair and went for it, only to make rather a mess of it all through his clumsiness in enlightening her about the different forms of contraception. Throughout the next four years this foundering relationship would blow hot and cold.

In April Brooke left Munich and headed for Florence to act as escort to his godfather and old Rugby master Robert Whitelaw – now elderly, newly widowed and in need of a travelling companion. In May Brooke returned to England, leaving Whitelaw with his mother in Rugby. He headed for the Old Vicarage where, in the coming months, he began to work at his dissertation on Webster and the Elizabethan dramatists to compete for a Fellowship at King's. Before the year was out, he would unwittingly captivate a young woman, unknown to him, called Phyllis Gardner, while sharing the same train compartment between London and Cambridge. This arbitrary crossing of paths would lead in time to their lives being altered forever [4].

Letters to + from Rupert Brook

Correspondence between Rupert
Brooke & Miss Phyllis Gardner.

Offered as a gift by Miss Delphis
Gardner, Reeves, Boxn Hill, Maidenhead
with reservation for period of
50 years from 13 Nov. 1948.

Deposit No 2141

---

2 November 1948

If when this Memoir is opened in
November 1998, the Trustees of the
British Museum consider that it should
not be made available for the public, I
give them authority to reserve it for a
further period of years or to destroy it.

Delphis Gardner

ONE

'A TRUE HISTORY.
WRITTEN DURING 1918'[1]

O nce, long ago, I was lying awake at night – or half awake
and I saw a kind of vision. It was a boyish figure, with fair
hair, and it was sitting in a corner. It was in a way like M[aitland].
R[adford]. as he was at that time, and in another way not in the
least like him, but a good deal like Christopher. I remember
vaguely wondering if that would ever be my son, and wishing
most heartily that it would be, but not with much hope of fulfilment of the wish. And then I suppose I went to sleep. But that
figure sitting in its corner haunts me to this day; and it was very
like someone I met since. ...

"You ought to keep a diary", said Uncle Stanley. The idea was
that one was able, by taking thought, if not to add a cubit to one's
stature, at least to control the direction of one's moral growth, and
that a record of what had passed through one's mind was a useful
asset in finding out the present direction of such growth, and
therefore helpful.

Accordingly I wrote spasmodically when it occurred to me. I
entered the difficulty of my relations with B[rian].R[hys]. I entered
the fact that I had explained to him, in the phraseology that he and
I used to one another, the feeling I had that there was someone in
the world a "potential B.", (I being A), before whom any claims of

his would be as nothing. It was a difficult thing to explain: this is a
business I have altogether mismanaged.

I do not know what exactly it was that made me stop keeping
the diary. The document stops suddenly at Nov.9. But I do remember that it was not mere slackness that made me stop keeping
it, but a definite unwillingness to put certain things on paper.
Moreover, I fell out of love with Uncle Stanley's plan of conscious
self-development. It annoyed me: it did not seem to me right
or suitable that one's inmost thoughts should be dragged to the
surface against their will and written down.[2]

And then on November 11 I went on a journey to Cambridge,
the occasion when I first saw R. It is an easy date to remember: it
was 11/11/11, and I took the opportunity to write a post-card to
my mother as soon as I reached Cambridge, simply for the sake of
heading it in that fashion.[3]

It was my mother who first called my attention to him. We
were having tea in the refreshment-room at King's Cross, I being
just on my way to spend a week-end in Newnham with my aunt.
"Look", she said: "there's a man a little like M[aitland].R[adford]."
I looked, prepared to feel resentment at the comparison, for
I thought a lot of M[aitland].R[adford]., and did not like him
compared lightly to strangers. But I felt no resentment; I was
interested in this newcomer. He had a red scarf knotted about his
neck – the evening being a chilly one in November – and he had
a mop of silky golden hair that he ran his fingers through; and his
face appealed to me as being at once rather innocent and babyish
and inspired with an almost fierce life and interest and keenness.
He was like Christopher, too, in a way.

We finished our tea, left our places and went to the train. I
chose a place in the right-hand corner of a carriage, bestowing my
bag on the rack, and stood in the door talking to my mother.

He came along the train, with another man who was apparently
seeing him off, searching up and down a little, and finally pitched
upon my carriage. He took the corresponding left-hand corner,
facing the same way as mine. My mother felt already that here
was an acquaintance, for she leaned in at the window and spoke to

me audibly of a good many of my Cambridge friends, – as I now know, she did this in the hope of discovering that he and I had common friends, – and soon the train started, and we settled down into our respective corners.

I had in my bag a sketch-book and some chalks, and as he sat in his corner and read a sheaf of manuscripts I took my opportunity. Except for a few moments that we spent in adjusting the windows because of the many little tunnels on the Great Northern Railway as it leaves London, I drew him steadily all the way to Cambridge, and the more I drew him the better I liked him. In the matter of the windows we exchanged no word, but each observed carefully what the other did, and tried to fall in with the other's wish. And then the train drew up at Cambridge (for which I could have kicked it, because I was just beginning to be pleased with my drawing), and we stepped out on to the crowded platform and, for the moment, lost one another.

I felt at the time that this was not final, that I should see him again. My aunt met me, and I went with her to Newnham; and when I got to my bedroom that night, I took the drawing out and looked at it. I realized that I had not the slightest right to sleep with it under my pillow, so I left the sketch-book, open at the place, on a chair by my bed.

The next day I began a campaign of showing it to people, with a view to identifying him by name. I showed it (this was unwise) to my aunt. I could not pluck up courage to show it to the students, though this would not have been a bad idea; I did not know any of them very well. There was a girl among the students then for whom I had a strong attraction. She was a dark, tragic-looking creature with great wistful eyes and some peculiar grace about her movements and the set-on of her head. She knew him, if I had but known it. I went and spent the evening in her room, but we did not happen across a mention of his name.

On Sunday my aunt took me to tea with some people. The lady of the house was an artist,[4] and I was emboldened to start forth with my sketch-book under my arm. As we turned into Sidgwick Avenue, himself on a bicycle, bare-headed, fled past us, and as he passed he gave me a look of half-recognition and a kind of wild smile. The artist lady was good enough to give a name to my portrait, may it be remembered to her credit; she was the first who identified it for me.

[Postcard, postmarked Cambridge, 5 pm, 11 November 1911]

Mrs E. A Gardner,
Farm Corner,
Tadworth,
Surrey.

11/11/11 Newnham

Thanks for your card. Have'nt knitted much sock yet= spent the time in the train drawing that man. Last night I saw Fanny Foster,[5] and Gwen Dyer; and an old Slade called Sargent-Florence.[6] Quite a jolly time. This morning called on Aunt Ruth. Annette[7] took me to see cousin Hugh[8] in his rooms, wh. Aunty Alice says is against all college traditions to do in the morning. Then I designed a border for lace which Annette wanted to do at once – then went with Aunty to the University Library and looked at illuminated ms of all sorts and early printed books while she looked something up. Saw my man again on a bike this morning but without a gown so he can't be "up"; very nearly recognized one another this time. Aunty has asked B. Bury, N. Adams and Hugh to tea: she would'nt ask O.R.[9] or GWK.[10] because she does'nt know them. Looked the latter up and he is B.A – Am going to Kings and to see Mrs Cockerell[11] to-morrow, and to some kind of a musical turn-up this evening, called an Open Raleigh: Fanny is playing in it. Everyone very bruised about the Magic Flute.[12] Aunty sends her love.
    Phyllis.

The second or corroborative identifier was the sister of the dark girl in Newnham, and was studying medicine at the hospital which abutted on the art-school, so that I occasionally saw her. I met her one day, and produced my drawing for her to see, and she gave it the same name as the Cambridge artist lady had done. So in triumph I appended this name, in black chalk, to my drawing, and showed it to M[aitland].R[adford]. and his sister M[argaret]. M[aitland].R[adford].,[13] who both agreed in giving witness to its correctitude.

Needless to say, it was Rupert Brooke's name that Phyllis chalked in beneath her portrait. However, she was unaware that the medical student she had approached was Noel Olivier, his ex-fiancée, who, it would become apparent, was annoyed by the captivated Phyllis's attentions. The 'dark, tragic-looking creature' happened to be Noel's sister Daphne, who was studying literature at Newnham.

In November 1911 Brooke was working at full stretch. He was engrossed in several demanding projects, including correcting the proofs for his first volume of poems, to be published on 4 December of that year, and completing his dissertation on John Webster and the Elizabethan Drama – his chance of a Fellowship at King's depended on its success. It is very likely that the 'sheaf of manuscripts' Phyllis mentions him reading in the train was his dissertation. He was also rehearsing a small walk-on part as the Seventh Nubian Slave in the very same production of *The Magic Flute* mentioned by Phyllis in her letter home. Conducted by Cyril Rootham at Cambridge's New Theatre on 1 and 2 December 1911, it was notable for being the first English language version of *The Magic Flute* to be performed in Britain. Brooke worked most of the week in London, going back to Grantchester at the weekends.

Some little time later, the dark girl had invited me to tea. After a day at the art-school I went in the half-dark and looked for her house in St John's Wood.[14] When I got there she was still out; there was a great fire blazing merrily up the chimney, and an inviting-looking sofa within easy reach of a table covered with books and periodicals. The room was only lighted by the fire.

I sat on the sofa, and began looking through the books. I picked up a little thin black volume with a white label on the back: Poems, by someone of the same name as chalked beneath my precious drawing. I opened it and read it a little, and the inspiration came to me to take down the name and address of the publisher.

I had not had time to read much when the dark girl came in. I asked her if she knew him, and she said "Yes"; and where he lived, and she said: "Partly in London and partly in Cambridge: but he's very difficult to catch!"

So I took home the name and address of the publisher, and mother ordered the book. And, having read it, she wrote a letter to him, care of the publisher, expressing a desire to meet him.

It is at this point that Brooke first mentions Phyllis in a letter written to Ka Cox:

> Oh, most exciting. You know about the Romance of my Life. I know I told you, because I remember how beastly you were about her – Miss Phyllis (is it Phyllis?) Gardner. Everyone was so beastly that I hadn't the heart to meet her. She went to tea day after day in St John's Wood, and I was always too sulky and too *schuchtern*[15]to go. So it all ended, you think. Ah! but you don't know Phyllis (?)! Today I received, through Sidgwick and Jackson, a letter. It was from an elderly woman, who said she had been led by a reviewer's hatred of *A Channel Passage* to buy my book, that she thought it all *frightfully* good (particulars) and would I go and see her, or her husband, a Professor at University College, or both, anywhen, anywhere.......addressed from Surrey and signed Mary Gardner. *Es ist alles sehr einfach, nicht wahr?*[16]
>
> Oh, I've put it in the hands of my solicitor (Miss Noel Olivier) who has been acting for me in this matter throughout.*
>
> Tra! la! la!
>
> <u>That's</u> what modern Mothers are![17]
>
> * in a thoroughly beastly manner, too, I must say.

Phyllis's attentions had evidently been an embarrassment for Brooke, his friends obviously finding the whole business very entertaining. It would also appear that Phyllis had not been as discreet as she had imagined in making her enquiries; if he is not exaggerating for effect, she had been persistent in trying to meet him before her mother wrote to him. As much as Phyllis's rash, feverish behaviour was what one would expect from a lovestruck young woman, her mother probably had other motives in driving on Phyllis's eagerness. It was apparent that, although lacking in any real talent as a poet herself, Mary Gardner longed to be a part of their literary world, so the slightest hope of having a promising young poet as a son-in-law would surely be the ultimate prize.[18]

Unknown to Phyllis, much had happened in Brooke's life in the short time between her first laying eyes upon him at King's Cross station (in November) and now (late January 1912). At that time he was a carefree, if a little overworked, postgraduate, excited by the imminent publication of his first book of poems. Now he was fully immersed in a messy love affair with Ka Cox and was a changed man – delicate, exhausted, damaged and raw-nerved. This relationship would inevitably end painfully for them both, leaving Brooke with a damaged, jaded view of women.

Throughout 1911 Rupert's relationship with Ka Cox had been moving on from that of platonic friendship. Ever since first meeting through the Fabians in 1907, they had enjoyed a good relationship; for Rupert, she was the first female outside his family he had become close to, her unthreatening motherly warmth allowing him to feel safe enough to have her as his confidante.

It was this closeness between them that led to Ka taking Rupert to one side during a reading party at Lulworth at the end of December 1911. She told him that she was in love with the artist Henry Lamb, who was already married, and was considering sleeping with him. Rupert, physically and mentally exhausted from having worked around the clock to finish his dissertation, was suddenly faced with the possibility that a woman he had come to care for might favour another above himself. He fell rapidly into a fit of jealousy and panic, accusing Ka of betraying him and, almost as a reaction, declaring that he was in love with her and asking her to marry him.

Totally bewildered by this reaction, Ka, not surprisingly, refused. Rupert, in a state of nervous breakdown, was dragged by his mother to Cannes for recuperation, but peace and quiet was far from his mind. His all-consuming objective was to get Ka to surrender to him. He bombarded her with desperate letters entreating her to meet him, and before long she gave in to his pleas through fear and concern for his fragile state. Reluctantly, she lived with him for a short time in Munich.

This proved a disastrous decision. It resulted in Ka's sleeping with Rupert largely through pity, then confessing to him that she wished she had not as she still loved Lamb. Rupert became repulsed by Ka, considering her 'dirty' for consenting to sleep with him while also holding feelings for Lamb. Equally he frightened and disgusted himself for becoming so out of control and sexually driven, anxieties that plunged him deeper into mental and physical collapse.

Quite unfairly Rupert always wanted to see his female partners in a pure, chaste light, yet pushed for sex with most of them. This aspect of his contradictory nature, puritanical and libertine in turn, brought him great inner conflict, often verging on self-hatred. After leaving Munich, Rupert's feelings towards Ka cooled – perversely just as she began to lose interest in Lamb and fall in love with him. The damage had been done, however, and any hopes of a future relationship were in tatters. It seems possible, based upon vague comments in letters between Brooke, Ka and their friends, that she may have become pregnant during this time, but miscarried.[19]

This affair was to cast a shadow across many aspects of Rupert's life and shape the way he perceived and reacted to many situations. It certainly had an impact on all his future sexual relationships. He carried new wounds and, more importantly, bore greater self-knowledge.

In March 1912 Brooke failed to win his King's Fellowship, but was fortunately given the chance of a second attempt. By April he was convalescing in a pension near Dudley Ward's flat in Charlottenburg, Berlin, with Dudley's fiancée (soon to be wife) Annemari von der Planitz and her mother staying nearby. Ward was a kind and steady friend to Brooke; his job as correspondent for the *Economist* meant that he now lived in Germany, which provided Brooke with a welcome bolt-hole. It was during this time in Berlin that Brooke's homesick feelings for his rural idyll found powerful expression in one of his most famous and best loved poems, 'The Old Vicarage, Grantchester', originally entitled 'A Sentimental Exile'.

> After a decent interval, during which I suppose the letter may have lain in the publisher's office, a reply came: yes, he would like to meet us. (I subsequently found out from him that he had heard who we were.) So my mother wrote and asked him to a lunch-party at her club.
>
> Bei Herrn Dudley Ward
Spicherns Trasse 16. /G.H.
[King's College, Cambridge]
Charlottenberg, Berlin
>
> June 1912
>
> Dear Mrs Gardner
>
> Your letter (which you wrote so long ago you must have forgotten it) came to me, through my publishers and many other hands, at length. It was very good of you to write like that. I ought to have answered long ago, and thanked you. I've been abroad and ill, nearly the whole year, and too lifeless to be answering any letter. – Oh but lively enough to have felt the keen pleasure of receiving a letter from someone, personally unknown to whom one's poems have appealed! It is rare and warming, to find such appreciation.

I don't know when I shall be in England again. And I'm afraid I shan't, anyway, be in London for more than half a day for a while. So don't see any chance for me to call on your husband in London (– of course I know his book on Greek Sculpture!),[20] though I should very much like to perhaps, if ever I'm walking through Surrey (I wander about England, sometimes) I shall be able to find Tadworth and ask for tea?

    With my many thanks for your kind praise of my book

      Yours sincerely

        Rupert Brooke

On his return to England, Brooke wrote to James Strachey that 'Solitude is my one unbearable fear'.[21] This probably explains his change of attitude towards the Gardners. What at first felt like embarrassing, unwanted attention might now have appeared as a chance to be seen with fresh admiring eyes, among new people who knew nothing of his troubles.

Referring to this time in Brooke's life, the author A C Benson[22] later recalled, 'I felt him to be oppressed by a great weariness of the life he had been living, and of a strong desire for a complete change of scene … he said that he found it easy to make friends, and enjoyed the idea of meeting strangers, who would take him just as he was, without any knowledge of his tastes or antecedents. … The prevailing feeling was that he wanted to break with his previous life a little, get a current of new thoughts and images, and obliterate by all possible means something which seemed almost like an obsession'.[23]

> The Old Vicarage
> Grantchester
> Cambridge

Friday, July 19 [1912]

Dear Mrs Gardner,

    I find I shall be passing through London on Monday – you asked me to tell you when I should be. If you're likely to be in London that day, I can get a train that gets in at 1.15, so I should be in time, and very willing, to meet you, as you suggested, at lunch. But please don't bother if it's a bad day for you. I have to go through then, any how–

    Yours sincerely

      Rupert Brooke

The appointed day of the lunch-party arrived. We were all as-
sembled and met together, a miscellaneous party of more or less
literary and artistic people of different ages and sexes. We had
invented a poet, Reuben Fell by name, and nearly all of those
present had contributed one or two poems which were gathered
together as his work. Some, however, were not in the secret; these
were told in glowing terms of his charming personality and interesting career, and also that he had written at the last minute to say
he could not come to-day. But he was not the idea of the moment
for me: the thing was that my friend of the Cambridge train had
written at the last minute to say he could come.

We all sat in a group round a window. Then the door opened,
and it was as though the sun had suddenly risen. Whether or no
he was really about a head taller than most of us there I am not
in a position to say: but so it seemed to me. Also I do not know if
other people found his presence as radiant and full of sunshine as
I did; it was extremely easy to see him in one's mind's eye with a
halo of gold.

He spoke not much at first, but looked serious and mild. We
went up to lunch, and all sat at a long table, I being next him
somewhere in the middle of one of the sides.

This all happened some time ago, and the details are blurred
in my mind between whiles, leaving only a succession of clear
pictures. The next picture finds the party reduced to four: he, my
mother, a friend of hers, by name Jessy Mair (a very charming
Scotswoman), and myself. We sat over the fire for hours and
talked. Mrs Mair wanted to outstay him, and being a woman of
great determination she succeeded, or nearly so: we all left the
building together at a surprisingly late hour and went our several
ways.

This was the second – no, if you count that glimpse on a
bicycle, literally third – time I had seen him. I could not get him
out of my head. There was his extreme beauty of physical type
to start with, but that was only a small part of the hold he had
on people. I felt as if I knew him well, wonderfully well, as if
I had always known him. I felt that here was a person cut out

on a colossal scale, one who would go much further than ever I could know of, and yet that I knew of it all the same by a kind of instinct. I was in love with him, to start with, but all love is not of that kind: there was "more to it" than that. "Potential B" had arrived: but I never thought of him as B to my A; he was A and all the others, Alpha and Omega of my life. I felt, from this time onwards for a couple of years or so, carried along on a kind of ir-resistible current. I could no more have done or thought anything else than a leaf whirling down an autumn torrent.

At the beginning of August 1912 Rupert finally ended Ka's hopes that they might salvage their relationship. 'It seemed useless to prolong the strain,' he wrote to Frances Cornford. 'It is incredible that two people should be able to hurt each other so much.'[24] Both were left in a shattered state, and each turned to Frances for comfort and advice. She told Rupert, sensibly, that he should leave the country to get clear of everything: 'Frances wants me to go to America or somewhere for a year for Ka's sake, for mine, and for everybody's. America means if possible, some physical work and little or no mental.'[25]

This was all happening just as Phyllis and Rupert were taking their first tentative steps towards getting to know one other. Not surpris-ingly, it appears that Rupert was keen this budding relationship was not known among his friends.

We wrote and asked him to come and spend a week-end with us.[26]

[Telegram sent from Kensington office]
September 14 1912
TO Gardner Farm Corner Tadworth Sy
Many thanks shall reach Tadworth 5.28 Brook

It was summer, and hot – the kind of weather when one lies in hammocks in the heat of the day, and goes out in the woods in the evening: if one is so fortunately placed as to be able to do so. But this was before the war. I suppose it must have been during the University vac, because there was a general flavour of my aunt in the offing. She, good soul, was a good deal of a nuisance to us, with the best intentions in the world. No man of any kind came to the house but she must needs suspect him of coming after me, and try her level best to put us off him; and, as I said to my father, it didn't matter as a rule, being merely funny, but it became a bore when there was anything in the supposition. So it came about that our household formed a sort of conspiracy to fool her in matters of this kind.

But this is a digression. To return to the subject; we all went down to the station en bloc to meet him, and when he arrived we fought over his bag, of which he ended by retaining possession himself. Then he and I lay in two parallel hammocks under the row of big elm-trees at the east of the house, and looked up overhead into long vistas of intertwining branches and delicate green leaves in perspective, with occasional spots of deep blue sky showing through. We lazed there awhile, and then went into the house.

I came on him and Delphis then aged about 11 in the drawing-room. They were both on the big sofa, sitting side-saddle-wise facing one another, in intent conversation. I overheard only one phrase: Delphis was saying "We poets". I should like to have heard the rest of the duologue.

He told us wonderful stories that evening. He told us a dream he had had. He was staying with two aunts in a house near the sea, and he more or less accidentally murdered one of them. Then, to avoid upsetting the other aunt, he had to find some means of disposing of the body. He had a pocket-knife. There was an immense cardboard box full of roses on the piano, and somehow with the pocket-knife he managed to cut the body into pieces so that it could all be hidden in the box of roses. Then, stealthily, when no one was about, he would cut off smaller bits and take them out and throw them into the sea…He knew that, sooner or later, the remaining aunt must ask him what had become of the other, and dreaded the moment when this should happen. And he came in from the beach after one of his expeditions to get rid of another piece, when at the head of the stairs he saw his remaining aunt.…He had the bloodstained pocket-knife in his hand, and hurriedly hid it behind his back. The aunt grew taller and taller till she towered over him like a giantess, then pointing down at him with one finger and fixing him with a terrible piercing look, she said; "The roses are bleeding!".[27]

And then there was the story of the Machine Messiah. There were once a community of religious people somewhere in the wilds of America, and one of their number had a dream. He dreamed that a new Messiah was to arise, and that he was its appointed prophet; and he had been warned in his dream of how he was to act. He called for the co-operation of the whole community, who placed themselves unreservedly at his disposal. Certain wheels, pulleys, girders, cranks and other assorted mechanical appliances were brought, and an angel regularly appeared to him in dreams, telling him exactly what to do; and daily the machine grew more absurd, complicated and unworkable. None of the community, it seems, were well acquainted with the principles of engineering, – nor, apparently, was the directing angel. But the construction went cheerfully forward.

At last the prophet declared that the angel had pronounced the work done. And the community ceased from its labours, and eagerly expected something to happen. But nothing did happen: and still the community waited.

And then from the other end of the States there came a woman, a member of the same sect, who claimed to be a prophetess of the Machine Messiah. And she said that nothing could possibly happen until It had been formally born of a woman, and she was the woman. And it was arranged that she should be shut into the shed with It all night. And in the morning the community gathered around the shed, and the Prophet opened the door, and the Prophetess came out and announced that the Messiah was now formally born. And still nothing happened: but the community did not lose faith.

And then another Prophet arose, who said: "This Messiah cannot do His work because He is not in the right place. His right place is as near to the heavens as possible. I have been warned in a dream that we must construct a trolley and haul Him up on to the top of the mountain".

So the community got to work again; and they made a great trolley with wheels, and with vast effort they hoisted the Machine thereon, and hauled it up to the top of the mountain. For this purpose they used neither horses nor mechanical power, but hitched long ropes to the trolley and hauled it with their own hands. It was a high mountain, and they took many days to drag the trolley to the top. And when they had done so the new Prophet had another dream of exactly how the Machine must be adjusted in its new position. And the community still waited: and still nothing happened.

And after a while yet another Prophet arose, and the course of action he proposed was a very drastic change. He had been warned, like all the others, in a dream, that the right procedure had not been hit upon, and, like the others, he had a positive proposal to offer. The Messiah, he said, ought never to have been placed on the top of a mountain: that was altogether a misconception of His nature. He must be in intimate touch with the heart of the earth, and in consequence must be as low down as possible. He knew of a place, in the bottom of a very deep valley some hundreds of miles away, and he had been instructed in a dream by an angel that this was the appointed spot for the Messiah.

So the community hoisted It on to the trolley again and hauled it down the mountain, and with infinite labour and pains they took it long distances across plains and prairies: and then they came to a lake. They waited here for their prophet to dream a dream, and he dreamed that they must take it across the lake. So they constructed a sort of huge raft, and wheeled the trolley on to it – all this took time, and the materials must be brought a long way off – and launched it on the lake, towing it with row-boats. And when they arrived at about the middle of the lake, there came a little flaw of wind and raised a ripple, and their cargo shifted, and the Machine Messiah fell into the bottom of the lake: and, so far as can be ascertained, is there to this day. And the faithful community departed their homes, saying that this must be all right, as It was certainly nearer to the centre of the earth than It had ever been before; and they are still waiting for something to happen.[28]

And then there was another story of a dream – someone else's dream this time, but the name of the dreamer was not recorded. He – the dreamer – was dead, and went to heaven, and at first an angel took him in through resplendent gates and into a vast shining hall: and then he was led by passages growing gradually smaller and less beautiful for a very, very long way. And then he began to notice niches in the walls of the passages, and dim figures standing in the niches. And still the passages grew smaller and less well-lighted, and the angel led him on and on. And the walls were covered with cobwebs, and the whole place looked dismal and deserted.

And at last the angel led him up to a niche in which no figure was standing, and said to him:– "This is your place: step up into it and stand there". So he did as he was told.

He waited two years, and nothing happened: no one passed, and all up and down the length of the passages as far as he could see the figures did not stir in their niches. And at last he grew impatient and leaning forward out of his niche he called to the figure that occupied the next place: "I've been here two years; is this all?" And the figure replied in a deep impressive voice: – "I've been here two thousand years: this is all." And then he woke up.

We told one another all kinds of stories, and talked of all kinds of things, till it was late, and then we went up to bed. I do not remember just where everyone was sleeping at this date, except that I had the east bedroom and he the room opposite the bath-room. Delphis must have been sharing my room, for I remember I was in the habit, especially on these late summer evenings, of going to bed without the gas, so as not to waken her, and this is what I did to-night.

My curtains were open, and the lights in the downstairs window threw long shadows out over the lawn and on to the oak fence. These disappeared one by one as my father turned out the lights. I leaned on the window-sill and looked out at the stars.

Then I heard the spare-room curtains being drawn, and a long ray of light shot out across the lawn; and then on the fence I saw his shadow clearly outlined, – leaning on the window-sill, like me, to look out at the night.

He stayed there a while, and then the shadow moved away, and I left the window and undressed.

In the morning, after we had idled about the garden for a little, I took him up to the attic and began showing him drawings and other things. There was one drawing representing a young girl riding out of a light place into a crowd of devils and darkness, and a young winged figure of rather the type of a classical Greek Eros turning away weeping into the light place. I am not quite clear now as to the exact symbolism of it, but I remember putting into the drawing of it all the passion and power I had at command.

He looked at it meditatively a long time, and then said: – "Yes; life is like that."

And I said: "Not always; it only seems like that sometimes." And he said: "It's always rather like that."

And I said: "Don't be so pessimistic."

And then we went into the west end attic, and leaned out of the north window and looked at the view, and he told me about when he had been somewhere up-country in Germany, and had heard a lot of people singing in the evening; and as they were a simple and religious people, and the general atmosphere of the place rather suggestive of the sabbath, he somehow assumed they were singing a hymn. But, again, there was something about their singing that seemed a trifle unlike the heavy pomposity of the average church hymn; it more called to mind some kind of a revivalist song. And there was in it a kind of sentimental flavour like "Home, sweet home." And he began to wonder what the words were, and came to the conclusion that they must be something like "Going home to Heaven." – No; on second thoughts, "Heaven" had not quite the ring of it; it might be something more like "Godville". Yes; that was absolutely it; "Going home to Godville." And he was rather disappointed when, later, he saw the very tune in a book, and heard someone sing it to a piano, and the words were nothing but about a rose in a hedge or something. It seemed all wrong, and after his taking so much trouble to catch the exact spirit of the thing, too.

And then we came out of the window, and I said: "Let me try and draw you." So I got out a sort of cushion and put it on the floor for him to sit on, and leaned a big drawing-board against a rafter for a back to the seat; and meanwhile he poked round and discovered a rough frieze I had begun to paint under the window-sill. It was in deep, rich colours, and represented a torchlight procession against a dark sunset; an old white-bearded man in a black cloak, a Knight on a black horse, a lady on a white horse, and certain page-boys and torch-bearers – and this he liked tremendously and looked at a long time. I had fallen out of love with it because it had not worked out exactly as I wanted it to; things never do! But after this praise I was encouraged and went on with it. But the surface was so rough that I never really finished it. One of these days I will, perhaps.[29]

Then he sat on the cushion and I began to draw him. He took out of his pocket a little book he had brought up with him from downstairs – A. E. Housman's poems –[30] and read a few things to me. The drawings were not altogether successful; At first I could not get a likeness to him, but the drawing would persist in looking like Margaret Radford. I said so, and he said "I should'nt mind: I should feel rather complimented." I went on drawing, but got on no better: and at last I got rather cross over it, and then had an interval during which I did not try to draw, but listened to him reading poems. He read "The quietest places under the sun", till the tears stood in my eyes: his voice was such an exquisite instrument, and his feeling for the poetry so exact: I have never heard anyone read as he read. He read "When I was one-and-twenty", and "Are the horses ploughing", and a lot of other things. And then I tried again at the drawing, but with not much better success.

And then we came out of the attic, and he and Daddy and I went a walk up to the Edge, otherwise known as Colley Hill [19]; and as we came back again we found a plant of white heather on the common. And we sat on a heathery bank and amused ourselves by watching the species golfer disporting itself on the Walton Heath links. There was one particularly fine specimen, in a loud mustardy tweed, that delighted our hearts by his perfect truth to the conventional type as displayed in comic papers.

In the early afternoon he and I went off to the hammocks. We lay silent for a while, looking up into the leaves, and then he said: — "I've rather a difficult thing to do, and I don't much want to do it. I've got to write to a man; his son was a friend of mine, and he's dead…That sort of thing: it reminds one — Did you ever read a story, a story of allegory, — all the people are walking along on ice, and one by one they fall through, and the others go on without them…But I've got to write this letter."[31]

"Would you like me to get you a pen and paper?" said I.

"Don't bother," said he.

"No bother," said I, and went and brought him writing materials. I got into the other hammock, and lay and watched him. He did not seem to mind: one of the pleasantest things about our relations with one another was that we were never embarrassed in one another's presence. He wrote calmly, without hurry, sometimes waiting a long time, pen poised, looking at the tree the hammock hung on.

I heard a click at the front gate. "Aunty," I said, and bounded out of my hammock. He turned slowly to me, and said: — "I never saw anything so quick! I didn't know one could get out of a hammock like that!"

I slipped quickly to the gate, met my aunt, engaged her in talk so that she did not notice him as we passed near the hammocks, and took her into the house.

Later on we had tea. He came in, carrying the writing things and his letter, and was introduced. He said very little, and when my aunt was going away she said to my mother: — "That certainly is an extraordinarily shy young man: he hardly said a word the whole time I was here!"

After my aunt was gone, when the sun was setting low and the evening cool, I suggested that he and I should go for a walk. "Where'll you go?" said my mother.

"Oh, Headley way," said I: and then, to him, "that is, if you'd like that?"

"I don't know," said he, "what 'Headley way' may be: but I should think anywhere would be nice on an evening like this."

"Be in to dinner at half-past-seven," said my mother, and we started.

Headley way is a beautiful way [21]. The path alternates between being a green tunnel between spreading hedges, their roots set about with an amazing profusion of flowers, and a track along the side of broad undulating fields of corn and clover with views extending over hills and woods to the farthest horizon. Later it becomes a dignified wide bridle-road between high woods of oak.

We walked along this path till we came to where a tremendous beech tree spreads its lower branches right over the path and the ground dips away suddenly, allowing a view of a foreground of steep fields and a further distance of woods, crowned by the solid little spire of Headley Church. The sky was all golden and rose-coloured, with vast towering clouds that sailed majestically in huge spaces. The woods were bluish with evening mist, and the valley at our feet lay in deep shadow. We sat down on the ground in the middle of the path and watched the scene before us. Then, so lucky were we, the Headley bells began to ring for evening service. They are not like ordinary bells: there is something silvery and ethereal about their timbre, and they ring a wild, irregular cadence in a minor key, that is more like the notes of certain Irish Keens than any other I know of. They mix wonderfully well with the songs of thrushes and nightingales and the hoarse call of pheasants. There was, moreover, a light breeze that stirred the leaves over our heads to a rustle which occasionally drowned the ringing of the bells.

This unearthly fitful music, ringing piercingly sweet in the clear air, and the great pageantry of sky in the west, held us mute a long time. A mouse came out of its hole, looked at us, bustled about a little among the roots of the tree, and vanished again. There was a little distant squeaking and fluttering of birds that quarrelled as they went to bed. The sound of the bells ceased, – it did not noticeably stop, but one listened and did not find it any more. The west sobered down a little: the wood and the spire were silhouetted solid and dark against the sky.

I turned to him. "We'd better be getting home again," said I. "If we're to be in by half-past-seven."

He got up: so did I, and we went back by the way we came, through the gathered shadows. Where the path is a little uneven and winds around the roots of trees he caught his foot in a gnarled bit of root that stuck up. I involuntarily put out my hand to save him: but he had already saved himself, and we both laughed.

We were not in by half-past-seven. But no one minded.

"Well, where did you go?" said my mother.

"Oh, Headley way," said I.

That evening he addressed me by my Christian name before my parents: it was the first time he had addressed me by it at all.

Truly life was very wonderful: I went about wondering if it were real, or whether I had stepped into some amazing fairyland. One night I leaned out of my window late at night to look at the stars and the dark trees, and let my dreams have space to expand into the skies. It was perfectly still, and I stayed there a long while. Then there came a sound – or was it a sound? So faint and far-off I could not be quite sure I was imagining it: it was like some music from another world. But, dim as it was, it was definite enough for me to notice the sequence of its intervals, and I forthwith got a pencil and paper and noted it down. Having done this, I went to the window again and leaned out, in case I might hear some more; but all was still. Then I thought I heard something moving near the house, and on looking carefully I saw a little dark object moving slowly along the edge of the grass under the lee of the terrace. I crept downstairs and out of the dining-room sliding door to look at it. It was no illusion; it was only a hedgehog. I stole in again and went to bed.

Next day we went to the Queen's Hall to a promenade concert. I had the habit I have mentioned before of searching feverishly among any large number of people in the hope of seeing R: I did so that evening, and found a possible candidate in the seats up behind the orchestra which were only occupied when there is a full house. But the atmosphere, charged as it was with the smoke of innumerable cigarettes, was not transparent enough for me to be at all sure about the matter.

The piece de resistance of the evening was Beethoven's Fourth Symphony, which was due to begin just after the interval. The conductor climbed into his stand and rapped with his baton, and a great hush fell in the hall. Then the first notes of the Symphony quietly stole in upon the silence: and they were note for note the same as what I had jotted down on a bit of paper while leaning out of my window. I have no explanation to offer for this. It was all of a piece with the magical atmosphere in which I was living at this time. No supernatural occurrence would have surprised me, because real life was all too impossible to be true.

Farm Corner,
Tadworth,
Surrey.

<u>Sep</u>. 26. [1912]

Dear Rupert

I am suffering under a vague wish to write to you, which is somewhat marred by the fact that I have'nt really anything definite to say.

In real life, one could go round and call on a person, and not say anything; but it would look silly to post a sheet of blank paper, even if one had stared it full of unsaid remarks. – Did you ever see Maitland Radford write a letter? He gives the task a vast deal of time and thought, and when he's finished it's very short. I was reminded because I'd just been staring ineffectually at this piece of paper even as he does at all his letters.

I've been trying to paint the portrait of a mare and foal; that meant following them about for hours in a field. I only came away because it was time to come home. They were very good company.

This night there's a wonderful full moon, and it seems a fearful shame to stay in bed. Yet there seems no object in not doing so.

Last Sunday I went off alone up to that place we took you to at the edge of the hill, and on getting there I was confronted with this:

it was somewhat of a shock, as I had always regarded that spot as more or less sacred: entirely not subject to the ordinary house-agent's evil machinations. I think it's high time to clear out of Surrey, really.

Delphis is muttering in her sleep: I'm afraid I'd better put out the light now, or it'll wake her up.

<u>Friday</u>. The aforesaid site is already bought: it is said, by an American.[32]

– I have come to the conclusion that perhaps after all life is rather like a valley full of devils. It is, by fits and starts: and whichever section one's in I suppose seems the predominant: like "But I am two-and twenty,
     And oh! tis true, tis true."
I shall be in a few days: and then we shall see.

I'm afraid the last post will go out in a few minutes now, and if I don't finish this up now I shall unmake my mind up – or make it down again – about writing this, and that will be labour lost, and a pity,
     So here goes.

By the way since you left I've discovered a whole lot of things I might have showed you. In particular, a silly face on the end of a house just near ours: and possibly some excursions of mine into verse. The latter with a view of calling forth criticism. I've no idea if they're good or bad myself.

     Yours ever
          Phyllis Gardner.

[Postcard addressed to Mrs Gardner.
Postmarked: Rugby, 2.30, September 27 1912]

                                                            24 Bilton Road
                                                                 Rugby

Sept 27 1912

I did go to Queen's Hall a week ago: but I couldn't see you all. And I soon got so wedged I couldn't seek. Alas!

It was very nice at Tadworth. Very many thanks for having me.

     Yours
          Rupert Brooke

                                                            24 Bilton Road
                                                                 Rugby

October 4–5 1912

Dear Phyllis

It's a good idea of yours – sending a blank, stared-on sheet of paper to someone, corresponding to a silent visit. I intend to put it into practice one day.

I gather you're twenty-two, just about now. A very fine and careless and beautiful age, I do faintly remember. I put off writing to you, for I've been meaning all this week to write a poem or two: and I thought as soon as I'd finished one, I'd send it to you as a birthday gift, of consolation. But the muse has stuck, horribly: so I write this unadorned metreless letter. If I do finish anything in the near future, I'll send it you – if you're interested in poetry.

I've been at home now nearly a fortnight: so today I'm off again on my wanderings. I do feel restless. When are you going to start for the West of America? Wire; and I'll join you in steerage! It's horrible – but nice, – wandering discontentedly and inquisitively looking for – one scarcely knows – round England and Scotland and France and Germany. But I shall continue doing so, I suppose. And, damn it, I've such a lot of work to do: – it's filthy having to do it in trains. I'm off to Sussex now for two days: then a day in London: then Cambridge: then Berlin: then...

I'd like to know if you're ever accessible in London. You implied you went up in the morning and came back in the evening. But I suppose you're liable to feed there, sometimes. Supposing I was suddenly dashing through London and wanted to implore you to have tea with me, – what should I do?

I'm glad you've come round to the devil view of life. Why?

It's so late at night: or early in the morning.

    Farewell, Rupert Brooke

        Please thank your mother for her letter.

TWO

'ALL NAKED,
FAIR TO FAIR'

A key person in Brooke's life at this time was Edward Marsh, who provided him with a means of escape from his old life. Marsh was a valuable patron to have; he moved among the most powerful and influential in society and politics and had, through his love of culture, collected about him talented figures from all fields of the arts. In addition, Marsh was happy to share his apartment at Gray's Inn with Brooke. This gave him an excellent base in London, with all his comforts tended to by Marsh's housekeeper, Mrs Elgy. It did not take long for Brooke, with his great good looks, intellect, charm and promise as a poet, to be eagerly welcomed by those in Marsh's world.

Over these last few weeks Brooke and Edward Marsh had come up with an idea to publish a book of modern poetry showcasing up-and-coming poets. A luncheon was organised in Marsh's apartment at Gray's Inn and a selection of those to be included were invited. Among them were the young northern poet Wilfrid Gibson, whom Rupert had only just met, John Drinkwater and Harold Monro, not only a poet but also the editor of the *Poetry Review* and proposed publisher of this new venture. Monro was also accompanied by Arundel del Re, who worked with him as sub-editor of the *Review*. Marsh decided this new volume would be entitled *Georgian Poetry 1911–1912*.

He had written to say he should be in town soon, staying for a few days; and, on the chance of meeting him, I had asked him, if he were free on a certain day, to wire to me and I would meet him. I did not much expect he would wire. I was going to the Rhyses for the week-end, and suggested that if he wired during the week-end their address would find me. This was silly of me. It never occurred to me that Mrs Rhys would think I was having my private telegrams sent to her house because I was up to some devilment that I was ashamed to let them know about at home. It also only half occurred to me that he would take me at my word and wire me at the Rhyses.

On Monday morning, before starting to go home, I went for a walk round the Garden Suburb with B[rian].R[hys]. As a matter of fact I had told him I might possibly have a telegram, only we prolonged our walk till it was almost time for me to go off by tube if I was to be in time to meet mother at the promised time. We had not started out till 11 a.m., and I did not think it worthwhile going back to the house, considering it was not quite noon yet, for a possibly non-existent telegram. I did not know Mrs Rhys. I saved about ten minutes that I should have had to spend if I had gone back to the house, caught the tube, and met my mother. We passed the National Gallery, and she suggested that we should go in: I forgot now what deterred us; I wish we had.

Next day, by the morning post, a letter came from Mrs Rhys, enclosing two telegrams. One was the one I had wanted; it had made the suggestion that I should meet R. at 12 noon in the National Gallery.

[Telegram sent from High Holborn Office]
Oct 6 1912
TO Phyllis Gardner 48 West Heath Drive Hampstead
Meet National Gallery 2.45. [*sic*] Rupert
care of Marsh 5 Raymond Buildings Grays Inn

I felt wild to think how nearly I had kept that appointment. The other was, and still is, a mystery. I do not know the name of the sender, and cannot remember what the gist of the telegram was.

This I posted back to Mrs Rhys. I was extremely vexed about the first. I thought she might, had she been really well-disposed, have posted it a little sooner, I thought. I don't know, though; it is possible she posted it with reasonable expedition. But we are on the telephone, and it would only have cost her twopence and a trifling effort to communicate to me the contents of the telegrams, both of which she had opened. But "that's all shove be'ind me, long ago an' fur away".

My mother and I took counsel what was to be done. I had the address he was staying at in London: it was on the telephone: we rang up, and it was arranged that I should go there and meet him. I consulted a map hurriedly, and set off by the next train to town. I found the place, and went up three pairs of stone stairs to a landing with a window looking out over trees and chimneypots. I rang, and was let in by a stoutish motherly housekeeper,[1] and shown at first into a biggish room with a view into that green place that has one side abutting on Theobald's Road. Then he came and brought me upstairs to another smaller room with the same view, where he and Eddie Marsh were having breakfast. It was latish, for breakfast, but Eddie was in a Government Office in peace-time, and R[upert]. was not by way of doing anything special at the moment.

I never saw a worse-assorted pair. To this day, I cannot think how they managed to exist together at all; R[upert]. with his wild golden hair and keen blue eyes and habit of going about in grey flannels and soft collars: Eddie with his man-of-the-world face and manners and his evident preoccupation with things of this life. They seemed to look upon one another with a sort of friendly amused toleration.

I had a squarish wooden paint-box of the kind habitual with art-students. Eddie said: "This is informal; but that," (pointing to my paint-box) "is a sort of passport." R[upert]. never gave a damn whether it was conventional or not, neither did I: but if Eddie was pleased to take my paint-box as a symbol of respectability, we were equally willing to let him do so.

The talk drifted on to contemporary art. They mentioned

some show then on in London,[2] and the work of one of the rising
geniuses of the hour: and R[upert]. said: "But surely one of his
things had to be removed to the basement or something?"

"Oh, why?" said I.

"It was supposed to be shocking", said Eddie.

"It could'nt be much more shocking," said I, "than some of the
things that do get hung".

R[upert]. took my meaning at once. "They may offend you as
an artist", he said, "but this one would offend you as a moralist. It
really was, rather, – for a public exhibition!"

Memory is a fickle thing. I remember excellently well the electric heater, made of two upright objects the shape of sausages in a
little iron and copper stove; but I am blest if I can remember how
I got away from the flat, or anything more at all about that day. I
suppose, from my having my paint-box with me, that I must have
at least intended to go to the art school. I very likely did go on
there after my visit to the flat: in fact I am almost sure I did. –Yes;
I remember that I came up in the train with my father, and he was
rather surprised at my getting out at Cannon Street, which was
not my usual route: but he was reassured when I said I was going
to see someone, and my mother knew about it. And the rest of
the day, I suppose, I drew a horse under the supervision of Frank
Calderon; and I am sure my mind had to be forcibly recalled to
the matter in hand. And when I went out in the street I looked and
looked at people, for fear I should miss a chance of seeing him,
were it only for a second as he flashed past in the other direction.
As he was large and conspicuous, and in addition had a habit of
going about in a Colonial hat that was rather unusual in peace-
time, it was not perhaps an altogether hopeless task; but, needless
to say, I hardly ever saw him unless I had actually arranged to
meet him. All the same, this fact did not deter me from a sort of
continual eager search for him wherever I went.

Phyllis was perhaps unaware that London was not Rupert's main haunt,
although he was spending increasingly more time in the city. The place
he considered home was his lodgings in Grantchester.

It must have already become apparent to Rupert that Phyllis's parents did not enforce the expected Edwardian practice of chaperoning their daughter while she was in the company of a young man, something not so very unusual to him in the light of the other females in his set, but he had yet to establish just how broad-minded Phyllis was in her views. Eager to see Rupert's rural retreat, Phyllis took the first opportunity she got to visit him in Grantchester, where she too, soon fell under the 'Neo-Pagan' spell.

A little while after this my mother and I were spending the week-end in Cambridge. He had asked me out to tea at the Old Vicarage on Saturday.

The Old Vicarage
Grantchester
Cambridge

Tuesday

This is nice: though I wish I'd known sooner. See here. Thursday's no good anyway.

Friday, I'm engaged 4.15 – 7.0 pm: also probably at lunch. Saturday I'm engaged 4.15 onwards.

In addition, I may have a poet staying with me all the while.[3] But he can be shunted.

Well: if you're here come out on Friday morning and discuss plans. (Or Friday at 3, less good). I'd like you to come out on Friday or Sunday evening for supper, if that's possible. But anyhow come on Friday morning and arrange. I'll keep Sunday open-

It's easy to find. Bicycle from Cambridge Barton Road through Grantchester. I'm the last house but one before the bridge

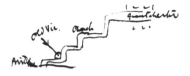

Come round the house, and I'm sitting on the lawn.
Say when and tell me your address.
I'm glad you're coming.
The post! Damn!
    R.B
I'll write again, when I hear

Cambridge

17 October 1912

Come before or directly after lunch on Saturday (I can't come to lunch, I've a poet with me).[4] It's ten minutes bicycle ride. Then we'll fix plans.

Don't, if you value your life, mention my name to Lady Mary.[5]

R.B

The Old Vicarage

Friday [1912]

Dear Phyllis,

I wrote my postcard rather hurriedly: – and perhaps this won't get to you. I hope to see you as soon after lunch on Saturday, as you can manage.

I am not doing anything special on Sunday. I shall have to look after my poet part of the time – and work! But you can decide when you'd like to appear here. The afternoon's lovely: but on Sunday afternoon's there's always the chance of a lot of people dropping in to tea. Which'd interfere with my showing you round my lovely grounds, and the neighbourhood. You could have supper with us – if you don't mind country food. It's infinitely romantic here at night. (But I will not meet you at 6.a.m. – your usual habit).

Will your mother be able to get in on bicycle and accompany you out here, anytime?

– Rupert

I got a bicycle and rode out to Grantchester: he had provided me with a little plan, but it was a foolish and inadequate little plan, because it misled me. I have it still, and it does not really state the facts of the case. On a postcard I had received a few days earlier, he had said: – "Come round the house: I'm sitting on the lawn." I found a house corresponding roughly to the position indicated on the plan, and went round it: but it wasn't the right kind of house, nor was there the right kind of lawn at the back. I walked boldly up to a French window, and looked in at it: no, the furniture too was all wrong. I gave it up. Luckily, no one was about in that house, or they would certainly have wondered what I was doing. I went out into the road again: there, too, no one seemed to be about, but at last an old man came along, and I asked him where the Old Vicarage was. He directed me to a much more likely-looking house. I leaned my bicycle against the ivied porch, and went round the house as directed. The garden was rather dank and deserted-looking: the grass on the lawn was not too recently mown, and was full of autumn leaves. In the middle of the lawn was a very peculiar sun-dial, in the form of a great open book with leaves half rolled in, the shadows of the corners of which indicated the time by falling on brass figures let into the stone of the pages. The house itself was a low structure almost entirely covered with ivy. A French window led straight in, on a level with the grass, to a room with a table in it, and books and papers scattered all over the floor.

He suddenly appeared within this room, and called me in. "Let's go for a walk," he said. "Let's go up to Byron's Pool." So we started off. We passed the weir of the mill, and stood and looked at the swirling and bubbling water. "I'd give you sixpence," he said, "to jump in there." "I'd like to," said I, "but you'd have to give me a bigger bribe than sixpence. The price of a new suit of clothes –"

So presently we went on along the Trumpington road. We were both hatless, he in a blue shirt open at the neck and white flannel trousers, I in a kind of blue-green muslin frock. It must have been warm for the time of year – late September – and the sun was shining. We went over a stile and up a field to Byron's Pool, and stood on the flood-gate that crosses the river just above it. He said: – "A man I knew once wanted to know what it felt like to shoot the rapids, and he did it here: and that wooden thing under the water is all full of little nails or something, so that when he came out again he was all covered with little longitudinal scratches. It was rather pretty, like some sort of a pattern: and it didn't hurt him much!"

And, having looked at the water a while, we turned back and walked downstream. And he told me about another friend of his, who had come out to sleep in the open in this field, under the impression that he was all alone and safe from intrusion: and he had been awakened in the very early morning by being licked in the face by a cow, which he did not appreciate.

"I should have thought," said he, "that it wasn't an unpleasant feeling really; and anyhow, it's nice and friendly!"

I have a certain uncle and aunt in Cambridge.[6] In a way they are very conventional people, and in any case they (particularly she) are critical. I had not told them of my intended visit to Cambridge, nor had we yet revealed our presence to them; because, had we done so, my every movement would have been enquired into, – and all meant in kindness. Also I knew that R[upert]. was certain to be in her black books, because he was in with an "advanced" set, who had wild theories, and that they would very likely do all they could to head us off him. In consequence I was not very keen on meeting them just at this minute.

We were just going along the open bit of road in the Grantchester direction from Trumpington when I was aware of a rather unwelcome appearance. My uncle is one of the very few people in this country who affect a tricycle, and he had chosen this fine afternoon to do what is known as "the Grantchester grind"; and his portly figure now came in sight round the corner of the wood, mounted on the tricycle, and proceeding at an exasperatingly sober pace. I wished I could dive into a ditch, or that my hair would suddenly change its all too conspicuous colour, or even that I had had a hat on; but all to no avail. He had to pass us. There were hedges and ditches on each side of the road. He was coming behind us, so I could with some show of probability appear to fail to see him; and this is the course I pursued. I do not know to this day what he thought. He cannot have missed recognising me. It is possible he kept the matter to himself; it is probable that, had he not done so, I should have heard more of it. I do not know if his code of honour includes the not giving away of the doings of nieces-by-marriage.

He being safely past, we went on to Grantchester without further incident. I mentioned that my mother was in Cambridge, and he asked me to ask her.

When we got in, Wilfrid Wilson Gibson was there. He came and looked at the sundial with us, but did not say very much. He was rather ill, and R[upert]. had been kind to him, he being down on his luck, and, I inferred, not in funds.[7] He explained that he was going away on a holiday for his health, and I suspected

R[upert]. of having contributed financially to that holiday. We began talking about various people: there was a young man by the name of Iolo Williams[8] among the coming poets, but R[upert]. said he had no sense of humour, and as an example of what he meant he quoted a poem in which the line occurred "My thoughts are like dim flies". "–He might have seen, if he'd any sense of humour," said R[upert]., "that one couldn't help thinking that what he really meant was that his thoughts were like damned fleas!"

Later, in a poem dedicated to Brooke, Wilfrid Gibson recalled these days at the Old Vicarage:

October chestnuts showered their perishing gold
   Over us as beside the stream we lay
   In the Old Vicarage garden that blue day,
Talking of verse and all the manifold
Delight a little net of words may hold,
   While in the sunlight water-voles at play
   Dived under a trailing crimson bramble-spray,
And walnuts thudded ripe on soft black mould.[9]

After tea I said I'd better be getting back. "Gibson can't bicycle," said R[upert]. "I suppose that's because he comes from the Midlands or something. Are you prepared to take your bicycle along the field path? He and I have both got to be in Cambridge this afternoon, and we might as well all go together."

So we all started off by the field path. We came to a stile. I am fairly used to negotiating all kinds of obstacles with a bicycle, and was picking it up with the intention of lifting it over, when R[upert]. said: – "Do you know this way of doing it?" – took the bicycle, did something like an arm-exercise which ended with it over his head, got over the stile holding it aloft, and deposited it gently on the ground the other side.

"It looks very nice," said I, "but I don't think my arms are equal to it."

"It's a knack," he said. "You'd soon pick it up." And we went on.

And then he began to quote: – "Why do you walk in the fields in gloves?"[10] because we met a very obtrusively gloved lady.

And then we came to Cambridge, entering it via Silver Street; and Gibson wheeled my bicycle, and he and it were very nearly crushed against the wall by a passing cart. And at the corner of King's Parade we all took our leave of one another for the moment.

On Sunday afternoon my mother and I went out to Grant-chester on bicycles, and rang quite properly at the front door of the Old Vicarage. He let us in himself, and led us to the room with the French window. I don't know whether he thought he had tidied it to receive company; there were less books and papers on the floor, and more on the sofa.

Gibson was there. We sat round the table and had tea, and my mother said we'd been to King's in the morning, and described the way the sermon had re-echoed round the vaults of the roof so that no-one could hear a word the preacher was saying: and yet, she said, "One couldn't help thinking one's own thoughts."

"Uncle is like that," said R[upert]., thoughtfully.

And then he told us about an interview he had had with his uncle. The uncle, it appears, had sent for R[upert]. with the intention of giving him something like what school children call a "pi-jaw" on the subject of his atheistic views and companions; and all that happened was that the uncle had shifted from one foot to the other and back again, and said: – "Well, you see – first there's a wave of religion, and then there's a wave of agnosticism. And then there's a wave of religion again." We laughed: we felt how the feeble conservatism of "Uncle" had been entirely unable to cope with this strong and brilliant creature – how the rightness of his own most cherished views had seemed doubtful in the presence of this rushing whirlwind; and also, how unable he had been to say anything that might hurt R[upert]'s hypersensitive nature.

Both Phyllis and Rupert contended with the unwelcome attention of their relatives who were part of the academic world in Cambridge. Ever since Rupert's arrival at King's, he had resented his uncle, the Rev Alan England Brooke, being the Dean – especially as Rupert, flying in the face of family tradition, was an ardent atheist. He had been taken to task on a number of occasions for his neglect of religious devotion, which was brought plainly to Uncle Alan's attention by his nephew never turning up for Chapel. After one such altercation Rupert vented his frustration in a sprightly written sonnet which was published – anonymously – in *The Cambridge Review*. It contained just enough biographical alterations to hide his identity:

Sonnet: in time of Revolt
The thing must End. I am no Boy! I A M
    No Boy!! Being twenty-one. Uncle, you make
    A great mistake, a very great mistake,
In chiding me for letting slip a 'Damn!'
What's more, you called me 'Mother's one ewe lamb,'
    Bade me 'refrain from swearing – for *her* sake –
    Till I'm grown up' ... – By God! I think you take
Too much upon you, Uncle William!

You say I am your brother's only son.
I know it. And, 'What of it?' I reply.
My heart's resolvéd. *Something must be done.*
So shall I curb, so battle, so suppress
This too avuncular officiousness,
Intolerable consanguinity.[11]

Then Gibson got up and said he must be going to catch his train: and my mother got up too, and said there were people in Cambridge she must go and see, but that there was no need for me to come yet. So I stayed.

And first of all we wandered round the garden, and there was something about it all that reminded me of when I was very little and we used to have a moss-grown bit of garden at Barton, not many miles from this spot: I think it was a certain Wellington pine that brought it all back so vividly to me. Especially in the look of the moss round its roots, it was exactly like our one, that I used to think was the tallest tree in the world, because it was tall enough to look over the top of the house. And I was suddenly reminded of a little song "O little moss, observed by few."[12]

And then we went and saw a little summer-house on the river at the far end of the garden. It was divided in two by a partition, half of it being within the garden and the other half outside it.

"I wish you'd seen this last week," he said: "a friend of mine had done some decoration on the walls. But the youths and maidens of Grantchester use this house to bathe from, and as the picture represented mixed bathing, nude, they didn't consider it decent, and we had to have it taken away. I gather that they wouldn't have minded the mixedness, or the nudity, but the two together were too much for them."

And then I saw a little paper boat the other side of the river, lying up against a little snag in a miniature backwater.

"Do you see that boat?" said he. "There's a prize being offered for the best poem, and Gibson and I were trying to make an augury and find out who was going to win it. We made a paper boat for each person we know who had gone in. Let's see: most of them went off out of sight. Drinkwater, Masefield, Abercrombie, – all that crowd, – went merrily … That poor deserted one over there, do you see? Is Gibson; that other, last of them all, stuck in the reeds, that's me. He and I are nowhere! I wonder who will get it?" (As a matter of fact, I believe Gibson got it.)[13]

Meanwhile the day was wearing on, and the sun had set. It was cloudy, and windy, and nearly dark, and the river was black and full of little dimples. We took off our shoes and stockings and walked about looking for chestnuts among the fallen leaves at the edge. He said it hurt his feet, and sat and watched me: and then said: – "Is it pure fortitude, or do you really not mind?" "I was brought up on a shingle beach," said I.[14] Then he suggested that we should go out, so I put on my shoes and stockings again, and so did he.

We went to Byron's Pool [18] and across the weir and into the wood. The wood was primeval and full of strange things that crawled unseen: and in the little stream through it were snags that looked like alligators. And as we went it seemed to me that we very nearly held hands: and we talked of strange old stories, of how the dead man steered the blind man home, and of the man who feared the sea too much to go on it, and yet loved it too much ever to lose sight of it. And there was a glimmer in the trees that I thought was an opening, and he pointed and said: – "That looks ghostly." And I looked again, and it was a white cow. Past the white cow we went, and out into the open, still by the river; and we kept on under the row of pollard willows by the waterside, sometimes talking, sometimes silent, till we came to the railway bridge. As we went under it, we saw two dark figures moving quickly the other side of the water, and they came clattering across the wood of the bridge and vanished away towards the lights of Grantchester. He said he thought perhaps they had come to murder us. I said I did not think they could see us. "They mayn't be able to see you, in this light," said he, "but my white trousers are rather visible." And we went on till we came to a fallen tree. And he was sad, and sorry because it was fallen, and said he would come and live under it where its roots stuck out in the air. And the heavy shadows lay under his brows as he looked away into the distance, so that he looked like a statue by Scopas.[15]

And we went on, walking and running, into the wind and up the river, till the river bent round at right angles to where we had come.

We were displeased a little: there was no way across. But we turned and went up this river. And we came to a place that was all pollard willows, and a notice that trespassers would be prosecuted: and still we went to cross, and could not. And we came to a gate, and sat on it. And he told me of a photograph of a friend of his, standing naked and ready to dive in the top of a pollard willow by the water, like a flower growing out of the old tree. And for a little a little silence fell upon us: and he broke it, saying: – "shall we bathe across?" We hesitated for a little: the field beyond the gate was dull, and the other side was lovely – wreathed in dim moonlight, and the soft wind coming over it: but the water was black and cold, and a little terrifying with swirling maelstroms on a miniature scale drifting down the slow current. However, at last we made up our minds, and very decently and in order we undressed behind separate trees, reappearing naked and each bearing a bundle of clothes. He took both the bundles and waded across, shoulder-deep, and I followed, carrying his boots. But my foot slipped on some mud, and the hand that held the boots was immersed in the water: and as I arrived on the other side, I held up the wet boots, and said: – "Look what I've done!" Will you kill

me?" and he answered: – "Perhaps." And I gave him the boots,
and turned and struck out in the black water: and he stood on
the edge, and said: – "goodness!" And he looked like a beautiful
statue, and I could keep away from him no longer, and came out
of the water beside him: and we ran and raced across the great
meadows, and in trying to catch me he knocked me over: and then
we came back to our clothes and sat by the water. And he offered
to dry me with his hair: it was wild and tousled and standing on
end like a mop, and I could see his keen eyes burning under the
shadow of his brows. And I said: – "Do you often do this sort of
thing?" and he answered: – "No." And after a long time he asked
me: – "Do you often do this kind of thing?" and I also answered:
– "No." And I tried to dry him with my hair, but it was still up,
and did not do very well, and he said: – "brown hair's much softer
than red: I had a friend that used to dry me always with his hair
–" "stop a bit!" said I, "till I let it down, and then we'll see." So I
let it down, and began to rub my head up and down his back: and
I understood how an animal that loves you feels when it rubs you
with its head, and I went on rubbing in a kind of ecstasy, while he
said: – "that's beautifully soft." And then we sat quiet for a little,
and suddenly heard a sound like music: and I said: – "What's that?
someone playing on the piano?" and he laughed, and said: – "That
is the good old English Sunday evenings sound of church bells!"
and I listened again, and so it was. "I'd forgotten it was Sunday,"
I said. And then he told me of some friends of his who were
bathing in this river not far from here, and a farmer and his wife
and daughter arrived on the scene in a boat: and the farmer was
highly indignant, and cursed the bathers roundly, saying he did
not know what England was coming to, if a man couldn't safely
take his wife and daughters out in a boat without meeting a lot of
naked savages, and much more to the same effect. And we agreed
that having nothing on was a very desirable and enviable condition, and that people were very silly to discourage it as they did.[16]
And then he crouched down and looked at me, and said: – "Aren't
you afraid?" – One's so primitive –" … I said I was not afraid.
And he seized hold of me by the throat and pressed his thumbs

on my Adam's apple, and laid me back on the grass, and said:
– "Supposing I were to kill you?" And I smiled up at him and
said: – "Supposing you did? Then I should be dead." And I began
to pat him on the shoulder with one hand, while with the other I
mechanically held on to his wrists to keep him from strangling me.
And he said: – "You couldn't resist – much – " But still I kept on
smiling and patting him: I was in a sort of heaven, although once
he made me choke. Then I said: – "How long would it take?" and
he answered: – "Oh, two or three minutes." And then I began
to shiver, and so did he, and we thought we'd better get dressed
again. But we didn't want to, and sat by the water's edge. And he
said to me: – "You are a fool." And I said: – "I can't help it – or
can I?" And after an interval I leaned down across his knee and
said: – "Are you cross with me for being silly?" and he said: – "A
little: … . It isn't fair to yourself, to be so silly." And I said: – "I
trust you." And he answered: – "But it's mad – to trust people."
And he emptied the water out of his boot on to me. And then I lay
down again, and he said: – "I want to see you," and lay me out
flat. And he looked at me, and felt me, and then said in an off-
hand kind of way: – "You've rather a beautiful body." And then
quite suddenly he bent over and kissed me.[17]

And then we got dressed. And we raced along by the river for
a long way, and water-rats plopped and little water-birds skittered
away in half-dozens at our approach. A long, long way we went, and
could not get across: and at the long last we came to the road, and
a bridge, and a milestone. And he lit a match and we looked at the
time, and at the milestone, which said: – "Cambridge I I I I miles."
And then we set off briskly along the road towards Cambridge.
There was no special hurry to cover the "I I I I miles", but as it was
beginning to be damp, and we to be hungry, we went at a good
swinging pace. – "Do you like stout?" he said, suddenly. I had
to admit I didn't know. "There's nothing like it," said he: "except
perhaps a good performance of the 5th Symphony?"

And still the rain fell faster. At length we reached Trumpington.
As we came within call of civilisation I realised how uncivilised I,
at any rate, must look: I had not troubled to do my hair up again,

and the wind had tousled it considerably. He had no hat, and his boots were dripping wet, however, we kept on our way, and hoped not to meet all our most respectable acquaintances.

We came to the great house in Trumpington that has huge wrought iron gates and iron palings facing the road, and we stopped and looked through the bars. It reminded us of the "Mezzotint" in Monty James's Ghost Stories of an Antiquary, and as we were saying so someone within began lighting up the windows. It was all very silent and mysterious-looking. And then, having spent about ten minutes looking through the bars, we went on. There is a place where the road goes by an over-hanging wood that dripped noisily into the road, and he told me about someone who had been murdered there. And later we reached the Old Vicarage.

I do not gather why, or what happened then, but the next thing I remember is that I was sitting on a doorstep of a side door, trying to get my hair under control, and he had gone away in by another door. Then after a while he opened the door outside which I was sitting: it opened straight on to the foot of a stairs, and I went up this, he following: and he lent me a masculine sort of a handleless hairbrush, and with the aid of this and a small mirror and a candle he left me to make myself decent.

And then we were sitting at a table by a fire, in the room opening on to the garden, and I noticed what wonderfully, piercingly blue eyes he had, and the beautiful clean-cut lines of him, and some quality of broad-builtness and fair colouring that somehow reminded me of a lion.

A woman brought us supper (and stout): and he asked her for the orange-coloured kitten, who was duly produced. It seemed preoccupied, though, and stared out eagerly through the French windows that opened on to the lawn, till at last he let it out.

"They get like that," he said. And then: – "Do you know about moths?"

"No," said I.

"They fly into candles," said he. "– Let's shut out the night." He got up and drew the long Venetian-red curtains, picking his way among the untidiness of books and papers that littered the floor. I noticed a photograph of the Demeter of Cnidus on the wall, and one of Rodin's "Penseur".[18]

"Do you know why they fly into candles?" he said.

"No," said I.

"Well: it's only the male moths that do it – the females have a sort of faint radiance: and so, you see – it must be rather like being in love, only much more so; we can't imagine in the least what it's like!"[19]

We were silent for a bit, I trying to think what it must be like. More so? Perhaps. But it takes some imagining. I did not tell what I was thinking. I wonder if he knew.

And then supper was cleared away, and we sat over the fire. The rain outside was pouring, drenching all that damp ghostly house and garden, and making sudden plops and spatterings outside. I suggested after a while that I ought to be going. "You can't possibly go in this," he said. "And yet, I don't quite see how to offer you to stay ... Yes! stay the night! There is another room."

I protested that my mother would probably think I was dead. And at last we rose and came to the door, and I found my bicycle and he lighted the lamp for me – and then suddenly we kissed one another again: and then he looked grave and said: – "—It would be so dreadful if you were hurt in any way ..."

"Don't you worry!" said I. "I shan't be hurt!" And I jumped on the bicycle and rode off in the pouring torrents of rain.

"I shan't be hurt." It kept re-echoing through my mind. I had not so much meant that I should not be hurt: I knew that there were in the circumstances the possibilities of untold and immeasurable pain – but I meant that it was worth it. If he should ever come to love me, I should be more happily placed than can well be imagined; if not, I had a little already of a wild joy that nothing could take from me. The whole world was reeling around me and bright with amazing beautiful colour, like some tremendous soap-bubble: the heavy drops of rain that whacked down upon my waterproof were so many precious jewels, and the sound of their falling a symphony in my ears. I could not believe that real life could be like this.

THREE

'BUILT OF FIRE AND FOR LIBERTY'

Phyllis was not to know that Rupert's fear of hurting her stemmed from his awareness of the pain he caused in his previous relationship with Ka Cox, the aftermath of which he was still trying to deal with. This probably explains why, following their time together at Grantchester, he exercised caution and waited until Phyllis made the first move.

Uncertain of how things stood between them, Phyllis cautiously took the plunge and wrote an emotional, somewhat distracted letter to him on her return to Tadworth.

Farm Corner
Tadworth

Tuesday [1912]
– It was all rather extraordinary to me: but now I know that in some other things I've been right as far as I can see.

D'you mind a bit of autobiography to explain. I won't write again for a long time in case it bores you but I just want to show that I don't misjudge you.

I went and fell in love. I got it bad. One always does, I suppose. The other person was, according to his lights, as nice to me as he knew how, but his lights were that giving anything much would ultimately cause suffering. Consequently I was very miserable. And I made up my mind that I'd do as I would be done by. So, when Brian[1] turned up, I proceeded to be nice to him according to my lights, and treat him as I had not been treated, and would have liked to have been.

And then we wrote a lot to one another: and a short while ago we began to make the experiment of not writing.

There was no pretence about any of it. I don't believe in pretence where it can be avoided. But some things are very difficult to say. They might hurt. But I've managed to say them. Only there are two schools apparently: and one has it that falling in love is a sort of once-for-all thing, and don't really quite understand when it happens to one again – I wonder if that sort of person might'nt perhaps be treated on the first plan of sheering off definitely at once: it's so difficult to put oneself in the place of a person with quite a different type of mind – suppose I do as I would be done by, and become certain that I'm right in supposing I really would be done so by – and find I've been quite wrong because I assumed all people to be more or less alike? – Is that what you meant when you said you didn't want to cause pain?

You need'nt have been afraid of it. I have a wild and extraordinary joy, and I feel sure I can work a vast deal better.

O Lord! Expression is so difficult?????

Wonder if I've made my meaning evident. Forgive me for trying to do so.

I'm sending you a bit of verse I'm generally too afraid of criticism to show anything in that line – not like Williams and his dim flies – I had it in my sketch book along with the music and c.

I don't want you to answer this: unless you've anything in particular – I mean don't bother about it – only I don't want to be misjudged either –
      Phyllis.

In bed: The Pink and Lilly.
Prince's Risboro'

Thursday [1912] –

I told you, on Sunday, I thought you were fine. You were. But I think so more than ever now, from your letter. I'm very glad you wrote it. I couldn't entirely understand it all – but I think I caught the main drift.

I've a lot to say, I shan't say it all now, I suppose I must sometime.

I feel proud – of both of us. It seems good to have got so swiftly and well down to things that matter – Don't you feel that – the relief at getting through the lumber. Now, though we meet only for a few minutes – and only rarely – we can talk and say things in a way most dull people can't get to in twenty years.

And there's a lot to be said – so we must meet, soon.

Last Sunday's a memory! It stands out so. Don't you find that? It's unlike everything.

Oh, I could say such a lot. – Tell me, can I write with utter safety to you? Will you, I mean, destroy or lock up in the ironest of unopenable boxes, my letters? If I know that I can write my mind…

I may be in London next week; I'll let you know. We could talk.

I think I see you do understand. It'll be good to understand each other. That's ever the foundation for building fine things. If you already don't misjudge me, I'm glad. I think I don't misjudge you. I had to say that as you rode off, because it seemed so terrible if I should by accident hurt you. I'm glad things are well.

I was surprised by your poem. It was quite extraordinarily better than I expected. It's got a sort of simplicity that's moving. You seem, somehow, to have a knowledge of how to write the stuff. – Things I don't like; ethereal, and some other things. But it's a devilish hard stanza. – I could talk for hours about the poem, in my role as expert. But I'll spare you.

I'm sorry your mother had the bother of coming out in a cab for you – perhaps it was for the best?

Goodnight Phyllis –

Rupert

What hair you've got!

Farm Corner,
Tadworth,
Surrey.

Saturday [1912]

Have just got yours. I am glad to have got it. – As far as safety is concerned you can write anything to me. I have a system of my own of keeping private papers: no one else would possibly see them. (I don't destroy.) So write whatever you have to say in security.

I know "ethereal" was bad, by the way, but it was the nearest I could get. I meant it all seemed unreal and like a sort of soap-bubble. Words are damned tricky customers. They slip round corners so, even in prose.

Yes, Sunday does stand out. So much so that it seems close up while everything else is foggy and distant.

I have'nt known what day of the week it was, because that giant of a day put all the rest out of perspective.

And then I feel to wondering if it could possibly be real: as you say, it's so unlike everything – But perhaps it's the rest that's not real.

Tell me, how did we cut all the things that did'nt matter? For me it started the second I saw you – I knew I would see you again, and I know that we should cut them: that is, I should have been hurt and disappointed if it had'nt happened so.

Partly I think it's this: you have the gift of silence. Unnecessary talk spoils a lot of things.

I mean the sort of talk people make to avoid silence. For silence is a test: it's such a sensitive thing, with such endless gradations, from awkwardness up to perfect harmony, not all acutely perceptible.

There does'nt seem much sense writing if you'll be in town next week. But I don't know: last week was years ago. I don't believe in time by the ordinary computations. For instance, how long does it take to play the 5th symphony? 5 minutes or a year? Time does'nt come into it. It's something like these "eternal moments" of yours.

Town as a rule is a rotten place for talking in. There's a noise, and a whirl, and a lot of conflicting "astral bodies" that don't give one a chance – That Gray's Inn flat was alright though: high up, not shut in, quite…

I must get to work. There are 2 sketch-club subjects to go in on Monday, and the time is wearing on. – I say, shall I ever show you any other of my writings? You were so surprisingly encouraging about that one.

– There is a lot to say. I can't somehow start – not on paper.

I think I'm a coward on paper, of a brand that I'm not usually off it. Things written are so irrevocable and you can't see the other person taking them and alter accordingly as you can with speech.

I've been horribly afraid 2 or 3 times lately: once, outside the door of Marsh's flat: I came in shaking: don't think you saw – once, outside Aunty's door in Newnham, for fear she'd cross-question me – she did'nt – ; and once, when I'd posted my letter to you. But that's all right. I was afraid I might have said something blundering and spoilt it all–

Joy be with you.
        Phyllis.

Brooke was inspired to write 'Beauty and Beauty' following his moonlit tryst with Phyllis at Grantchester. This poem, and four others of his, was published in *The Poetry Review* in November 1912.[2] All but one gave insight into his life at this time, not only his feelings of bitterness and loss over the affair with Ka Cox, but also the new romance he was enjoying. According to Wilfrid Gibson, who noted 'Rupert is hard at work on new poems',[3] Brooke was in a particularly industrious phase. Gibson was impressed, writing to Marsh that 'I rather marvelled that poems could be written because Monro wanted them, and to catch posts, and telegrams about them being sent off between the verses. It seemed queer – but never having seen poetry being written before, I didn't know – and anyhow from the spectacular point of view it was superb!'[4]

The November edition of *Poetry Review* also contained an article written by Harold Monro, announcing the opening of his new venture, The Poetry Bookshop, on 1 January 1913. Arundel del Re acted as his right-hand man.

Phyllis was not the only woman with whom Brooke would soon be arranging clandestine meetings. Elisabeth van Rysselberghe had recently come to study at the Royal Horticultural College in Swanley, Kent, and he wasted no time in organising a weekend at a hotel with her. Brooke seems to have made no pretence of romance in their relationship. Practical matters dominated: he sent Elisabeth a book on contraception and told her to wear a ring on her wedding finger to help with the pretence of their being a married couple.

Rugby

Tuesday [1912]

Dear Child,
　　I go tomorrow to stay with E Marsh
　　5 Raymond Buildings
　　Grays Inn
Till Saturday, and again Monday–Wednesday. Will you be in London on Thursday or Friday, lunch or after till just before dinner? If not, next week. – So I won't reply to your letter now. Thanks for it, and for the poem – Will talk–
　　Rupert

Grantchester
In bed

Tuesday night. [1912]

　　Well, you strange Phyllis, what I'd wanted to say was this: you are incredibly beautiful when you're naked, and your wonderful hair is blowing about you. Fire runs through me, to think of it.
　　You devil, I remember every inch of you, lying there in that strange light. "Primitive" … did you know what you were saying, child, when you said "Why shouldn't we be primitive, now?"? God, it was a hard struggle in me, half against half, not to be. Sudden depths got moved – But it wouldn't have done. It's fine to be "primitive", in a way: finer than merely a modern person. But there's something finer yet – the best of each – beast and man.
　　Oh, it's difficult writing. But you seem so queerly to understand – and face things. Sometimes I think I know you right through; better than anyone in the world knows you – I'm going up to London tomorrow (Wednesday) evening. I think I shall be staying with Marsh again (5 Raymond Buildings Gray's Inn). If so, I shall be in his room, working, alone, on Thursday. If you were in London you could come at 11.a.m. and we could lunch together and sit there afterwards – or meet at lunch – or anything. I'll leave Thursday open – can you persuade them you are coming up to your drawing?

Friday's less good; because I go away at noon or soon after.
I go for a month next week.

I hope something on Thursday is possible. We can sit and talk. – If I'm not at Marsh's I'll wire my address.

Send a wire or card there, Wednesday evening.

Till Thursday!

Rupert

[Postcard addressed to Rupert Brooke c/o Marsh, Gray's Inn. Postmark: Epsom, 10.15.p.m. 30 October, 1912]

Farm Corner,
Tadworth,
Surrey

Wednesday evening

I'll appear at the flat sometime before lunch – sometime's probably between 12 and 12.30 – Am going to try and ring you up to-night: this card in case I don't get through. I've got a tamasha [show] to go to at Kensington in the evening, and I daresay a tea engagement – we can lunch and spend the afternoon–

P.G

It was a few weeks later when I knocked at the door of the flat. He opened it himself: he was alone for the afternoon. He showed me some poems in proof – "A Night Journey" was one – and we stood one each side of the fireplace, elbows on the mantelpiece. There was a little china plant in a pot there: one of us, I forget which, knocked it over, and the tip was broken off one delicate green leaf. I demanded seccotine urgently, but he said there wasn't any, and gently placed the broken tip in the pot beside the plant.

There was a large armchair. I sat in it. He wandered about aimlessly for a while, and then came and sat on the floor near my feet. And then the next thing I know is that his head was on my knee and I was running my fingers through his hair.

This was a wild minute. It would not be true to say it took me by surprise: after the incident of swimming the Cam nothing would have surprised me – but, for all that, there was a strange gripping of my heart, and the feel of him made my blood run fire.

"You don't know how your touch burns me," I said: and for answer he rose up a little and put his arms round me.

I remember looking up at the ceiling and noticing the electric light, a kind of inverted bowl of encrusted glass in the middle of the ceiling: also I noticed the table in the window, and the zebra-skin under the table. I remember these things in a sort of rainbow whirl – little irrelevant things put in, as it were, to give relief, foreground, contrast, or whatever you like to call it. The chief part of the picture is himself, radiant, beautiful, at once pathetically helpless and full of a wild irresistible driving force. I "didn't know if I were on my head or my heels:" the Cambridge affair might have been an isolated accident, but here was his beautiful silky golden head on my knee to prove the contrary. My hands trembled violently. He lifted his head off my knee and took one of my hands in his. "Your palms sweat," he said. "The Elizabethans said that was a sign of a passionate disposition."

I do not remember exactly how or when I left him. I met my mother by appointment somewhere or other: I found her rather anxious and worried about me. Any strong emotion on my part always has that effect on her. She had half thought I was run over or injured: but understood completely later on, when the facts reached her knowledge. I did not, as far as I remember, tell her anything: she guessed it herself. "Were you hurt?" she said. I said not. "Or nearly an accident or something?" "No." "Has R[upert]. been making love to you, then?" "Yes." And that was all that was said.[5]

I often met him in town these days. Usually we would begin by going out to lunch somewhere and retreating to the flat for the afternoon. I sometimes came to town on purpose, and at other times I cut an afternoon of art-school work to go and see him. He took precedence of everything else in all my thoughts and actions. When I went about town it was always with a desperately eager watching, as I have mentioned before, of all passers-by in the street and in conveyances, in case one of them might be he.[6]

Another day I went to the flat with him. And I do not remember how, or why, but we discovered that we wanted to see one another again with nothing on. So, very decently and in order, we undressed in separate rooms, even as we had before behind separate trees, and then foregathered in the room where we usually sat. He was (how queerly that "was" comes in! I nearly wrote "is") an exceptionally beautiful figure of a man, like some exquisite statue: grand and noble in the general conception, yet with no pains spared in matters of fine detail. He appealed to me as a work of art. And apparently, though with little justification I am no competent judge, he felt the same way about me. He must have idealised me to some extent: I do not pride myself upon possessing delicate ankles, but he complimented me thus: – "You've got nice legs, just like a rather pretty boy – and nice ankles: Most women have such thick ankles!"

We made a heap of cushions in the middle of the floor, and sat on it, and in a mixture of affection and curiosity we gently ran our hands over one another, tracing the outlines of forms. I stroked him all down his back, and he said: – "Do that again – keep on doing it! I wonder why it feels so nice?"

I replied: – "Perhaps because of what it feels like to me."

And the time wore on, and we thought of getting dressed again: but before we did so he picked me right up in his arms like a child, and kissed me. Only I hope no one does pick up a child in exactly that fashion: because he did not support my head, and I thought I should break my neck through it falling off backwards, as he lifted me rather suddenly – However, I said nothing.

I began plaiting my hair to do it up. "A pity you have to do that," he said. "Couldn't you go about with it just like that, I suppose not – But I hope you aren't going to leave hairpins about, because Eddie might find them, and wonder what had been happening!"

"You needn't mind for that," said I: "I've only got four, and they're all structural."

Marsh's flat was now a favourite with Brooke for entertaining his friends. Christopher Hassall later wrote of an anecdote Marsh's housekeeper, Mrs Elgy, enjoyed telling him, although it cannot be certain if the young lady in question was Phyllis:

She used to tell what she had always treasured as a shocking story, about how she was coming down the stairs one day to open the door when Mr. Brooke got there first and a young woman burst in and flung her arms round his neck exclaiming, 'Oh you gorgeous piece of flesh!' Then she went on: 'Fancy greeting a young gentleman like that, and in Mr. Marsh's hall!'[7]

On another occasion I had arranged to meet him at the flat. I went up the three pairs of stairs, and waited on the landing. There was a view out into the mews up Jockey's Fields, as well as up and down past Raymond Buildings. A woman came out of the door of the flat opposite with a little dog. I knocked at Eddie's door, but no-one answered, so I stuck my head out of the window and went on looking out. A postman came along: I saw his top view come in at the door immediately beneath me, and heard his footsteps coming clacking up the stone stairs. When he got to the top he took from his bag a parcel containing apparently a book, and tried vainly to insert it in Eddie's letter-box. I watched him for a while, and then he gave up, and said to me: – "Anybody live 'ere be the name o' Brooke?" " – Should be," said I: "I'm waiting to see him." So on this the postman quite calmly handed over the parcel to me, and clacked away down the stairs again. I felt rather complimented by his trust in a complete stranger, and fell to looking out of the window again.

At last R[upert]. came in sight. He was walking rather dreamily, looking up in the sky, and he did not see me until he was close underneath. Then he waved his hand and quickened his pace a little: and then I heard his step on the stairs, and wondered whether I should have known the sound of his step without having seen him first. And then he came up, and we went in, and I gave him his parcel.

We sat by the fire. I took off my hat and fur, and we were just sitting peaceably chatting when we heard a sound at the door. We looked at one another in alarm.

"Eddie," he said.

Eddie was the last person on earth I wanted to see just then: let alone the fact that we weren't particularly keen on being found in his flat, I hated his eyeglass, his buttoned boots, and his general air of sleek and self-satisfied prosperity: his whole personality jarred on me like the sound of cutting slate with a hack-saw. However, we had to put a good face on it: there was no time to hide, nor anywhere to hide if there had been time: and Eddie was in command of the only way out, which was through the door on to the landing, via a sort of central hall into which all rooms opened. It was Eddie: and he had brought with him a man about whom I had a difficulty in deciding whether I should put him down as a retired colonel or an art-dealer. He had apparently been brought for the purpose of being shown all Eddie's pictures and curios, of which there were a good many.

It was not a pleasant time. We stood one each side of the mantelpiece and looked embarrassed. When the others had gone, we went back to our seats, and I said: – "Well?" meaning "What will Eddie be doing in the way of gossip and backbiting on finding us two here like this?"

"It might have been worse," he answered. "We hadn't got our clothes off!"

[Postcard from Rupert to Phyllis.
Postmarked: Exeter, 9.p.m. 1 November, 1912]
Do you naturally see The Poetry Review? If not, I'll make them send you one –
    Reply to Grantchester.
    R.B.

Farm Corner,
Tadworth,
Surrey.

November 3 [1912]
    Thanks, but I'll get one sent me quicker if I ask for it myself – I tried to ring up Arundel del Re on Saturday, but no one answered. Shall you be in town on Tuesday? Did'nt you say that was the day you went? I have to be in town, and go to the Slade crit at 3.30–
    P.G.

Brooke went to stay in Berlin with Dudley Ward and his wife for over a month, needing to distance himself from all distractions – Phyllis being one of them. He was trying for a second time to win a Fellowship at

King's, but the clock was ticking and time was against him. He needed to complete his Webster dissertation and hand it in before Christmas.

Bei Dudley Ward
Charlottenburg
Berlinerstrasse 100
Berlin.

November 7 [1912]

Dear Phyllis

I didn't get your card till too late to reply. And in London on Tuesday I was too rushed to be able to find you. – I only got there late in the afternoon, and had to fly to the Grafton Gallery to write a notice of the show for a Cambridge paper.[8] Then register luggage, a swift dinner, and off to Folkestone – now I'm ensconced in Berlin: a hideous town, but, for me, quiet. Only two people I know here. I mean to work like anything for a month.

Then I shall see you again–

I'm leaving you, at your direction, to get The Poetry Review. But I copy out here Beauty and Beauty. I told you about it, I write from memory, so it might not be quite the same as the printed version. But I wanted to give it to you–

You might send me out a few others of your verses …

I hope the Slade criticisers were appreciative of you–

Do you think poor Eddie Marsh's room is haunted for him now? I rather figure him stirring uneasily in his chair, with wisps of voices about behind him.

In Berlin everybody's hair is muddy-brown.

You're a fine creature. It's funny, that you should be blown together by the winds, to be like that. One day you'll die.

Write to me. Tell me how you are and how London is …

I shall write you a letter soon.

    Good bye golden one–

      With love Rupert

October 1912

Beauty and Beauty

When Beauty and Beauty meet,
   All naked, fair to fair,
The earth is crying-sweet,
   And scattering-bright the air,
Eddying, dizzing, closing round,
   With soft and drunken laughter,
Veiling all that may befall
   After – after –

Where Beauty and Beauty met,
    Earth's still a-tremble there,
The winds are scented yet,
    And memory-soft the air,
Bosoming, folding glints of light
    And shreds of shadowy laughter,
Not the tears that fill the years
    After – after –
        R.B. [32]

Farm Corner
Tadworth

Nov. 8. [1912]

Bless you – I wanted you to write first, and I'm glad you did.

Thank you for the poem. The Review is'nt out yet, and there does'nt seem any immediate prospect of it, so I'm glad to have it.

– The Slade noticed my picture officially exactly as much as I supposed they would: That is, they did'nt say much about it. But I was encouraged because the Pro said there was skill in the drawing of the horse: and he owned to be puzzled, always a hopeful sign. And Harvard Thomas the sculptor liked it.

But I know I've taken a twin: and it's encouraging to be told it from an unprejudiced source. The other day, quite unprovoked, Calderon was decent enough to say to my mother that I was doing very well and had "The root of the matter in me". I don't know what that means, but praise is sweet.

I want to do well, – partly because I want you to understand. I don't think you did quite understand my work. People don't at first, but the best people do after a bit. I know you're different and ought to understand at once, but the imperfection is doubtless in my unformed expressions.

Also I want to get on in a worldly way and earn money. The question is can I do that consistently with learning step by step in exactly my own way? The buyer expects certain things I suppose: the thing would be to accustom the hanging-committees of exhibitions to some style or other of mine and get a look-in. It's hard.

I'm sending you some verse. Dating them. Tell me without mercy if they are bad, and roughly why: possibly I'm not selecting the right ones.

It's weary work not seeing you. But I dare say a month won't take long. And things take a little while to settle into their places again after that.

Yes, some day I'll die: so will you. But I'd rather not think of it. I'm not afraid for myself. I don't think I'm afraid at all, only puzzled. Why should things be arranged together in the way they are? death, and life too?

– I went up a mountain this summer. And when I reached that which from below I had supposed to be the top, I saw before me another mountain double the size. And from a little higher up, that tower top revealed itself a puny foothill. Even so with people. There are those that I have idealised, caught up, and passed. One discovers by degrees. Nothing to do with falling in or out of love.

I wonder if you're the top, as far as I'm concerned. You look like it. That's a bad metaphor. But I can't find a better one, and it'll do to illustrate my thought if it is'nt too deeply prized into.

And you are so fine: bodily, mentally, spiritually. It's a wonderful thing for you to tell me I'm fine: I can believe it easier from anyone who's demonstrably not so good a specimen as myself.

You're built of fire, and you must be perfectly free. You belong to nobody, as you said. But when all's said I feel as if I too were built of fire and for liberty: if circumstances say the reverse I must acquiesce I suppose outwardly.

But if I were'nt built like that I could have no sort of sympathy with you. Don't you see that?

Oh damn – this is all so hard to put. I can't. I'll wait till you write and see what you say.

Meanwhile, best beloved, blessings be on you: a curse be on any evil thing that dare touch a hair of your head. – I could be an avenging savage for your sake: and I always thought I did'nt understand revenge. There is a saying "every woman is at heart a savage" – every man too I suppose–.

I love the poem. It has a way of ringing through one's head. You're a fine singer. Write soon.

Phyllis

Bei Herrn Ward.
Charlottenburg
Berlinerstrasse 10
Berlin.

November 20? [1912]

I write in bed; late.

Thanks for the poems. I've written some cold impersonal stuff about them on another sheet. I do like them – or rather, the most part of them. Do go on labouring at them, when the fit comes on. I'd like to talk about them: because writing's so lengthy. I want to know how some things seem to you–

I've been working and idling here; rather forlorn. I've been rather distraught – sleeplessness and headaches and things. These things go in waves. One hour I feel as if I could carry the whole world on my little finger. The next, as if I should shoot myself for misery, if anyone said a harsh word to me. Fool. But for the next week or so I'll have to work hard.

Yes: life's arranged badly. But one can mould it. We have, in past: haven't we? But I wish you were independent and studying painting in, say, Munich. I'd rush down and carry you off for a week. A week's eternity. But an afternoon is damned short.

Yes, you're made of fire and made for liberty: you too. To have burnt together is something, – isn't it? I know when I get before God, and am asked what I've got to show for it all, I will begin by saying "Well. I wrote twenty seven books; I was undersecretary of State for India for six years; I was J.P; I managed a theatre; I … " And They'll say "Stuff and nonsense": and then I shall think, and say "There was … this … and that … and one night Phyllis and I were naked and mad and wonderful in a great wind in a far field …." Then they'll respect me, and say "Oh, well, you were worth while"… -

Pooh! I think too much of ultimates. You don't even think about death, you say. Good, Lord! [*sic*] I think about it continually.

But I also think about you. And dazzle to think of your beauty: you naked; we have shown each other wonderful things; and shall show – wonderfuller. What a world! There are joys unimaginable –

The halo about your beauty is strong. It carries across Channel and over Holland, here. I'm in a whirl of golden dazzle when I think of you –

I wish you were here, this moment.

One catches fire, from another.

I'm glad you're whirling about England. – I'd rather you were in Berlin, indeed: but I'm glad you're not nonexistent, I mean.

I put my hands on your cool lovely sides; and my lips to yours, and kiss you goodnight.

Rupert

[Notes by Rupert to accompany the previous letter.]

I'm writing in bed: so pencil's comfortabler –

The poems (I'm keeping them; unless you drag them from me.)

I don't like "A Reawakening". I can't get hold of the metre, happily, these tumtity metres are the devil. (Do you know about metres? I'll explain one day.) And the whole thing doesn't touch me. – I'm only saying I don't like it as it stands. One's always, I know, making experiments, trying at things, starting off … They're useful, only not good. Perhaps this is like that.

"Where flows the start" you also don't bring off (years ago, though!). I like one or two things in it. But it runs not quite well. Rather jig–jog.

"Colley Hill", I like. You seem to understand that metre: which is very rare to do. Remarkable.

"But o what horror have we here" I don't like. It doesn't come off. You blend the two ways of talking – the lighter and seriouser – perfectly, later. But not here. I wonder if you feel that too? It's uneven. I like lines 20–22 fairly, 23 and 24 quite; 25 and 26 less: and then it gets better and better and it seems to me to end really lovely. If you get the whole up to the level of the last couplet it'd be a perfectly beautiful thing. But lines 13–16 (e.g) aren't up to that level. But I like it.

The triolets all right, but not really much worth while. I don't like running <u>straight</u> on to line three.

"<u>Your face was like</u>" I think was interesting but unsuccessful. I'm bothered that lines 5 and 7 in the stanza don't rhyme. (Still more when "<u>one</u>" and "<u>down</u>" <u>do</u> [underlined three times]. Of course, you handle it all rather well. But the expression's a trifle … academic. Not always – .

"Despondency" has an extraordinarily nice movement. It has faults. – I don't like the last two lines of the first verse. – But the last verse is good: and you have got the lilt of the stanza and metre in an amazing way – and contrived to fit the words naturally in. In that sort of metre people either twist the words, and so spoil the movement, besides sounding affected; or they fit the words to the metre and achieve a jingly empty effect. You've somehow got between the two.

The longer poem's very attractive. I can't make up my mind if I like it better than <u>Colley Hill</u> or less well [19]. It's a nice stanza form. I keep liking bits – e.g. the last couplet of the last verse. It has a simplicity in its loveliness … otherwise the beginning's less good than later. Verse 4 I like, and feel that "heartless human jeer" rather mars it. The next page is better. Verses 7 and 8 I like best, and 9.

It's rather good on the whole – the atmosphere.

What keeps surprising me is how capable you are at handling metres, most people are so wooden.

It does look as if you're getting more and more whole poems only of your good lines: and without blemishes or padding. It demands toil. None of these are perfectly so. When one is, it should be very good.[9]

Brooke continued to hammer away at his 'resurged Dissertation'.[10] On his return from Berlin, however, it was still not finished – probably not helped by distractions such as making plans to publicise the launch of *Georgian Poetry*. Brooke therefore holed himself up in his room at King's, working around the clock, in an exhausted state, until his deadline was up. Throughout this time Phyllis longed for them to be together again, and made plans despite her fears that their romance might no longer be a secret.

Bei Herren D Ward
Berlinerstrasse 100
Charlottenburg
Berlin —

Dear Mrs Gardner,

I'm afraid I shall be very disconsolately having a wretched <u>Tee mit Sahne</u> (<u>und kuchen</u>) in the <u>Café des Westens</u> on Friday afternoon. I shan't be in England till the middle of the week after that, at earliest. I'm sorry I can't come to the Ball.

I hope you'll all enjoy the Greek play.[11] It's very kind of you to praise my poems in The Poetry Review. I'm afraid they're a little incondite.

Yours

Rupert Brooke

Farm Corner
Tadworth

Nov. 23. [1912].

I've been working at a bookplate till I'm stiff and stupid: and now know why trees on Greek vases, red-figure, of the best period, are so few and far between. Perfect monument of patience. But a good effect.

When are you coming back?

The time is drawing on.

Look here, when Arundel del Re was down here he was damnably sly about something: we had had a hoax on about an imaginary poet of ours[12] and when we began to own up about that he thought it was something else we were talking about: I don't remember exactly how, but I had a very distinct impression that Eddie Marsh has said something, I could'nt quite gather what, to him – about me.

I suppose it was odd to invade his flat at breakfast: no one could have known about that other time? One has to be so beastly careful – I feel a trifle shy of his flat now. Those things that were going to haunt him – might'nt they have peached?

Would you, could you, come down here for a day or two? Mumma and Daddy go out a goodish deal, we'd probably have the place to ourselves some of the time anyway and I know of some splendid places around, lonely enough, that we could go to, specially on bikes – and no comment would be excited at all. I often take my friends for long walks, or get left in charge here in the evening – I don't know what you think, but it seems to me that that way we'd get more time at the cost, on my part, of less fuss and c, than the other.

You'll be writing about plans? By the way I think not a week-end would be best, there are fewer people about everywhere. They come out like flies on Saturday and Sunday. Also, this place is quite different for us with no Aunty around. You only saw it under her regime, and at a rather unpropitious moment of that.

On a Monday or a Wednesday I could meet you in town. Otherwise I'd have to come up. I could. Oh well, we'll see.

I'm glad you took the view you did about those poems of mine. I think in pretty nearly every case I know what was bad. I mean my judgement coincided with yours. I'll tell you more afterwards. As you say, writing's lengthy.

And it is difficult. Things one could make understood so easily have to be cooked down brutally in writing, or run risk of missing fire altogether.

I've spent another long while staring at this paper.

I was glad to get your letter. There had been just been long enough for me to begin to imagine things of various descriptions, happily untrue – I hope, untrue.

"O I carenae for the love that is written on a caird" – but personally I like to be reassured at intervals of your existence.

I do think about ultimates. I should be an ass if I did'nt. Sometimes, not often, they come on me with a sickening fear. And then I say to them, "Get out, you're not here yet: when I have to worry about you you can come". They don't always go, though.

I wish you were with me. Apart from the mere joy of having you near, there are things I want to discuss with you.

– This world of ours is a very beautiful place. To look at to begin with. I was at Woldingham to-day, playing hockey on top of a very high hill, and all around was strangely beautiful.

And I'll perhaps be seeing you soon. Sometimes I can feel the direction you're in. I can't if I try as a rule.

Lord! When I see you again will the world not suddenly blaze up?

It does'nt do to live in anticipation. It's generally untrue, and exciting in a stupid kind of way.

Sunday morning – They're all in a hurry. All rushing about. I will post this I think.

Bless you. Be back soon.

 Phyllis.

          In the train. Monday

I could'nt find any stamps yesterday – Have re-looked this through – I'm sorry that in my hands words become such dull unmanageable tools. The thoughts are clean enough, but I think they all go off into what I don't write, and the leavings look very disjointed.

The thing is, I don't want to express wrong and also I am a little shy of expressing at all – But at best writing's unsatisfactory.

The only thing is it's a jolly sight better than nothing at all.

King's, (my address) – Tuesday [1912]

I got here on Sunday. I'm working all day and night till Wednesday midnight. Then I stop, I shall be here till Friday. I probably go off for Saturday and Sunday, London Monday or so for a week. Then home, I can see you in, or come from, London?

I'm frightfully busy and tired –

Good luck to you

Rupert

London – Friday – [1912]

allerschouste!

At length I'm clear of that damned stuff: and can think clearly –

I'm in London for the moment. I have to be in Cambridge till Tuesday morning (address King's): in London Tuesday evening, and probably, Thursday evening, but that's not certain.

I go back home about the following Monday –

I can't come down, then, on Monday with you. Can I come on Wednesday dawn? I don't understand about your flat (I think your mother's letter hasn't yet reached me). I could stay till Thursday afternoon. Then I should see you on Friday in London? and Saturday? I don't gather, if you're all living in London continually for a fortnight. – I'm not doing anything for the weekend – but you said that wasn't a good time –

Write to King's and say. My only two engagements are Tuesday 8.30–12. Dispose of any other time as it seems easiest to you. Marsh's flat is at my disposal and empty all day – I shall be staying there. I think Arundel's slyness can be neglected. If I don't come to you on Wednesday; you come to me? Perhaps you'll even be in London Tuesday afternoon and evening –

There. That's fairly clear – for an exhausted brain like mine.

I shall be on a sofa and look at you for seven hours; and then be entirely refreshed again.

Rupert

Farm Corner,
Tadworth,
Surrey

Sunday [1912]

Sorry you did'nt get Mamma's letter: she sent it, I believe, to Grantchester. I suppose you were fearfully busy on Friday. It's annoying to think I was in town on Friday too and might have seen you.

We have taken the flat from Thursday for a fortnight.

We shall be moving in on Thursday, – What time'll you be in town on Tuesday? – Yes, come down on Wednesday any time: I wish, though, that it was'nt going to be all muddly about packing and c: but that ought'nt to matter.

I mean we shall have packed and shall be all ready by then.

We shall be in town for the week-end. It'll be possible to see you then. We can arrange when we meet.

I'll come to town on Tuesday. Tell me when. 5 Raymond Buildings I suppose. And tell me soon, because posts are horribly slow and always letters reach me later than people think they're going to. Better wire.

Now look here. An awful thought has just struck me. Aunty [Alice Gardner] is coming to Tadworth latish on Tuesday and will probably expect us to devote the whole of Wednesday to her. Either I must really go to town – in which case I'd come to you and not trouble Calderon – or if you come down, which I'd infinitely prefer, seeing as how I shan't see country for a whole fortnight, it must be pretended that I've gone to town.

We can develop plans on Tuesday. This Wednesday business depends largely on the weather.

No time now. The post is going. Till Tuesday.

(I say, you could'nt catch the 11.40 p.m down here on Tuesday night by any chance?)

    Phyllis

[Telegram sent from Cambridge,
postmarked: Tadworth, 7.30 pm, 16 December 1912]
TO{ Phyllis Gardner Farm Cnr Tadworth

King's Cross 1.15 or Grays Inn 1.35 tomorrow then lunch super

FOUR

'ACTING ON INSTINCT'

Some time about now he went for a while to Cambridge, and on his return I went to Liverpool Street[1] to meet him. I found the arrival platform, and skulked behind the tall brick pillars to watch the train come in. I went on skulking there till I had taken stock of the people disembarking, because there were people in Cambridge, possibly coming to town, whom I was not keen on meeting, at any rate in company with him: Cambridge is a perfect hotbed of gossip. However, he was on the train, and they were not, so I came out of hiding. We found a taxi, bundled his bags into it, and got in ourselves. As it drove away from the station he placed his hand right over mine, and said: – "Well: it's a long time since I've seen you." And then neither of us said anything for a little while.

The driver was a hustler, not to say reckless: he cut it very fine through traffic, and once when we narrowly escaped a collision I felt a little start in the arm that was resting against mine.

"I wish I didn't jump so," he said. "Since I was ill – this last year or two – my nerves seem all on edge. I'm not a coward – at least, they never used to think I was one when I played football at school!"

"It isn't the people that have nerves that are the cowards." said I.

Not very long ago I happened across a thing he had written to someone else: it was apropos of his experiences during the retreat from Antwerp. It stated that he was glad to find that facts bore out the theory that he would prefer, – that it isn't the highly-strung people who are the cowards. At Antwerp – his first taste of active service – he had found that it was the stockish, unimaginative men who had suffered abjectly from terror. He, in common with other nervous thoroughbreds, had apparently not felt fear, at any rate not that kind of fear, and this was a great relief to him. He had been afraid of being afraid, and was glad to have this bogey dispelled once for all.[2]

My grandfather (who was offered the V.C., but refused it) once said: – "There are two kinds of being afraid: any man is talking nonsense who says he has never felt afraid – but in the one kind you run away, and in the other you don't, that's all."[3]

The taxi journey to Marsh's flat did not take very long. We got out, and I helped him drag the bags up the three pairs of stairs. He had a key, and let himself in; he seemed distraught and bothered. He was either very tired or ill, I am not sure which. I would have given anything to help him, but I didn't know how.

"I'm tired," he said. "You must be kind to me." And he showed me a few poems in proof, and we talked a little. He said he wanted the Poetry Bookshop to take up the matter of publishing "rhyme-sheets." They have since done so, but I do not know whether it was at his instigation. He said he was going to give a reading there. This annoyed me: I had once attended "Evensong" there; (it was really called a reading, but del Re jocularly christened it Evensong, because of the quasi-religious hush that was preserved, and the dim light in the back shop;) and the atmosphere of it seemed to me charged with some poisonous spirit, I know not how to describe it, so that I wanted to get up and knock the whole away, – heave out all the forced "intensity" of the audience, the unhealthy self-consciousness of the reader, and let in a breath of the "free air of heaven".[4]

I do not believe I told him this at all. He was tired, and I could not dispute things with him. He lay down on the floor, and I sat down beside him and took his head on my knee, and he simply lay still a long time, and said: – "that's nice and peaceful." I got incredibly stiff through sitting in a cramped position, but the mere fact of enduring any pain or discomfort for him was an acute joy to me. He dropped off asleep, and, after the manner of nervous highly-strung people, at the moment of falling asleep he gave a violent convulsive start. After a while he woke up again, smiled up at me, and moved off my knee, and we went off together to lunch to the Inns of Court Hotel. As we sat at lunch, I thought I saw a man I knew and rather disliked; I pointed this man out to him, and he said that he was very like a man he also knew and rather disliked; but, on comparing their names, we found we were not alluding to the same man. "He must be the devil," said R[upert].

And then he came with me to Cannon Street to see me off. As we walked along a street, we saw a great crane lifting a block of stone to the top of a building. It swayed dizzily about, and dwindled into the upper air, and we stood and watched it. "Supposing that were to fall," he said.

"I don't think that's very likely," said I.

But his mind seemed to like to dwell upon gruesome possibilities. I saw him shudder a little at the thought of all the crowd in the street that were, like us, watching the stone ascend, being squashed into a red mess: and then we walked on.

We came to Cannon Street a few minutes too early for my train, and we walked down a narrow street with high walls to the river. "Don't these places make you feel afraid?" he said. "They look sinister; you never know what mightn't be lurking in them."[5]

We looked up into the narrow bit of sky. There was a thin drift of blue smoke in a golden afternoon glow. "Look at that," he said. The beauty of it somehow counteracted the horrible deep-down dinginess of the street with its blank walls of dun-coloured brick. But it was only a temporary puff, and when it disappeared we thought it was time for me to go back to the station.

In the station, too, everything was strangely pictorial. The arch of the roof had made itself into something like a coloured wood-engraving by Emile Verpilleux, and the smoke made itself into odd schematic patterns as it curled round beneath the roof. The man at the gate, an old acquaintance of mine, let him come up the platform with me. He, too, noticed the woodcut effect, and the way the signals with their red and green lights stood out dark and flat against the browny-gold of the sky. And then I got into the train, and it moved off.

Not long after this we arranged that he should come down to Tadworth. On the day appointed my aunt supposed me to have gone to town by an early train; this idea had been tactfully conveyed to her the night before, so that she should not ask embarrassing questions. I set off to the station to meet him. It was perhaps not an ideal day for a long picnic expedition such as we had planned: yesterday's snow, half-melted, lay in dejected-looking streaks and patches where the full sun had not fallen upon it: the sky was full of low clouds that raced and let through fitful glints of sunshine, and the roads were damp and slushy.

Knowing as I did the usual lateness of the South-Eastern trains, I was no doubt ill-advised to come down ten minutes before the train was due: but so I did. And then it came over me that Aunty was very likely going to town by the train that left a few minutes before the arrival of his train. This was a moment of swift action, as she might at any moment come in sight round the bend of the road. I walked past the station, struck aside into a field, and doubled back on my tracks under cover of a hedge: not a minute too soon, for there was the little grey hurrying figure just at the meeting of the roads. My hedge suddenly seemed hopelessly inadequate with its bare black twigs and wide gaps: I dared not lie down, for fear of attracting the attention of a cottager who was busied in her garden not far from me: I hoped violently that Aunty would not look my way, for she must assuredly have seen me. But, luck being with me that day, she did not.

As soon as she was out of sight, I began coming back again to the station, and before I reached it her train puffed away into the cutting. I came down on to the platform. It began to rain. The rain was mild and sweet, the sky utterly beautiful; the shining twigs in hedges and trees, and the large luminous drops of water that hung everywhere, gave an almost unearthly beauty to the landscape. Moreover, anything looks lovely when one is awaiting one's beloved... The train rounded the bend in a shower of sparks, and shot past the place where I was standing, but not too fast to let me catch a glimpse of a familiar fair head and red scarf at one of the windows.

We went up to the house together. He had a long easy swinging stride, with a touch of a slouch in it, very characteristic – but it was not much effort to me to keep step with him.

We decided to have lunch quickly at the house and then walk to the Edge. It obligingly stopped raining, and we swung off together in waterproofs. I do not remember all we said: I remember more the radiance of him against the black bare slopes of wet heather, and the blowing of the wind round us as we went.

We came to the Edge. This, perhaps I should mention, is our name for the place where the North Downs slope southward to the Weald. It is a good place. The ground dips away suddenly, and the Weald is spread like a map below one's feet. On this day the distant hills were amazingly clear; there was a faint roseate look of low winter sunlight over everything, and the surface of the Weald was picked out here and there with snow still unmelted. The wind swooped up the amphitheatre below us with redoubled force, laying the grass flat and quivering round our feet. He said: – "This is where Meredith used to walk:" then, gathering his coat about him so that it looked like an Italian cloak, and pushing his hat down over his face sombrero-wise, "I've just remembered that I'm a Victorian poet!" (referring to Q's "Oxford Book of Victorian Verse.")[6]

We turned westwards and followed the brow of the North Downs for miles and miles and miles – mostly along the crest of a bare grassy slope with the whole Weald spread at our left, some-times by a forced detour through little wet lanes and narrow paths. Once he stumbled in a wood, and laughing asked me: – "What would you do if I were to break my leg here?" "I'm sure I don't know," said I. "I couldn't carry you far, that's one thing certain, and we're about a mile from any house that I know of."

We came out on the high road not long after this. Night falls early on these winter afternoons, and it was already half dark by the time we reached the lonely little inn that bears the sign of the Hand in Hand. So here we went in, and sat by a blazing fire while a tiny little girl brought us tea, and a candle that could not really hold its own against the firelight. This was a good time, but all comes to an end, and we seemed not to have been there much longer than a few minutes before he summoned the little maiden and paid the reckoning, and we were on the road again. A half moon had come up, and a few stars looked through fleeting white clouds. There was a black wood at our right and a wide field at our left, and the road went shining wet between them.

After about the first mile, I remember I found without surprise that we were walking hand in hand like a pair of children. There is a place on that road, with high thin fir-trees at the left, that grips my heart now whenever I pass it for the vivid picture it calls to my mind of us two that evening. I could have wept aloud for the very beauty of everything. Who was I that God should give me such piercing joy? The remaining miles flew as in a dream: time was as nothing, and we might have been a moment or an age for all I knew or cared.

Somehow or another we reached the house. It was lit up within, and some of the curtains were drawn. I wondered what the time was, and then suddenly if Aunty had come back from town, and were perhaps there…

We crept round the end of the house like cats, tiptoeing on the grass. The drawing-room curtains were shut, and we vainly applied our eyes to the sides of the windows in the hope of seeing through the slit between window-frame and curtain. We gave that up quite soon, and crept past the drawing-room to the dining-room. The table was laid, – the curtains here were open, – and the clock stood at five past seven. We stood awhile in doubt, flattening our noses on the window. Then Christopher drifted aimlessly in from the hall, and I succeeded in catching his attention and asking him if Aunty had come. She had not. And we came in and dried ourselves.

The next morning we were moving for a fortnight into town. It was too much to expect that we should get clear without running into Aunty, but we were setting forth for the station in hopes that, once there, we could pass him off as a person accidentally met, or even a stranger. We took up each a bag, and left the front door. But Aunty was too smart for us: we met her in the drive. And the scene that ensued was comic. Delphis, surely innocent, looked unspeakably "caught", but bravely walked on. My mother fell in behind Delphis, I behind her, and R[upert]. behind me, so that we must have presented the odd spectacle of a row of persons each taking refuge behind the next smallest in series to himself. But, the cat once out of the bag, the embarrassingness of the situation gradually cleared away, and Aunty saw us peaceably off by the train.

He came with us to town, and to stay a few days in a funny little flat in Chelsea. Having seen the others safely into the flat, he and I went out for a walk, with no particular intention of going anywhere, and wandered about streets. As we went I was suddenly seized with a sort of sickening fear that he would not stay with me, and I said to him: – "I'm afraid; you might turn round and begin to hate me!" And he looked up at a high house beside which we were passing, and said: – "Yes: and so might a brick fall off the top of that house and kill you, and yet you don't worry about it!"

And then somehow we were discussing, I think, "Flat Earthers", and he propounded a theory that the world was not a globe as it is thought of ordinarily, nor yet flat, but a hollow sphere inside which we are living: which would bring out New Zealand somewhere over our heads. "Horrible", said I; "I can't bear the stuffiness and shut-in-ness of it: it reminds me of the points in Abbott's "Flatland"." "O, I don't know," he said: "it's rather nice and comfortable!"

He was altogether perverse in his theories that day, and in a freakish humour. We crossed the Albert Bridge. I said something about its delicate spidery framework, and we felt it tremble to our steps. He would have it that the central portion of it was constructed like the Tower Bridge, to lift up, and that by just pressing a spring somewhere one might set the machinery in motion.

And then told me a story about a man who went for a walk across a bridge, and saw a man throw himself into the water and then begin calling for help, upon which the first man, whom we will call A., jumped in and rescued him. When they were safely ashore, and B. had the water shaken out of him a little, B. said to A.: – "Now, you have saved me from death; you are just as responsible for my existence as if you had been my parent. I jumped into the water because I had not a job. Find me a job."

So A. found him a job. But at the end of a fortnight B. turned up again with the unwelcome news that he had lost his job, and wished A. to find another. This he accordingly did, and not once only. And then he began to get tired of the process, and hinted as much to B., who forthwith threatened to jump into the river again.

However, B. gradually led their steps towards the bridge; and when they were about over the middle, he jumped upon the parapet. A. knew perfectly well, from what he had seen of B.'s general behaviour and character, that B. had not the necessary courage to jump again; so legend hints that he gave him just that small push that upset his balance, and completed the work that was already begun.

"That's all very well", said I, "but don't you see that that's not the end of the story? Do you suppose A. looked on in cold blood while that wretched B. was drowned?"

"No," he admitted. "A. almost certainly jumped in, acting on instinct, and saved him again; and then of course he wished he hadn't! And there they were at the beginning all over again."

And then we came to Battersea Park, and sat on a seat facing the river; and we saw a tram going over Battersea Bridge – at least such is my recollection – do trams go over Battersea Bridge? And as it breasted the rise and began to descend on the other side the movement of it struck him as being beautiful and he proceeded to versify thus: –

"Curtseying, gliding,
Queenly riding, – that isn't the beginning – it must come
    somewhere in the middle, I think –
Over the ridge
Of Battersea Bridge,

Rose the 'bus, the Hammersmith 'bus,

The Putney, Wandsworth, Battersea, Hammersmith.

Fulham and Kensington 'bus!"

I objected that it was really a tram, but he waved this aside as irrelevant, quoting the Limerick: –

There was a young man who said: "Damn.

I have recently found that I am

A creature that moves

In predestinate grooves,

Not a 'bus, – not a 'bus, – but a tram!"

"The pathos of that last line," he said, "with its repetition, is very good! It's the only Limerick in the world, except perhaps this one: –

There was an old lady of Dijon,

Who did not believe in religion; (pronounced as in French.)

In the hour that she died,

"God is not!" she cried;

Ni le père, ni le fils, ni le pigeon!"[7]

He was in rather a versifying mood that day. He went on to lay out a scheme for a longish poem about a young couple who began life

"in a heavenly abode,

Somewhere down the Holloway Road;"

I wish I could remember the whole of their career, gradually rising as it did in the financial and social scale, and meanwhile becoming less heavenly, till in the last couplet,

"Now we live in Westminster,

Life is dull as ditchwater –

A good Pre-Raphaelite rhyme, that!"

We sat on the seat in Battersea Park a long while, talking nonsense and watching the river flow past, and then we went along through Battersea Park and began coming across Chelsea Bridge. We walked along the eastern footpath of it, and then we came to the little exedra [an outdoor bench in a recess] at the south piers; we sat on the seat there and went on looking at the river, and at Victoria railway bridge. It was getting dark by this time, and

different coloured lights of the railway and on the river banks sent
down little tremulous spears of light for an infinitely long way
into the darkening water. Lighted trains came over the bridge,
sometimes crawling, sometimes quick as a flash: electric trains
struck bluish purple sparks from overhead wires. Under the bridge
there hung bundles of straw or other material of varying shapes
and colours; I do not know their purpose; it may be to warn the
bargees not to hit their masts under the bridge. We fell to discussing what they were for, but got no light on the subject; and then
his freakishness came to the surface again, and he said: – "they are
really the scalps of evil-doers, hung there as a warning to others
… . Look at that one! The owner of that one was a fine representative of the Anglo-Saxon race. (It was a large bright yellow
bundle of straw.) – and what a giant, too! And that little dark one,
was he an Italian?" And so he rambled on. And then he fell silent,
and we sat and looked at the water, which was a deep wine-red
beneath the after-glow of a brilliant sunset, and at the lights that
grew proportionately brighter as the sky deepened.

And then two men, wrapped up in black cloaks and with
broad-brimmed hats shoved down over their eyes, came hurrying
past behind us. And as they passed the one said to the other in a
voice deep and fraught with a kind of sinister significance: – "The
fire is kindled."

And we suddenly caught each other's eyes for a second. "Yes,
all right," thought I: "it is." But that was probably not the same
one that they were meaning.

And then we walked home. I do not remember that either of
us spoke another word. We stopped on the way to look in at the
giant rockers and wheels of the Pimlico Pumping Station, but we
did not need to explain about this to one another. We each knew
that both of us loved to look at powerful machinery, and there was
nothing more to say.

That night he and my parents and I went to the theatre. It
was Granville Barker's production of "Twelfth Night". We sat
at the side of the upper circle, next to a kind of brass railing on
which he leaned his head most of the time. He enjoyed the play

tremendously, remarking softly at intervals, "It is good." And when the play was over we went and walked across Hungerford Bridge and looked at the lights in the river. And then we went back to our little flat, and went to bed.

And then, who knows why? I was irresistibly overcome with love of him, and it seemed ridiculous that he should be one side of the wall and I the other: and I got out of bed and very softly stole out of my room. His door was not shut: I slipped round it, and stood by his bed. I did not know if he were asleep at first, but then he whispered: – "Well?" I sat down on the bed, and he put his arms about me, and I laid my head on his shoulder. He pressed me closer, and something in the touch of him made me suddenly feel afraid, and I began to tremble violently from head to foot. "Are you frightened?" he said. "Yes," said I. "You need'nt be," he said: "I wouldn't do anything you wouldn't like." (This very quietly.) And then: – "I suppose everyone's like that – at first."

I lay down on the bed beside him for a few minutes. Somehow he became more reassuring, and my first unreasoning terror disappeared. We lay quietly in one another's arms for a little while.

Then I thought I heard a sound: so did he. I bounded up off the bed, cold and stiff with fear of discovery. In my own mind, I was not doing wrong: but, all the same, I had no mind to have to explain my presence in his room to anyone. Particularly I hoped my father would not know … A light appeared. My heart began to thump very loud against my ribs. I put my hand down and felt that his was beating an equally powerful tattoo. He pulled me down nearer to him. "Knock on the wall to tell me you're safe back in your room!" he whispered.

I crept back again as I had come. The light was in my room, and there was my mother. "What are you doing?" she said. "Oh, I just went to say goodnight to R.," said I. "You should'nt have done that," she said, simply; and then she went off to her room. When she was safely away I knocked on the wall, and heard an answering tap.

In the morning we all pretended it hadn't happened. I knew mother would not give me away. She told me afterwards she found out, more by thought-reading than actual hearing, what was happening, and had started moving about herself partly with the object of preventing my father, who was awake, from hearing anything.

At breakfast he had a letter. He read it, and then said: – "I must go home". And Mamma said: – "Don't go. Stay over Christmas with us." But he turned the letter over and over in his hand, and muttered something about his mother. "That poor woman," he said. And he was bothered about when he would start, and how he would fit in some appointment he had made. So Mamma arranged that he should go off to this place, I forget what, and I should meet him at the station with his bag. At first he would not hear of this, but finally he gave way.

After breakfast I went out with him to help him do some shopping. As soon as we got clear of the house, he said: – "I was relieved this morning! I didn't know what sort of faces to expect … My heart was beating so that I thought I should die! But it was worth it!" "Yes," said I.

We went to some shops, and he bought various presents for Christmas. We went to a bookshop, and he wandered round aimlessly. It occurred to me that I was probably only in his way really, and I said: – "Shall I go home?" But, rather to my surprise, he answered helplessly: – "Don't leave me!" So I stayed with him, and we went on to other shops. We went to the Russian shop in Duke Street, and it was there that I bought the satinwood cigarette-case with a compartment for matches that I have now. And then he went off to keep his appointment, and I went home.

When the time came, I set off with his bag to see him off at Euston. The Lord knows how I found the station: I went as in a dream, and only half saw things about me. I had a sort of sickening sinking feeling. I didn't want him to go away. Life with him was too beautiful to be true: without him, even temporarily, I didn't care to imagine it.

I met him, and he took his bag. We had tea in the station, and I saw him off in the Rugby train. There were other people there, seeing other people off: I remember how kindly one of them

looked at us. And then the train moved off, and I saw his lion's
mane sticking out of the window, and his hand waving to me,
till the train rounded a bend and I lost him … and then I turned
and went. I saw nothing. My eyes were blinded with tears, and I
almost think I may have wept aloud as I went. But if I did no one
heard, for the roar of London mercifully hid it.

4 Cadogan Court,
Draycott Avenue,
S.W.

[1912]

O thou most beautiful –

I drifted back here, unseeing, wakened abruptly at intervals by a taxi
behind me or the ridiculous annoying thought that I ought to look about
me to observe. I found Christopher in bed and Delphis limp. I went on
with the little wood carving: you shall have it soon, as soon as I can
do it – I'd give you anything of mine if I thought you wanted it. I was
intending to offer you the illumination – say the word and I'll give it
you – or the flower thing when it's done. But what's the good? The only
things worth giving you are ones I have'nt done yet and probably shan't
for a long while, if ever. You go away and my standard's lower. I begin
to see other things: I begin even to see good in my drawings.

But the things I've seen with you are burnt in. The tremendous silent
machinery and the long red dart of light under that black bridge – and
the trains…

I wish there had'nt been that beastly alarm and ending that night.
There had of course to be some kind of ending, some time. I'd face
the same risk over again, though. Pity it came so close on the heels
of my stupid little fear – which was a mere nothing, only I was afraid
you'd despise me for it and think I did'nt after all trust you. I do, most
completely, in every way. And having said so I'd better abandon the
hopeless task of trying to explain first, how much I love you and want
you –

second, how often I seem to understand your thoughts so that they
almost seem to have been mine –

third, how horribly I fail to make you see that I do understand.

Silence is best, and here I am wasting words, which "fit about the
truth like a loose garment" concealing rather than making clear.

Another thing – for you I have the "spirit of service". I would'nt care
how beastly or how difficult a thing was. Do, if ever you can, let me
serve you – it'd show me you do trust me.

I saw your fetch [a servant, probably Marsh's, who did chores for
Brooke when he was staying at the Gray's Inn apartment] in town.

Back view, looking in a window, and only for a second. As it was in the evening, it was presumably all right.

I hereby promise not to be afraid again. I want you every bit as much as you want me, and you know it.

– By the way, from the impression in general that I have about my parents I should rather imagine that if mamma had found out she would'nt have said much to me and nothing to any other soul – if Daddy had–: unthinkable, to begin with, he'd be so horrified: he'd tell Mamma. But oh my, I'm glad he did'nt!

I'm going to post this. Then I'm going out to have another look at the power-house.

Joy be with you. Lot of use wishing you a merry Christmas and a happy new year when I'm wishing you as well the whole time!

Phyllis.

Farm Corner,
Tadworth,
Surrey.

At 3, on Monday. [1912]

Sorry my hand's so shaky. I've just been carrying very heavy things to an empty house I'm going to use as a studio.

Housewarming of a sort to take place on Sunday.

Beginning to look inhabited.

I've got

A large room with 3 doors, and access to the open air on 3 sides.

An oak table (this came on a wheelbarrow).

My square cushion.

A fire.

Two rugs.

A chair.

Paints, drawings, paper, and materials for tempera backgrounds.

An immense drawing-board.

I shall be undisturbed here. It will be beautiful, I shall do a lot.

You must come and pay it a visit one of these days. Sunday if you don't go after all.

What I need in the way of accessories will gradually accumulate. A fender is coming, also a comfier chair.

Mumma does'nt seem to have done any thought reading yesterday. The beastly people didn't come to dinner after all.

Phyllis.

You might ring up if you've not gone.

Brooke must have only gone to Rugby for a day or two, because by 20 December he was back at Gray's Inn attending a party put on by Marsh, at his request; he was eager to make the acquaintance of

Cathleen Nesbitt, the striking young actress who had been playing the part of Perdita in *The Winter's Tale*. The evening turned out to be a great success for Brooke: he met Cathleen and they had instantly hit it off. On 23 December Brooke headed back to Rugby to spend Christmas with his mother; on his arrival he wrote to Marsh, describing his happily distracted state the morning after the party: 'What else could a young man say with his eyes full of sleep and his heart full of Cathleen?'

In spite of Brooke's increasing involvement with Phyllis he remained at odds with himself, unable to get clear of the sense of restlessness and lack of fulfilment that continued to nag at him. A desire to flee from all that haunted him set in, and he decided to try and exercise a more extreme version of Cornford's suggestion of going abroad to do manual work, to purge himself.

At this time several parts of the world were suffering unrest, and the thought of becoming a war correspondent appealed to Brooke's sense of adventure and the dramatic. Like most boys at that time, he had been brought up on books that spun good yarns about gallant battles, and men of war who died a hero's death or returned a legend. Back in September or October 1912 he had approached Henry Nevinson of the *London Nation* and asked if he would take him 'out to the war then *threatening in the* Near East' as his 'squire'.[8] Nevinson refused, however, for both financial and technical reasons.[9] Brooke was aware of the increasingly critical situation brewing between Germany and Russia, so asked John Masefield if he would recommend him as a war correspondent should conflict come about.

When all these attempts proved fruitless, Brooke's thoughts turned to another grand plan, about which he wrote to Rosalind Murray[10] at the end of December, 1912: 'I've a plan for making a fortune in the South Seas. Absolutely certain. You and Denis,[11] if you assist, could have a quarter share each – about £200,000.'[12] However, we are not enlightened as to what this scheme involved.

A few weeks later, in a letter to his trusted friend Gwen Raverat, Brooke touched upon how his relationships with Phyllis, Cathleen Nesbitt and Elisabeth van Rysselberghe conflicted with his desire to escape abroad. He wrote, 'I have such a passion for various women in

London, that I shall live mainly there, for a bit. I want passionately to go to the South Seas: and it's <u>awfully</u> difficult tearing myself away'.[13]

After spending Christmas with his mother in Rugby, Brooke returned to London, just in time to catch the opening performance of *Hullo Ragtime* with Marsh. He became enchanted and intoxicated by this thoroughly modern, brash and colourful show, apparently going to see it ten times. It greatly appealed to his desire to see stuffy cultural convention shocked into action: the same effect he tried to achieve with some of his poetry.

Brooke left that night for Cornwall, where he spent the next two weeks with his good friends Frances and Francis Cornford. This proved a very productive time for him – as often seemed the case when he was removed from the temptations of London's social whirl. He nearly completed his play *Lithuania*, which he had been working on since the spring, penned the poem 'Funeral of Youth' and wrote two reviews on a newly published edition of *Donne's Poetical Works*.[14]

c/o Mrs Cornford
Inglewidden
Cadgwith
Ruan Minor
Cornwall

1913 [Postmarked: 6 January]

My dear,

I should have written before, I suppose. I suddenly fled down here, and I've been resting. And resting takes up so much time that I've never written.

I shall be here for some days more, so I shan't be at the Poetry Bookshop when your mother seems to be going to a party there. I'll write to tell her. I hope everyone'll buy lots of books.

I write in bed.

I'll be in London in the next three weeks – I'll let you know.

Yes, it was a shock, that night. I hope it hasn't permanently strained my heart. I never heard it thump so! I agree (in my slight knowledge) with what you say about your parents. Still, it's not worth finding out if it's true! I feel that night meeting business is awfully risky. That's why Gray's Inn is so much better. I wish to goodness you were free and could get away when you wanted. If ever you get a chance of getting away for a night, let me know.

Thank you for the wooden man and horse. I like it a good deal and I like having it. It's so much nicer to have, you see, than any drawing and painting, because it's carriable about with me, and the others aren't so conveniently – and I'm a wanderer. The horse's left hind leg, in spite of the packing, – but a little selotine remedies that, I find. The railway's fault.

Service, child, – that'll come soon enough, one way or another. Feelings are queer, I sometimes want to make you serve me –

You're three hundred miles away. Goodnight.

   You're very lovely.
      Goodnight
      Rupert

[Letter from Phyllis to Rupert.]

You need'nt explain not writing, blessed one. But it was good to hear from you. I'm sending you a thing about the power-station, to tell you a little what it was like. I wished all the time you'd been with us. It was wonderful. I'm sending 2 other things: one I unearthed among some last year's things by accident, and another recent one.

I rather agree about night-visits being too risky. O Lord! Modern civilisation! And yet I suppose it has its uses. It gives one a sight more liberty than some kinds of other arrangements. What does one do about it? Do you believe in a) Everyone keeping rules: b) No one keeping rules c) Some people keeping them and some not? The last does'nt seem to me nohow fair: the second's chaos, and "devil take the hindmost", and as for the first, it depends entirely on the rules, and I suppose that's why one's a socialist.

In this (I hope) transitional time, presumably we're each to adjust outward conformity with a sort of minimum-wage of liberty, and so if possible steer between being persecuted and outcast and being perfectly passive in one's conformity.

– I went to the Poetry Bookshop's at home yesterday. Never saw such a crowd in my life. The whole house was bursting. Newbolt talked a little, and read out "Is there anybody there?" said the traveller", and your "Dust" – The room he talked in was quite full and all of us were on the stair – up and down which no one could get. Some quite distinguished people – Maurice Hewlett and so on – came late and were disgusted and fled – Monro says no-one bought things but he hopes they'll come back. The fact is that, till this talk began, all the people who did'nt know what to do stood in a row round the shop with their backs to the shelves. They did'nt read the books, as sensible people in their case would have done: and they prevented possible buyers from getting at the shelves. I introduced Eddie Marsh to Mamma, and he told her with jubilance that Georgian Poetry was sold out of its first edition and was going into a second.

And now I'm busy preparing tempera backgrounds. I want to get taken in some exhibition. I have'nt tried yet. By the way, the

Westminster's accepted a sonnet of Mamma's about the power-station, over the signature Delphis. This is because I've a cousin Mary Gardner who never does write anything – and Mamma's afraid she'll get the credit. Wonder when it'll come out. A proof with one line left out appeared this morning. That may have been their fault, or the fault of too enthusiastic home typewriting.

It'll be good to see you again. So much so that the other night it suddenly came into my mind and I was afraid. I don't know what of.

Wonder if I could get off for a night. But if the Rhyses or anybody were to ask me for 2 nights it might be done by changing one of them. Only they're not very likely to just now; Brian goes up to-morrow, and Megan is still very newly engaged and probably has no use for me – The Radfords used to ask me at intervals, but now they're in the country. It's all a chance. I don't know. Besides, going off unbeknownst for a night is as bad to be caught in as anything. I think I'd have to do it more or less in the square or not at all.

– My mind is running on potter's colours, size, copal and whitening. The attic also is full of them. Painting as an art has the advantage that you can amuse yourself by making a hell of a mess; and the nicest techniques are often the messiest. Powder colours, when they get out of control … Work done in this technique is indestructible save by main force.

– The reason why I generally answer a letter at once is the longer I leave it the harder it gets to write. If I write the same day I want to cover ten sheets at one go. After a week I take a piece of paper and look at it in vain.

Glad you like the little horseman. He came with a blessing. The legs and reins of course are brittle. I hope the cottonwool did'nt stick to the varnish, or if it did that you scraped it off.

Goodnight. Not finally, for I'm going to creep out in the dark to post this. Are you within sound of sea? I wish I were. I get homesick for the sound of sea-water. May it sing you to sleep.

Phyllis.

Forgive this if it's stupid, uninspired, beastly – I have'nt been alone enough. Don't hate me.

Phyllis's longing for the sea culminated in 'The Dykes', a poem which conjures up the landscape surrounding her old school in Southwold. Appropriately it was published in the July edition of *The Felician*.

The Dykes[15]

By an Old Felician.

In the grey of the east there is a battered shore,
And marshes down to the edge of the stormy sea;
And the river winds in an endless curving line,
And the breeze that blows is heavy and salt with brine
As it speeds and sweeps in the open bare and free –
And I'd dearly like to be walking there once more.
In the grey of the east there is a long straight road
That leads inland from the breaker's swirl and roar,
And the hedge by its side is thorny and wild and low,
And in it the rose and the frail sweetbriar grow,
And wayside herbs in an endless varied store –
And happy I was when that was my abode.
In the grey of the east the plovers wheel and call
The whole day long as far as the eye can see,
And mists roll up, when the summer nights are still,
To die breast deep at the foot of the rising hill,
And day breaks over a blinding silver sea –
And here, inland, I am homesick for it all.

    P.G.

                                Cadgwith

                                Cornwall

10 January 1913

Dear Mrs Gardner,

Many thanks for Travels with a Donkey.[16] I read it in the evenings when work has palled upon me and I'm (as ever) too lazy to write letters. I've, queerly enough, never read it before: having something of a contempt for Stevenson – only I think, because he has been set too high.

I was sorry I couldn't appear at the gathering at The Poetry Bookshop.[17] I hope the institution is getting on, and taking in money hand over fist. I leave here tomorrow. I'm going home for a bit, and after that I shall be in London again: so I may see you. I hope so. I've been working a little here – nearly finished a play.[18] It's so quiet and remote here, it seems almost out of England.

I envy you having been over the power station. I wish I could write about machinery. Alas, there aren't words!

    Yours ever
      Rupert Brooke

The Power Station

The four tall chimneys stand against the sky
Where faints the sunset in a fairy dream,
A mass of masonry beyond which seem
River and trees in delicate outline shy.
Inside, the vastness of machinery,
With shining metal rods that dip and gleam
Makes a soft purring and a blazing stream
Of light from out the furnace burningly.
This is the city's heart, the man in blue
With the dark patient eyes, the ultimate soul
Who holds the balance between power and power,
Silent he governs all from hour to hour,
While we two, looking dizzily on the whole
Conceive how Power can fashion all things new.

    Mary Gardner[19]

FIVE

'THE CENTRAL POINT...'

A constant inner conflict for Brooke was his need both to be free but also to belong and be loved: not a comfortable combination of emotions. He told himself it was a matter of finding the right woman. However, the reality was he enjoyed the heightened emotion he felt when embarking on a new romance, but always, in time, the magic wore thin and he became bored and felt trapped. Brooke touched upon such feelings in a letter to Ka Cox, written while he was staying with the Cornfords in Cornwall:

> you'll have to put up with my views on 'women' and love. I can't unlearn what I've learnt … I see – not only through you – a lot of things about women … Also, I know about love. It's all right if one can be taken in, enough; and all happens to go happily. But one can't <u>keep</u> it at that. Love <u>is</u> being at a person's mercy. And it's a black look-out when the person's an irresponsible modern female virgin. There's no more to say.[1]

Jacques Raverat later wrote of Brooke's ability to compartmentalise his life:

> he had two sets of friends that he was not interested in bringing together; for a long time, he even tried to keep them apart. Was this because of his natural love of mystery, from fear of too great an incompatibility and mutual disdain or did he fear a rapprochement at his own expense – that both sides might be exposed to a dangerous influence?[2]

Ultimately the thin divide that Brooke had tried to keep between his relationship with Phyllis and the torturous mess of his past affair with Ka was starting to slip away; bitter emotions from one began to spill into the other. Phyllis's idolising Brooke and his keeping many major parts of his life, both past and present, secret were the real threats to their relationship.

I rang the bell of the flat. He had been away for a while, first to his home, and then to some people in Cornwall; people whose point of view I did not like, who liked in him only parts that I felt to be an excrescence and a marring of his perfection, – the perversions and bizarreries that were superimposed upon his childish receptive nature by this queer world he had fallen into.[3] It was nothing unusual for my knees to tremble violently and my hands to sweat profusely if I were going to see him: but they did it with redoubled force to-day. The last time I had seen him was when I had seen him off at Euston and come away with my cup of bitterness flowing over. I was afraid. In all this part of my life I seem to have been gifted with a strange foresight: I knew, to begin with, before I met him, that something was going to cross my path, – witness my words to B[rian].R[hys]. on the subject, and the incident of the diary; no, I may even be more definite, and say that I knew that some person corresponding in all particulars to him was coming into my life. I knew, when I saw him, that I was going to see him again; I was not afraid of losing him in the chance stream of passers-by. And now, not for the first time, a sickening fear came upon me. He it was that made life not only worth living to me, but incredibly beautiful, so that I would lie awake and enjoy the mere beauty of it for hours in the night, and wake in the mornings half expecting to find it all unreal after all. I did not choose to imagine what life would be like without close intercourse with him. My mind refused the idea, while secretly dreading it. I knew that he had been drawn into a vortex of would-be original people, who to satisfy their own base natures had made inconstancy a principle and went as much as possible on the negative morality that he who breaks a rule is greater than he who makes it. I also knew that I was totally incapable of convincing him by argument. To be honest, I did not try; or it seems to me now that I did not try, at any rate enough. When he enunciated any peculiarly enraging doctrine, I merely stated my disagreement. And if I offered reasons, he brushed them aside as being founded on phantasms. Perhaps he was right; perhaps my foundations were phantasms; but I, and not I alone, would die for such.

"Be ye perfect, even as your father which is in heaven is perfect." All love wishes that which it loves to be perfect. My love saw in him many perfections, but it could not be blind to those things that were not perfections.

There were evil things abroad in the air; spirits of unrest, precursors of war perhaps. He was young, unformed, feeling about; and somehow I always felt that even his feeling about and being wrong was greater than the neat small rightness of most people who are more or less right. He was a sensitive barometer; any idea that was in the air was as likely as not to find expression through him; and the kind of childish perverseness of his mind led him to catch on to ideas, irrespective of right or wrong, that were out-of-the-way and fantastic. In short, he had not found himself; and when he had found himself, he was not much longer for this world. But I anticipate.

I always felt as if he were some poor lost angel that had come by mistake into a world of inferior beings that did not understand him, and that he only dimly understood. I wanted him to be perfect; if by undergoing nameless tortures I could have compassed this end, I would have undergone them without the slightest hesitation; but somehow I always seemed either to be fighting shadows or running my head against a brick wall.

Here was a person of noble, generous impulses, looking askance at these impulses because they savoured of a rather hackneyed form of chivalrism and romanticism. Here was a person whose strength lay in his personal charm, in his sensitiveness, in his power in the world of ideas, receiving hospitably into his mind the notion made in Germany that might is right: a person who could not bear to hurt another allowing house-room to the idea that love is nothing but a plaything and very temporary at that. These are specimens of what he occasionally expressed in conversation. They left me dumb with rage; they were so unlike what I knew in my inmost soul he was really like.

Up till now I had sometimes felt all this vaguely, in the background; he was so sympathetic and could so little bear to hurt me that the question had not really arisen. There were after all, so many things we had in common that we preferred to keep to these. I suppose it is bad to enjoy the present to the full without thinking about the future: all I can say is, I don't suppose I should do differently if the whole thing were to happen again. I knew that there were things about him that I could not go much further without running against. In the back of my mind, I suppose I wondered where we were going to. What would he have? One of two things: keep me for good and all, or throw me away. He was inclined to let things drift. I casually mentioned the future to him one day, and he said: – "There is no future. No past. Only the present. Isn't that good enough?" – A comfortable doctrine, perhaps...

Meanwhile, here I am shivering outside the door of the flat. The housekeeper, good matronly body, let me in; and there I found him deep in a chair, snowed under with papers, and the floor all littered with papers according to his custom. He extracted himself from the chair and greeted me. He seemed to be trying to write letters; two or three unfinished ones lay about. He seemed bothered, and asked me how one would set about finding I forget what address. I suggested the telephone book, and we found it, and set forth with the addressed letter to the post-office at the end of Warwick Court. I felt him in a way dependent upon me for support and protection; I almost forgot what had been in my mind before. And if it did cross my mind, I was unable to say any part of it as it seemed to me, for fear of hurting him, he seemed so little able to bear unpleasantness, so sensitive, so delicate an instrument that my rough hands did not know how to handle.

Having done what we had come to do at the post-office, we went back to the flat. We began talking about when we were at school. I described some of my school life. "It sounds very like a boys' school", he said. "And did you develop sudden passions for one another, like boys do?"

"Oh, yes," said I: "it was quite a part of the curriculum! One wasn't considered fully fledged until one had been 'gone on' at least one person."

"And were they very merciless to one another?"

"Absolutely. They teased me one day till I got under the table."

"What did they tease you about?"

"Mostly about this same question of being gone on people."

"Again, like boys. But I don't imagine they were as violent as boys."

"I don't know. I had a fight with one of them once."

"Who won?"

"I did: she was soft. Besides, I was angry with her. We were playing planchette, and she said we were cheating, and we weren't."

"Yes, it's all very like our school. – I remember, they wanted me to cut my hair, and I wouldn't and I had to fight a lot of them for it. – I didn't cut it."

"Good," said I. "But, all the same," – this after a little interval – "I don't like violence. I had to slap Christopher the other day."

"And didn't you rather enjoy it?"

"Enjoy what?" said I indignantly.

"Oh – the feeling of power, I suppose."

"No. It made me feel all trembly in the knees."

"I don't know – violence is rather refreshing in some ways."

"But there's no sport in it if the other party is so much smaller!"

"Or if he's too much larger! – There isn't enough violence; if there's a war in Russia, I think I shall go to it. I could pass myself off as a Russian if I could learn a little Russian: at any rate the people in Germany always took me for a Russian spy! By the way, as you're so fond of Greeks, why don't you go to the Balkan war[4] and nurse them?"

"I don't know any nursing," said I; "only a little first-aid."

"You could learn," said he.

He was sitting in the big armchair, and I was sitting on the arm of it. We both stared out of the window for a while.

Presently he said: – "I think I shall go to the South Seas. If I do, and wire for you, will you come?"

"Yes. When are you going?"

"Oh, I don't know. Some time. Future ... there is no future."

I leaned my head down on his shoulder, and said: – "I wish there weren't." I loved him fiercely, wildly, but with a little shade of annoyance to-day. However, the touch of him put that out of my mind, leaving room only for a feeling too rapturous and extreme to be called by the name content.

Then: – "Do you understand about things?" said he.

"Things? – I don't know. I know about some things," said I, with a glimmering of a guess at his meaning.

"I must have you, here," he said, laying a hand over what is delicately referred to by artists as "the central point of the figure."

"Yes – some time," I said. "It had occurred to me."

And then we kept silence for a while. And my mind projected itself who knows where, and I thought of myself as the happy mother of his child, – our child, – perhaps more than one, lovely, passionate creatures, the offspring of our physical and spiritual selves; and suddenly there leaped into my mind the image of that boyish figure sitting in a corner that had come to me long ago in a half-waking dream.

Then suddenly I happened to look at the zebra-skin under the table in the window; and there I saw a point of brilliant green liquid radiance.

"What on earth's that green thing?" said I.

"I don't know," said he.

I dived under the table, picked it up, and handed it to him. We both looked at it curiously for a long time. It seemed to contain more light, and greener light, than seemed possible for the size of it. It was egg-shaped, about a quarter of an inch long.

"It's a green ruby," he finally said. "You'd better keep it, since you found it."

I had in my pocket a large piece of India-rubber. I drew forth this and a pocket knife, made a little hole in the India-rubber, and squeezed into the hole the 'green ruby'. It glinted at me like a wolf's eye in the dark. There was something uncanny about the way it shone. I put the India-rubber, with the jewel embedded in it, back in my pocket.

Another thing that had been bothering me for a long time was that he did not take my drawings in the right way. He who under-stood some things so well – why should he not be able to know, as some people were able, exactly what I was striving after, even when I had least succeeded? This hurt me. I was keen to prove to him that even if he did not know what I was trying to say in art I had something to say.

"I don't think I shall come and see you again", I said, "until I've got a picture into the New English."[5]

"There were people", he said, "who vowed that they would go without their dinners until they had accomplished some feat or other – – "

"Yes, I daresay it is rather like that, but still … . Shall I come the day after to-morrow?"

"Yes, do. Here, if it suits you."

"All right."

I left him, feeling sore and rubbed up the wrong way. Nothing was definitely wrong, but I felt his attitude and mine coming into collision. This I could have borne had I felt that his attitude really was his, but I most definitely felt that it was nothing of the kind, that it was extraneous and undesirable, and that it was my duty to combat it. I also felt singularly powerless to do so. I took the green thing out of my pocket and stared at it senselessly. It still looked hopelessly unreal, but it felt solid all right.

The day before Brooke went to stay near Croydon with his friends, Gwen and Jacques Raverat, he sent a postcard to Mrs Gardner arrang-ing to turn up at a party she was holding.

[Postcard from Rupert to Mrs Gardner.
Postmarked: London W C. 2– am. 23 January 1913.]
Wednesday
Many thanks, I'll turn up at five –
    Rupert Brooke

1 This photograph of Lieutenant Rupert Brooke was taken at Blandford Camp in February 1915. On 1 March Brooke and his battalion left England for Gallipoli.

2 Rupert Brooke in unusually formal attire, c. 1911. This is the only known photograph of him wearing a dinner suit.

3 A broadly smiling Rupert Brooke with (*left to right*) Evelyn Radford,
Margery Olivier (holding dog) and Dudley Ward, outside
Mrs Primmer's Cottage at Bank, New Forest, April 1909.

4 (*left to right*) Noel Olivier, Maitland Radford, Virginia Stephen (soon to become
Woolf) and Rupert Brooke camping in a field near Clifford Bridge, Drewsteignton,
Devon, September 1911. Two months later Phyllis saw Brooke for the first time.

5 *(left to right)* Fellow undergraduates Geoffrey Keynes, Rupert Brooke and Gerry Pinsent in a boat at the May Races, Cambridge, 11 June 1908.

6 Members of the Gardner family, *c.* 1912. Phyllis is second from left in the back row, while Delphis holds what is believed to be the Gardner family's dog. Their mother, Mary Gardner, is second from right. Also present are Major Wilson and Elizabeth Wilson (third from left), the girls' grandparents.

7 Christopher, Phyllis and Delphis with some of their Irish wolfhound puppies in an advert for their kennel in the *Irish Wolfhound Yearbook*, c. 1932.

8 Professor Ernest Arthur Gardner, Phyllis's father, a respected archaeologist and author on ancient Greece. This photograph must have been taken when he was Yates Professor of Archaeology at University College, London, from 1896 to 1929.

9 Phyllis with one of her beloved Irish wolfhounds, 1934. By this time she had become a respected name in the wolfhound world, following publication of her book on the breed in 1931. The image appeared in an advertisement for Virol, a malt-based supplement, with the line: 'His [Cannavaun of Coolafin's] life was saved by Virol and Milk before his eyes were open.'

10 A watercolour sketch by Phyllis of her sister Delphis drawing. Phyllis refers to painting this in a letter of 1917.

11 *Fairy Gold* by Phyllis Gardner, 1913. The work was exhibited and sold at the winter New English exhibition in the same year. Although Phyllis considered this painting significant and refers to it in her memoir, she fails to mention that it is clearly a self-portrait. The painting is packed with meaning: the woods behind are believed to be the beeches at Reigate where she and Brooke walked, while the title reflects her feelings after the breakdown of their relationship.

"So sinks the day-star"   ΦΥΛΛΙΣ

12 (*left*) *So sinks the day-star*, 1921. Phyllis created this woodcut, clearly a self-portrait
of her mourning for Brooke, at the same time as those used in Stanley Casson's
Rupert Brooke and Skyros. According to Phyllis only two prints were made, one pasted
into her own copy of the Casson book and the other given to a friend for her copy.
The pose is strikingly reminiscent of the woman in Vincent van Gogh's *Sorrow*.

13 (*right*) **Phyllis's woodcut of Rupert** Brooke's grave. Along with ten
other woodcuts, she based it upon photographs taken by Stanley Casson
in April 1920. It was reproduced in *Rupert Brooke and Skyros*, 1921.

14 A wood engraving of a mare and foal by Phyllis. She loved horses and
they often featured in her art. In a letter to Brooke she tells how she had
followed a mare and foal around a field for hours, painting them.

The Old Vicarage, Grantchester, around the time that Brooke lodged here.

15 (*above*) The house front in the overgrown state Brooke loved so much.

16 (*below*) A view from the back garden showing the sundial
in the form of a book, described by Phyllis in her memoir.

17 The Orchard Tea Garden in Grantchester, *c.* 1909,
very much as Brooke would have known it.

18 Byron's Pool, Grantchester, *c.* 1914. This was one of Brooke's favourite
places for naked bathing, where he took his friends and Phyllis.

19 Colley Hill, Reigate, Surrey. Phyllis loved this place, which she also referred to as 'the Edge', with its spectacular views across the North Downs. She took Brooke to this spot in 1912, and later sent him a poem she had written about it.

20 A military camp at Tadworth, in a photograph of c. 1915. The camp was rapidly established in 1914, and used by various London regiments and the King's Royal Rifle Corps during the First World War. After Brooke's death Phyllis threw herself into helping to run its canteen, grateful for the long hours and distraction from her own grief. However, she and the local women found the unwelcome attention of the soldiers embarrassing.

21 Phyllis describes taking Brooke on the 'Headley way' walk when he visited her at Tadworth in 1912, and refers to 'the solid little spire of Headley Church'. It was a favourite walk of hers.

22 Farm Corner, Tadworth. This old postcard view does not feature the Gardners' family house, but instead shows the view that would have greeted them coming out through the front gate. It led on to the Common, the route Phyllis often took for her walks.

23 St Felix School, Southwold, 1907. Phyllis is in the third row from front, sixth from the left. She clearly enjoyed her time at the school as she joined the Old Felicians and often attended reunions with Delphis.

24 (*left*) Mrs Mary Ruth Brooke, Rupert's mother. This portrait by Elliott & Fry belonged to Miss Tottenham, governess to the Brooke boys.

25 (*right*) A studio portrait of Rupert Brooke, aged just 19. It was taken by Burrell, The Cosway Studio, Bournemouth while he was staying with his Aunt Fanny in late September or early October 1906. A few weeks later he was installed in rooms at King's College, Cambridge.

26 The Brooke brothers and the family's Jack Russell. Miss Tottenham, Brooke's childhood governess, owned this photograph, which she inscribed: 'Dick, Rupert, Alfred and "Trim"'. It was taken by E H Speight of Rugby.

27 Rupert Brooke in the back garden of the Old Vicarage, Grantchester, 1911. This photograph was taken by Estrid Linder, whom Brooke helped to translate two plays by Gustave e Collijn from Swedish using a German translation. The French doors behind Brooke led to his sitting room, while the window above was his bedroom.

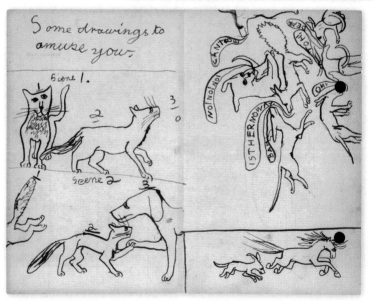

March 1st, 1899

RADNOR COTTAGE,
SANDGATE, KENT.

Dear Mr Kipling,

I am very sorry you are ill, and hope you will soon get better, as it is uncomfortable being ill.

your loving
Phyllis Gardner

Bagheera on a tree, my idea

Some drawings to amuse you.

Scene 1.

Scene 2

28 This charmingly illustrated letter, written by eight-year-old Phyllis
to Rudyard Kipling in 1899, when he was gravely ill with pneumonia,
is her earliest known surviving letter. *The Jungle Book* had been
published five years earlier and was clearly an inspiration to her.

29 A section of **rib bone** depicting Pegasus on both sides, carved and gilded by Phyllis. She gave the piece to Maitland Radford.

30 A beautiful illuminated page illustrating 'Lyke Wake Dirge' from Phyllis Gardner's *Scottish Ballads*, 1919. This unique book, painstakingly written out by Phyllis and featuring her watercolour illustrations, is a true labour of love, finely detailed and quite exquisite. The blond man depicted throughout its pages bears a strong resemblance to Rupert Brooke.

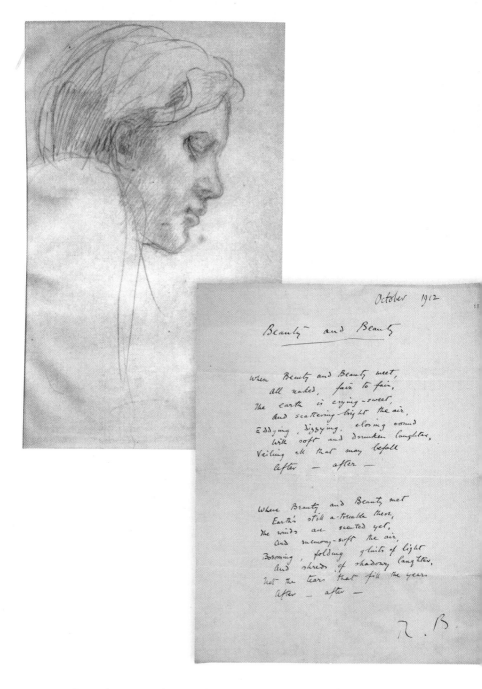

31 (*above*) This previously unpublished pencil sketch by Margaret Ethel Pye, a Cambridge friend, shows Rupert Brooke reading poetry at the Old Vicarage, *c*. 1910.

32 (*below*) The manuscript of 'Beauty and Beauty' which Brooke sent to Phyllis, a poem inspired by their naked moonlit tryst at Grantchester. This draft starts with 'The' in the third line of the second verse, whereas all later printed versions of this poem are 'And'.

Two days later I went to the flat as arranged, but I went with mixed feelings. If it had not been for the almost irresistible attraction he exercised over me, I feel sure I should not have gone. I was punctual to the minute: he was a little behind time. He set me on edge to start with, because he gave me the key and asked me to unlock the door while he did something else, and I found it a little stiff, whereupon he took it from me, started fresh, and unlocked the door without an effort.

"Why did you do it so easily when it wouldn't go at all for me?" I said. And his reply was: — "That's because you're a rotten female."

"It is nothing of the kind!" said I. "You make me want to knife you."

When we had got in I showed him the rough draft of a poem I had been writing since our last meeting. He came to a phrase "When the shadows flit", and said: — "I don't like 'flit'".

"It rhymed", I said weakly.

"Yes." said he, "and so would 'spit' or 'hit', but I shouldn't like them either!"

And then he fished out some German comic illustrated papers.

"I should love you to read these to me!" he said.

"But I hardly know any German," I objected.

"Then that'd be all the funnier," said he.

After a while I said to him: — "Why did you call me a rotten female?"

"I don't know," said he. And then, ruminatively, "All women are beasts! And they want a vote — but they'll never get it!"

"Never's a large word," said I, inwardly boiling with rage, and wondering whose ideas he was reflecting now. "I suppose your friends in Germany have been stuffing your head up with that rot!"

"Germany's rather a nice place", said he, "At least, Berlin isn't; but Munich, — and Dresden —"

"What's the attraction?" said I.

"Good music, to begin with: and beer-gardens."

"Too soft," said I, "as an existence."

"Why not be soft?" said he.

"I like to keep in condition," said I, "so as to be able to run a mile if necessary."

"Oh, but ... to listen to good music and drink beer all day, and gradually grow lazier and softer, – and never anything unpleasant to happen –"

"It doesn't appeal to me. Except that of course I like the good music. The rest seems rather a heavy price to pay."

"Beer – all day," he crooned, dreamily. He must have been trying to provoke me, I think. And yet his demeanour was affectionate, and his voice soft and gentle like a caress.

Then somehow we found our arms about one another, holding close. After a long caress, he said: – "I must have you. If you could come away for a night somewhere – "

"But – it would hardly do!" said I.

"The world need never know," said he.

"What'd you mean?" said I.

"There _are_ ways – "

My heart sank within me. Where was my castle in the air, where my visionary child? Was this the way to look at things? Was this what came of holding the doctrine that there is no future? I said nothing. It was not enough that he should have been seized on by evil ideas that were nothing but ideas, here he was about to bring them into relation with practical facts ... and still it seemed not possible that any evil thing should go hand in hand with the glory of his personality.

"There are ways"... I dimly remembered that someone had begun to tell me of such "ways" long ago, and I had been mildly repelled and put the subject from my mind. That they were necessarily evil I felt by a kind of instinct. I did not think collectedly. I do not know what I thought.

After a while I looked at my watch. "Are you remembering," said I, "that we're due at the Vienna Café at half-past four?"

"I must go and dress," said he. "I'm going out to dinner afterwards with some people at Golder's Green, and I think I ought to put on at least a black coat." He was dressed in a blue flannel shirt and grey flannel trousers.

"But," said I, "I didn't think to allow time for you to dress, — and I ought to start now, or they'll wonder what's become of me."

I kissed him good-bye, and started off.

There was a large party of us at the Vienna Café. There was, among others, M[aitland].R[adford]. The sight of him was like an oasis in the desert to me; I felt I could trust the kindly sanity of his outlook on life. And later, when R[upert]. came, arrayed in a white shirt and black suit, he sat the other side of M[aitland].R[adford]. from me, and they began to argue on I forget what subject; but I knew that I felt myself in agreement with M[aitland].R[adford]. and in disagreement with R[upert]. and that I felt sore and miserable and torn in two. I took no part in the discussion. I was rather dazed, and wondering whether the foundations of all things were really as precarious as they seemed.

I loved R[upert]. passionately, but with equal passion I hated parts of his recent attitude, particularly since he had come back from Cornwall. What did I consider the end and aim of life? I do not know, definitely, but it embodied some sort of a striving after nobleness. And what did he apparently consider it? An opportunity for pleasure-seeking. Or it would be fairer to say that this was the way he made it appear to me. There are certain things to be held in mind: first, he had not long ago been seriously ill, and been sent to Italy for his health. While there, he had received news of his brother's death, and he had not long been home when his father also died. This had left him in an extremely depressed condition, nervously exhausted, and only asking to avoid further pain.[6] Further, some sort of shame or reticence, an exaggeration of the presumably British quality that makes the Tommy sing music-hall songs where other nationalities of soldier sing national anthems, prevented him from ever owning up to noble ideals, — at this time, that is.

I was born, and I suppose shall die, with an obstinate belief in the ultimate rightness of things. In vain I tried to communicate this feeling to him. I tried to explain how it comes to me in flashes even in the midst of despair; and he answered me with a verse of imitation Tennyson: —

"The sun goes down into the west,
And, after, rises in the east;
And why, we know not in the least,
But only know it for the best."

And said in a slightly superior way that he supposed that that represented my philosophy.

I drew an illumination thing with all manner of little details woven into it whose meaning he could not fail to see; the text was: – "I shall not die, but live, and declare the works of the Lord." This was because the idea of death seemed to weigh so heavily upon him. I suppose he imagined that the human soul goes out like a candle when the body dies...

I did not imagine this. I believe that he has since had the error of his ideas demonstrated to him. But this again is to anticipate.

He looked at my drawing, and said: – "that's a very optimistic view of things."

"I am an optimist," said I. But I felt him despise me for it.[7]

In the way of thinking about death, he was much more bothered about the future than I. In all other matters he seemed to me to have a tendency to let things slide. He neither pushed nor strove for his literary success. I think it was mainly the charm of his personality that gave him such a good start; and, as the quality of his work steadily improved, this initial success was not wasted. To say that he did not care about it would not be true; but he certainly had none of that long uphill fight that is so often the lot of budding genius. Success came his way, and he accepted it as his right, with a good grace. His attitude on a good many things was: "Time enough for that, says I." "There'll be plenty of time," he said to me once, "to have all the children we want."

But to return to my narrative. The talk of the tea-party flowed round me and over my head: I was more or less stupefied, because I realised in a dim way that the breaking-point had come.

The tea-party broke up and went to its respective homes.

c/o J. Raverat
Croyden
Royston

4 February

Dear Mrs Gardner,

   Many thanks for the Westminster with the sonnet – I wish I'd been inside the power-station. It must have been fine. I'm sorry I couldn't stay longer at your party a fortnight ago. I had to get up to the far north for dinner – I was late, as it was. I liked the Americans, and the admirably and grimly humorous Professor Ker.

   Rumours reached me in London that an illustration to Dining-Room tea was completed! I hope to see it soon – I'm going to be in London again shortly, I think: and I'll try to slip down for a little to Tadworth. I've been trying to work here – not successfully – I think I shall go to Grantchester – ten miles away over the hills.

   Yours sincerely

   Rupert Brooke

In uttering 'There <u>are</u> ways' – understood by Phyllis to be a reference to using contraception – Rupert crossed a line that Phyllis hadn't really known was there until faced with it. Her earlier assertion of 'Why should'nt we be primitive, now?' was all right in theory, but not in practice. When it came down to it, Phyllis really wanted conventionality and commitment.

Brooke was sexually frustrated, angry with the female sex and not keen to commit to anyone. Such frustration was doubtless increased by Phyllis's tempting night visit to his room, so rudely interrupted by her mother, while his continuing correspondence with Ka was disastrous. Each kept the other's wounds open and fanned the flames of anger, blame and self-recrimination, giving neither of them a chance to move on. Rupert was to sum up the result in a letter to Jacques Raverat: 'Suffering's a dirty business. It only weakens and destroys, at best – and worst, poisons.'[8]

In early February Brooke read a paper to the 'Heretics' in Cambridge.[9] Officially meant to be on the contemporary theatre, he actually used it as a guise to vent his own rage at the two main issues needling him at the time: feminism and sex. Those present, including some young women from Girton, and Newnham, must have been taken aback by the apparent personal anger in his verbal attack on the playwright Henrik Ibsen. Brooke had much admired his work back in 1911, before personal experiences had altered his views. Now he saw Ibsen as deplorable because of his support of feminism, a movement that Rupert held largely responsible for what had happened between himself and Ka. In contrast, August Strindberg had come to symbolise his champion in the fight against feminism, his nemesis. 'He is out to declare that men are men and women women. It sounds an easy thing to say, but it's not. The pain of the statement nearly drove him mad.'[10] Not only this, but Strindberg, he declared, also taught us that we as humans are driven by a far greater power, unconsciously, helplessly, to behave as we do:

> When lovers first kiss – I am told – they feel as if, almost physically, two gigantic invisible hands were softly, irresistibly, pressing their heads together. By such vast and uncomprehended compulsion are Strindberg's people in part moved; as people are in real life, as we are driven, with or against each other, to life or death, to pleasure and pain, but mostly pain, by forces we never quite understand.[11]

The more time elapsed, the more I felt that in his presence I was as wax in his hands, and could refuse him nothing: and that there was thus the choice before me of going on on his terms or of withdrawing from my intimacy with him, at any rate for a time – I never dreamed of withdrawing permanently from it. Even the thought of temporary withdrawal drove me mad. I tried to think in the train on the way home. I could not. I wrote a letter, – a silly, angry letter, – which I threw in the fire, only to replace it by another not much better.

Farm Corner
Tadworth
Surrey

My mind works slowly, as you may have discovered. – When I got in I wrote you a rather angry and disjointed note, which I burnt. I thought I'd wait and see what you said. But that would'nt make my point clear to you.

"All females are beasts" you say. That means probably that you've only come across females who are beasts. I don't see how any female who is'nt a beast can consent to the things which you asked me to consent to, practically the murder of her possible offspring. Also, where does this path lead, in which you expend on a little paltry pleasure of your own, which I don't think improves the general aspect of the world for you to any degree worth mentioning, the large part of the energy and joy which ought by rights to go to the making of the next generation?

I'll be no party to it.

Anyway, apart from this, you did'nt seem to me to be taking me at any valuation I was going to stand.

I don't like the feeling that you might bully me into something. You would'nt intimidate me into anything, I'm stubborn, but your superior strength renders it possible for you to compel me to do things against my reason: the result of which might be to make me turn on you, perhaps kill you by treachery. I like people you can reason with. I give way easy to reason.

But if you drown your reasons in pleasures, if you deliberately take up this hedonistic attitude – which in the end spells growing hateful, coarse, devoid of any excellence, literary or otherwise, and even after a while ruins physical beauty, because having no ideals is plainly written on the face of those who for a long time have had none – then what is there to appeal to?

The gist of all this is, you must not come down here, nor will I come see you in town; I don't like the prospect, but there it is. If you write and say you're coming here, then's the day I've arranged to take Margaret Radford away to the sea, or to do some other thing that'll take me out of the way for a bit.

I did'nt realise at once how much I disapproved – not only of this one thing, but, for instance, your description of life in Munich followed up to its end. The only thing I can think is that, having been through a terrible time, you clutch feverishly at any pleasures. Even that does'nt excuse giving up all "Striving towards the light". For a time I tried to think you were striving towards it in a difficult way, but I really can't think that.

It all makes me feel a little sick – I wish I could make you see.

– I told you Mamma's a reader of thoughts: she knows I'm offended with you about something, and she is'nt very keen on your coming, consequently. So, as I can do nothing, I suppose you must just go to the devil your own way. But you're not going to take me with you. I have work to do.

Phyllis.

(a train)

Monday

My dear Phyllis,

I just got your letter before leaving Cambridge today. It disturbed me, as no doubt it was meant to do; as no doubt I deserve –

I've been continually thinking about writing to you, but it always seemed so much easier to talk, so I put off writing till I could see a chance of arranging to talk. I'd meant to write about it this afternoon, in this train, – but now your letter's come.

There are times (and now is one) when I entirely sympathize with any body not wanting to see me or have anything to do with me. But not in the way that, and for the reasons that, you suggest.

I wish to God I hadn't been weak and tired last time. I'm afraid I made a bad impression. And I didn't put things clearly, or nicely.

But, my dear child, your letter – it hurt. It sounded so extraordinarily unlike your voice I could scarcely believe you'd written it.

I mean, the thing's quite clear. There are things we might do or not do; we might decide to part or meet; it is for us to decide. I'm willing to decide reasonably, and abide by the decision. But, Phyllis, even if it is parting – don't let us do it like this.

You write so strangely – you must have misconceptions about some things. Let me tell you what you seem to me – somehow – to be wrong about.

For one thing, you seem to think it probable I might insist on coming down to try to see you, although you asked me not, O Phyllis, why on earth do you think that of me? If you won't see me, you won't; and I abide by it, what have I done to give you the impression I'm such a cad?

Then the idea that you stand for reason and I for bullying. It's really unfair, child. Have you forgotten that I could have used my strength and opportunity, and didn't try – just because I wanted our relationship to be on a different plane? You must know that's what I've done all the time. My good Phyllis, all I want to do is tell you reasonably my view of things, to hear yours, and to agree on the best and least mean course of action we can jointly adopt. Be fair to me, child, even if I am going to the devil! Also, you don't quite seem to understand what I suggested. There's plenty of life left for either of us to have all the children that we want, even if we did what we thought of for now.[12] The next generation doesn't suffer at all from what we experience and emotions we leave them. If you think (as you seem to) it only leaves ugliness and horror – "hedonism", you're right enough to refuse, and I'm not content, but acquiescent – but if you think there's anything more in the effects than that, you're wrong.

The real point is my attitude towards things, and yours. If you really think mine impossible, – well I'm sorry, and goodbye – as clearly and as kindly as we can manage. I am not ashamed of my feelings. I think your beauty fine; I'm not ashamed to think so. I don't think or pretend to think, that you have only a head and hands. I know that you begin at your hair and go down to your toes, a human being. We have given (or I thought so) each other fineness and beauty. We could give each other more, I thought: but if it hurt or harmed either of us more than it was worth – then we wouldn't: –

Phyllis, I had a spasm of fear once lest my drifting life should hurt you. I was afraid – I didn't know if you were strong enough to stand unconventional emotional life – how is one to judge of another soul? I warned you; and you promised not to be hurt. Well, judge how not to be, and abide by your decision, and I'm satisfied. But don't think me beastly.

You have suddenly judged and condemned my life and me, without, I think, knowing what they are, and certainly without discussing it with me or reasoning at all –

There is so much to say, and it is hard to write it. I wish you would come and talk. I won't be unpleasant. If you're still so mistrustful of me, you may bring a police rattle or a revolver. I don't think you'll need them. I'll reason. I want to make you understand. And I'm far too fond of you and respect you too much, and admire, to want to hurt you. (Though you don't seem – after all these months – to understand that.) Please come and meet me somewhere. Then we'll know what to do. I've some work as well as you. I hoped to give beauty and glory to both. If we think we can't – we can retire on what we've got from each other already – if there is anything. I, at any rate, have got something.

So write, Phyllis, and say what afternoon and where. I'm here this week. If you don't like the idea at the moment, wait till you feel readier to be fair. But I can't think you can help being what you've been, brave and reasonable. Come and talk here if you like (I'm finishing in Marsh's. 5 Raymond Bgs, Grays Inn). It's probably most comfortable. Please let me know – I want to see you –

Goodnight child.

I'm sorry.

Rupert

In the train

Tuesday. [1913]

If I wrote in haste and put things brutally, I'm sorry. But the things were there. I assure you it could'nt have been conventional morality (sorry to write so badly the train's jiggling) because that would have prevented a whole lot of things that it did'nt. It's something inborn and inbred into my character. You say "be fair to me even if I'm going to the devil" – what makes you admit that you are? You've told me awfully little really, and I have'nt asked because I did'nt want to bother you – But if you'd tell me a few things I might have a better chance of understanding – I can't bear the prospect of a deteriorating you. Do tell me what you mean.

But if going on seeing you means that: intercourse without result – I do definitely refuse it.

I would'nt of course come to see you with a police whistle or a revolver – if it came to that I would'nt come to see you at all: you need'nt have said that.

You must'nt imagine I don't want to have any more to do with you. That hurt frightfully.

But as I don't consider you to be there only for my pleasure, so I expect you not to consider me only there for yours – I wish I could explain.

Why don't you want me enough to do so much as consider the possibility of marrying me? Are you ashamed to own me? You'd never find a person fonder of you – nor one more ready to go through suffering for you – you may'nt believe it, with me saying what I do, but I do care about your ultimate interests: I wish you would'nt accept hedonism with acquiescence: I know you're tired, but I wish you would'nt. There are better things.

If you definitely commit yourself to it, though, I'm afraid I'll have to say I won't see you. Not for a while at any rate. If you think I don't care, you're very wrong. It's about the hardest thing to say I've ever said. It'd be less trouble to be dead –

You who say you care whether you hurt me, tell me your whole attitude – write it out like a creed if you will – tell me a little more of your history – it might help me to understand more – and for heaven's sake don't keep things back because you are afraid they'll hurt, it'd hurt far less if you told me them –

What was worrying you those last 2 days? (also, why did you say all women are beasts? That sticks in my head, it's so palpably unfair.)

It's better to write in some ways. One's more dispassionate. One forgets things less. – not much less, it's true.

I would really much rather talk to you about it all – but I know I should say even less of what I mean than I do now. And I apologise for saying you'd bully me: I did'nt mean it. I wrote in rather a disturbed condition, and may have said things I did'nt mean. Forgive me. And do try to see my point of view: don't call it conventional, for I don't believe there's an atom of convention in me – call it ascetic, puritanical, if you like –

Look I have chosen the harder path. I could have leaned on convention, or thrust aside my feeling. I accept no authority. I stand alone, and try to do what I feel to be right, and it's very difficult: for I get blamed by both the upholders and by the destroyers of convention: or would if I gave them the chance of criticising me, which I don't –

I must stop now.
    Phyllis

c/o Marsh
5, Raymond Buildings.
Gray's Inn.

My dear Phyllis,
    London's bloody. I never have the energy to think...
    It's very difficult writing.
    Don't gloom over my saying that all women are beasts. I've quite forgotten saying it, and apropos of what I said it. They mostly are, I assure you. So are most men. All men, I think.

You're less of a beast than any I've seen, I'll admit. Look here, it's horribly difficult to get one's ideas straight on paper. I didn't mean to insult you, child, by saying you were "conventional". I don't think I should think it an insult even if I did call you "conventional". But you seem to think it is.

I think it's partly right, what you say about you being "puritan" and not me. Though I'm not sure what "Puritanism" is.

And my view of life is roughly, this. – And it's what I meant about "conventional" – but I'll use less misleading words. There are two ways of loving: the normal and the wandering. Different kinds of character are drawn to each. The normal is to love and marry one person, and only him. The wandering is to take what one wants where one finds it, to be friends here, lovers there, married there, to spend a day with some, a week with others, – possibly a lifetime with others.

Neither is a' priori better than the other. The wandering requires the shallower temperament, perhaps. Well. If one's made for one, one can't do the other, without risk of smashing. That's what I find about people. I don't know why it's so. It is so.

My dear, I'm a wanderer. If you are, too, – if you're satisfied with taking what you can get, and going on or not, as it happens – then we can give each other things. If, as I suspect, you're disposed to normality – then I shall harm and hurt you too much.

O, there are so many thousand subjects rising out of this. It's impossible to enter into them all.

Isn't it really, just a question between people who'll have all or nothing, and people who take what they can get?

My dear, I'll talk about myself, if that's what you want! It's not very enlivening – I wish we could talk together. It's so much quicker than writing. I may be able to explain to you that I'm not a brute: and you may be able to explain to me that you're not a coward, but a Puritan.

If there's a war in Russia, I shall go to it. But I shall be here, alone, next week –

My dear child, please don't be hurt. I do want you to be happy –

    With love
      Rupert

Thursday.

Forgive me if I write angrily, unreasonably. This is my share of hell, even as the beginning was of heaven.

I don't think it's really quite fair to say I'm not strong enough for what you call "unconventional emotional life"; it really seems to me as though I've needed a great deal more strength to say what I've said than to go straight on: I'd have had to tell you my feeling in the matter sooner or later, as well now as any time, I suppose, though – Any fool can sit on his or her conscience. Because I don't choose to, you say I'm not being strong enough.

Now with worrying about this I have grown so tired I don't know what I'm doing. I shall be ill in a little if I can't see my way through it better than this.

I would call out to you for help, only that I don't believe you understand my point of view: I thought you did, once.

I wish to heaven we could turn to one another for help and the re-gathering of strength.

But if I were dying of tiredness I would not do anything I had a rooted instinct, or prejudice, or what ever you like, against – I'd burn at the stake. People have been known to do such things.

Can't you see that I would'nt write so vehemently if I was'nt distracted and the battle ground of two passions? Therefore forgive me and try to see, or I shall go silly. I won't condemn you unheard, only do write, and say – oh, anything you will –

No, really, that was a relapse. It won't break me. Only it's disturbing.

Wonder how much more of it would lead me to accept hedonism and the line of least resistance. Personally I think I'd die first.

"God help us all" – I'm a fool.
Phyllis.

c/o Marsh

Friday –

My dear, it's all right. Don't trouble so about it. I can explain my feeling's and position, I think. And I can explain what I think of yours – I'll write at greater length in a day or two, when I have time to ponder it. It's not so easy to write one's whole position out on paper! I think it'd be much better if we could discuss it together. We'd get clear sooner.

But any how I'll write in a day or two, trying to explain one or two things – meanwhile, don't tire yourself, child.

With love
Rupert

Both Rupert and Phyllis had been playing a part. Now that both were being honest, they could hardly recognise one another. For Brooke it must have been obvious from Phyllis's last letter that if he did as she asked and discussed his past with her, she would be horrified. Phyllis knew she could not trust herself to stand firm in his presence, and so insisted on a discussion via correspondence. These two factors meant little if no progress could be made. The more they argued their positions, the more it became apparent that they were poles apart: each antagonised and insulted the other at every turn, escalating the situation rapidly beyond retrieval.

It was evident that Brooke had quite a different agenda than Phyllis. At least now, to his credit, he was being intensely frank about his intentions towards her. It would seem that this, a landmark in his relationships with women, was ultimately because he did not want to inflict on Phyllis the damage he felt he had both caused and received through his relationship with Ka. In addition, for more selfish reasons, he was keen to avoid any further unpleasantness and messiness in his life.

My mother could not fail to notice something wrong. One evening I tried to explain to her. She loved him too, and felt the extraordinary charm and power of his personality in the same way as I did. But she had an even stronger feeling than I had against the tendencies into which we saw him drawn, including "There are ways."

The next little while was a while of utter agony to me. I would not go and see him – I suppose partly from the fear that I should see all things from his point of view, and surrender myself unconditionally to him. But the effort of making the break was too much for me, and I fell ill. This was partly due to mere misery, a fruitful cause of illness, but partly also to the purely physical side of things. I was working at a screen, and I worked from morning till night in a cold room, working being the only thing that could take my mind off the utter unbearableness of things, and I must thereby have lowered my vitality. One day I crawled home from the empty house where I was working, went to bed, lay flat on my back, and thought of nothing. And by the time I had recovered a little I heard he had gone off to the South Seas.

[Postmarked: London W8, 3.15 pm, Mar 8.13]
5.3.13. – 8.3.13. London.
My dear Mrs Gardner,
   I don't know what you want me to say. Nothing, perhaps –
   It's all horrible –
   It hurts me very much that Phyllis is ill; and that she, and you, should hate me in that way –
   You hate me for my general character and for my behaviour towards her. Rightly, I suppose. For I've always known that I'm entirely an "ordinary" kind of man. And for her – in regard to individuals one has to be judged by results. And if she is ill, in any way through me, – I have failed; and deserve any blame.

Yet, I'd hoped to give her something, – as acquaintance with her was a thing I was glad and proud to have. I have always admired her fineness of mind and of all sides of her – But if I have only given her pain, I have done evil –

But I can't understand it –

I cannot bear the thought that she should be ill because, in any way, of me – if I could say or do anything, to make her better –

It's no good, writing.

Rupert Brooke

As is so often the case with Brooke, there are two contrasting pictures of his life at this time: the public and the private. It was during March that he started writing overblown letters of admiration and ardour to Cathleen Nesbitt – in great contrast to the tone of correspondence he was now exchanging with Phyllis. He was also keeping his options open with Elisabeth van Rysselberghe, taking her out to lunch and to the ballet. In addition, while receiving Phyllis's distressed letters, Brooke was writing in flippant, light-hearted style to Noel Olivier about his life in London society, into which he had wholeheartedly flung himself – no doubt partly as a distraction:

But you, poor brown mouse, can't, in the dizziest heights of murian imagination, picture the life of whirl glitter and gaiety I lead. A young man about town, Noel, (I've had my hair cut remarkably short –). Dinners, boxes at the opera, literary lunch-parties, theatre supper-parties (the Carlton on Saturday next) – I know several actresses. Last night, in the stalls at the Ballet, Eddie and I (I'd wired for my white waistcoat) bowed and smiled – oh, quite casually – at

Queen Alexandra
The Marquis de Soveral
The Duchess of Rutland
Countess Rodomontini (or such)
Mrs George Keppel
and a host more.[13]

Brooke was certainly making some influential new friends. Most notable among them were Prime Minister Asquith and his family, who were invited to a party held on 11 March to celebrate Brooke's being elected a Fellow of King's – all his work on the Webster dissertation had finally paid off.

Beneath this frivolity, Rupert's health suggested that the guilt he felt over Phyllis was taking its toll. Around the time he had written this last letter to Mrs Gardner he became ill with flu, an ailment to which he always fell victim at times of emotional upset. He also wrote to Ka at this time, 'I'll be all right in California. I'd better go, you know. I'm not doing anyone any good here, myself nor nobody'.[14] He had already broken the news to his mother.

As far as literary achievement was concerned, Brooke was going from strength to strength. *Georgian Poetry* had been a great success, and at the end of March 1913 he won the prize for best poem of last year in the *Poetry Review* with 'The Old Vicarage, Grantchester'.[15]

It was also about this time, one foggy day, that Brooke went and sat for the American photographer Sherril Schell at his flat in Pimlico. Some years later Schell was to recall his first impressions of Brooke in vivid detail. He paints for us a compelling picture not only of the man before him, but also of his thoughts and mood at this time:

> He spoke too that afternoon of his forthcoming trip to America and asked many questions about California, keen to know all about different trails to the high Sierras, about the natives of that part of the world, the animals and the big trees. He thought he would stay in the west most of the time and possibly try to get something to do in the way of work out there. He seemed all eagerness to be off on his adventure, but now and then a wistful expression would pass over his face that gave me the impression that he was not entirely happy at going away. Friendship meant much in his life.[16]

The 12 frames were taken using only natural light, Brooke having to hold his position for a minute each exposure. For the final portrait Brooke suggested one in profile, bare-shouldered, for which he stripped to the waist 'revealing a torso that recalled the young Hermes'. On seeing it Brooke wrote 'I think it's rather silly'.[17] He did not realise that with this single image he had helped bring into creation a portrait that, when used as the frontispiece to his posthumous *1914 and Other Poems* in just over two years' time, would help fuel his fame ... and later mockery.

Brooke was finally regaining his strength. Determined not to let emotions get the better of him again, he explained in a letter to Ka, written on 25 March:

The queer thing is, that now I've hardened myself a good deal, and
cut off other emotions, fairly short, ambition grows and grows in me.
It's inordinate, gigantic. It's no use; it doesn't even make me work. I
just sit and think ambitious thoughts. As I used to sit and think lustful
thoughts.[18]

Throughout April and into May Brooke continued to live life amid the
glamorous whirl of society, the highlight of which was being invited
to 10 Downing Street on 15 April for the birthday party of Violet
Asquith.[19] Here he found himself in impressive company: George
Bernard Shaw, J M Barrie and John Masefield, to name but a few.
At the event Naomi Royde Smith, literary editor of the *Westminster
Gazette*, learnt of Brooke's desire to go abroad. She offered to pay all
his expenses plus four guineas per article if he was prepared to travel
through the United States and Canada, writing a series of articles for
the *Gazette* as he went, recording his impressions of the places he passed
through. He, of course, accepted, and wasted no time in preparing to
leave. 'I have been rushing all day, buying outfit and making bloody
farewells,' he wrote to Marsh in May.[20] In the same month, Brooke revealed his mixed emotions to Frances Cornford, who had first proposed
the idea of travel to him:

> I don't really feel going off to be nearly as 'Hellish' as you imagine.
> I've really got quite callous in my feelings by now. I'm not excited by
> travelling. But I've the feeling of shaking the dust of a pretty dirty period
> of my life off my feet. And that makes up for any tear there may be.[21]

[Postmarked: Liverpool, 5.15 pm, May 22]

24 Bilton Road
Rugby

Wednesday May 21. 1913

Dear Mrs Gardner,

I am leaving England tomorrow for six months, or eight, or more.
As you said you didn't want you or Phyllis to be bothered by coming
across me again, I thought you would like to know this. Though even
if and when I return I shan't bother people who don't want me. I didn't
think you wanted me to answer your last letter. Some of it I could not
understand. And I had nothing more to say than I had already said. But
I was sorry you said nothing about Phyllis's health, for you had said she
was very ill, before. But I have gathered she is better now.

I enclose a note to Phyllis, telling her I am going away. I feel responsible only, or almost only, to her and to myself, for what I say to her. But as she may still be ill, and as I do not want you to think I am "deceiving" you, I send the letter through you. I hope you will give it her. But you are at liberty to send it back, or to read it.

It won't upset her, I think.

I am sorry it has all been like this; and that you think me disgusting.

Goodbye.

Rupert Brooke

24 Bilton Road
Rugby

Wednesday May 21 1913

My dear Phyllis,

You ceased writing to me, and your mother wrote instead, and conveyed the message that you didn't want to hear from me. So I didn't write. But I was sorry. If I'd seen you I think I could have explained things that hurt you. But it is impossible to explain any relationship between two people to a third: even if it was desired –

I gather you think me evil. Well, I'm sorry. And I think you're wrong. But that doesn't so much matter. But if I hurt you: if you have suffered pain in account of me, I am deeply sorry. You were good to me. I'm sorry for what pain I gave you: and glad of any good I gave you.

I won't write about any thing now; as you don't seem to want it. I'm writing to let you know – it may be a relief to you – that I'm leaving England tomorrow, till the end of the year, or till next Spring. If ever you want to hear of me, you can; but as you do not seem to, I will not bother you by letting you know I exist. If ever you want any thing, or want any help, please ask me. I should be glad to give it you. I owe it to your fineness, and the good you gave me. (Oh, I shouldn't give it as a debt! But because I should want to.)

I wish you good luck, and happiness.

Goodbye.

Rupert

SIX

'ACQUAINTANCESHIP'

On 2 May 1913 Brooke climbed into his train at Euston station. On the platform to see him off were Geoffrey Fry and old friends from Rugby days, St John Lucas and Denis Browne, who had hunted down at the last minute the 'most tasteful notepaper Euston could produce'[1] as a parting gift. On arriving at Liverpool Brooke, feeling 'a trifle lonely', paid 'a dirty little boy' called William sixpence to wave him off.[2] He then boarded the SS *Cedric* and set sail for the United States of America.

It was not until nine days later that he arrived in New York, in a depressed state of mind:

> I don't know a soul in New York; and I'm very tired; and I don't like the food; and I don't like the people's faces; and I don't like the newspapers; and I haven't a friend in the world; and nobody loves me; and I'm going to be extraordinarily miserable these six months; and I want to die. There![3]

Before long, however, he started getting into the spirit of this new adventure. Soon Brooke was travelling from New York to Ottawa and then on to Toronto, Vancouver and San Francisco. From here he sailed to Hawaii, Samoa, Fiji, New Zealand and Tahiti.

Back in January 1913, the Gardners had become friends with the poet Robert Frost and his family after meeting them at the opening of the

Poetry Bookshop. Frost had come over from the USA in September 1912 in the hope of making his name as a poet in England, something he had so far failed to do in his home country. He brought with him his wife Elinor and their four children, Lesley, Carol, Irma and Marjorie. In July 1913 Elinor Frost wrote to a friend back home about their new friends:

> We have become very well acquainted with the family of one of the professors at London University – Professor Gardner. His wife is author of a Greek grammar[4] and is very kind-hearted, clever and impulsive. There are three children, a daughter, 22 years old, who is an artist, and two younger children, Lesley and Carol's ages. We like them all very much, and they have been very nice to us, but they live on the other side of London, in Surrey, and we cannot see much of them.[5]

Soon after this, things between Robert Frost and Mrs Gardner became strained, largely due to a clash of personalities. This was further exacerbated when in August, at the Gardners' invitation, the Frost family went and stayed near them for a holiday in Fife, Scotland. Robert Frost came away harbouring contempt and ill feeling for the whole family. The sentiment was not shared by his wife and children, who remained in contact, particularly with Mrs Gardner and Delphis, for several years.

> I set to work and produced a picture which was accepted, and hung in a good position, at the New English. This was the first success of this kind I had had. The picture was called "Fairy Gold". [11] And represented a young woman standing in an autumn wood, sadly looking down at a lapful of dead leaves. Some person unknown bought it, and I have not seen it since.
>
> He wrote to me once or twice from the other ends of the earth. I also wrote to him. Across such great distances our letters were not exactly answers to one another. By this time I was more or less recovering myself, and had decided that I would try, when he came back, to hold my passion in check and be friends with him – as an experiment. I doubted very much whether I should be able to manage it, but I meant to see whether I could. Really, I think, my mind welcomed any subterfuge that would allow me to make

terms with him at all, because I was overpowered with longing to see him again. When I reread my letters to him about this time, I see that they are the letters of a passionate lover. I remember thinking them very cold and severe when I wrote them. – He kept every word I wrote him, even post-cards, and these are all now in my possession.

Farm Corner
Tadworth
Surrey

My dear Rupert

Of course I know I've made a fool of myself and expressed myself extremely badly: but it's really quite a misapprehension to think that I don't want to hear of or from you: and it is'nt a relief to me for you to be gone away. But can't you see that the way things were I could not possibly take the initiative in writing to you without tremendous loss of self-respect? I hated leaving as the last of it all a letter to Mamma in which you assumed that I wanted to have nothing more to do with you.

I can't say how glad I am you've written. – What I wanted to happen was that I should meet you by accident and then we might have explained: and in Cambridge and in London I looked hard for you, but uselessly. I might almost say that, fearing I never should, I've tried to be unfaithful to you and did'nt seem able to manage it: even when I thought you did'nt really mind at all – I thought if you really minded at all you would write, and if you did'nt I'd better forget all about it if I could –

But I don't think you need have accused Mamma of ever keeping back my letters or reading them against my will.

Of course it is'nt really possible, as you say, to explain any relationship to a third person; but I could not manage to hide that I was suffering under something, and as I had to tell something I tried to explain the truth. It's no use whatever – telling lies to people one's intimate with: they always find out.

And when Mamma said I was too ill to receive letters the fact is I had received yours: and was'nt in a condition to use either brain or hands and could'nt possibly have written myself.

I wish I had known a little more about your movements.

I recovered in time to get to work on a thing for the New English. You won't be surprised to hear they did'nt hang it. But I am consoled, because they did'nt "reject" it, they only "excluded it for want of space".

Mamma and I have a volume coming out with Dent. I did the woodcuts. It's called "Plain Themes". 1/– I think.

– Where are you gone to? I wish I'd seen you, even in the distance, before you went.

Write about things. You know perfectly well I do want it. I don't want anybody's help just now: I want to work. But I do want to know that you exist. (how could I help knowing, with your things coming and hitting me in the eye in all the papers?)

Write and explain, as you said you could, the things that hurt me. Don't be afraid of hurting me any more. I promised that I would'nt be hurt, and I've broken my promise: nevertheless in hope I will renew it.

[Blessing][6]

That is an Erise[7] blessing for you, to take you over the sea.

Phyllis.

A happy Christmas to all of you

Pango-Pange
The beginning of Samoa

November 1913

My dear Phyllis,

Your letter, of May or June, found me wandering somewhere in Canada. Now I'm here, in the South Pacific, for how long I don't know.

For nearly two years I have planned to get away like this. I think it is a good thing. One sees more clearly. Perhaps it would have been better, had I done it sooner.

Your letter assured me that you are better again, which is what I chiefly wanted to know. I was anxious about your illness, all the more because I felt responsible for it.

My dear child, there are two ways of approaching these relationships. One is only to allow love in the supposition that it may lead to marriage: the other is ... the wandering way. And there are people made for the first way, and – perhaps – people made for the second. But to introduce those made for the first to the second way is to invite pain and endless trouble and confusion. That's what I dimly foresaw, when I said I hoped you wouldn't be hurt. You said you wouldn't and I agreed – but the laws of things were too strong for us. I ought to have seen that then and prevented all this. But I was selfish.

I think you are the first kind. That need not imply that you are better or worse than the second kind. Only different. Though, as a matter of fact, it is the better kind, I think. – So you may know that I am not trying to insult you!

You are meant for love and marriage. There isn't anything better. Nothing I shall do or know of, anyhow. I'm a wanderer: and the more I have to do with you (beyond a certain degree of friendliness) the more trouble and pain I shall bring you.

That is my conclusion about it all: that I did wrong trying to lead you along a way that wasn't fitted for you. I am sorry I hurt you. I guess I'd better stick, in my wanderings, to people who are meant for wanderers. There are many such in the world. And I shan't do harm.

– I hope I made my meaning clear in all this. It's so difficult, eight thousand miles away. The sense of communication is lost. Put it like this. There are some people for whom it's always a case of all-or-nothing. They are made to enter the game on other terms. Others play for a little each time, win a little or lose a little – well, it's not fair of the latter to play with the former.

I did wrong (though not without warning you! – for what that's worth!). You made a mess of it from my point of view by suddenly landing me in that situation. But you were ill and couldn't help it.

For the future (which is very dim, at present) I don't want to see you – in your home, at least, – if it means that I'm to be regarded as a very disgraceful and objectionable character (as I was soon reported to be regarded, I remember – before I left England – mutual, or semi-mutual friends, are very obliging in such matters). Nor do I want to, if it means pain to you. On the other hand, it's nice to be friends.

I shan't be in England anyhow before March, I think. And I may not return for years. So the best thing for you would be to dismiss me from any prominent place in your thoughts, and give yourself up to your work and anybody else you may find. And if I do come back soon, we might meet once for a discussion, if you wanted: but otherwise leave communication to letters for a time. (By the way, a letter to Rugby or to Kings, will always find me in the end – if it's not lost –). There's too much in you to waste on unsatisfactory dealings with a person like me – as they have been recently.

Child, don't love me.

I'm very much in the dark about your state of mind. But I hope you won't feel any dislike or suspicion of the male half of mankind on my account. They're mostly better than me, – though some, I must admit, are worse. I wouldn't have you trust them: but like them. And realise – which is very hard for a modern young woman – that they are entirely different from woman, and have different problems to face. They often have a hard time in their way, and deserve pity.

I have misgivings of whatever plan of behaviour I think of. It seems so silly to sacrifice "acquaintanceship" – it's so very rare for two human beings to be within hailing distance. Yet I don't want you to be hurt by seeing me: and I know from experience that that often happens. –

Oh well, it's a long way ahead. And I may get swallowed up by a shark. I suppose the chief thing is that London (I suppose you're there?) is a fine place and that Samoa is a very fine place, and there's a lot to be got out of life. I hope you're getting it. You ought to. (Only, don't let pride get in your way, my good Phyllis. If, as you say, you wanted to write to me before I left and pride prevented you, why, you were foolish. There's a place for pride, but not there.)

God be with you, my dear. Are the streets of London full of mist and fairy lights and shining taxis and the smell of wet English people? I suppose so. And here there's blinding sunshine and white sand, and cocoanut [sic] palms, and strange brown people.

I hope you're doing a lot of work, + I hope you're happy.

Damn these mosquitoes + bless you!

Manina! – there's a Samoan answer to your Celtic greeting.

Rupert

P.S. Please tell your mother that you've heard from me and that I'm alive and well and some distance away –

It is not known if Brooke ever saw a copy of Mary Gardner's *Plain Themes*. If he had, it would not have escaped him that at least one of her poems, entitled 'Quits', was unquestionably about Phyllis and himself.

Quits

I loved you? – No, I only loved your face
Your tall, fair beauty and your well-knit form,
Your voice's music and your body's grace,
Your keen, bright glance, too piercing to be warm.[8]

And you loved me? – You loved the outer shell,
The masses of bright hair, the melting glance,
The delicate flower of maidenhood's sweet spell,
And the aroma of untouched romance.

And now all's gone, our hearts have gone asleep,
I turn to work again with added zest,
In colour and in form I laugh and weep,
And through Imagination seek life's best.

You wrap your naked thoughts in garments of verse,
And rhyme about joy and sorrow, youth and art,
In different keys your varying theme rehearse –
The infinite potency of mind and heart.

Shall I have other models as fair as you?
Will you find other maidens to admire?
I'll paint the background sky a deeper blue,
You'll write another poem on desire.

Brooke was right to believe that there were those among his literary circle who frowned upon his treatment of Phyllis. Robert Frost, who had frequent contact with the Gardners, touches upon this whole business by way of notes written in the margin of a December 1913 copy of *Poetry and Drama*,[9] sent to his friend, John T Bartlett, in the United States. A collection of Brooke's poems had been published alongside some of Frost's in this issue; next to Brooke's 'The Funeral of Youth: Threnody' Frost comments: 'This boy I have met once. He is near you now, in Calif. He effects a metaphysical sarcasm and would be a later John Donne.' And then over the page, alongside 'He Wonders Whether to Praise or to Blame Her', he continues: 'We know this hardly treated girl oh very well. Her beauty is her red hair. Her cleverness is in painting. She has a picture in the New English Exhibition. Her mother has written a volume of verse in which he gets his. Very funny. No one will die.'

He wonders whether to praise or to blame her
I have peace to weigh your worth, now all is over,
　　But if to praise or blame you, cannot say.
For, who decries the loved, decries the lover;
　　Yet what man lauds the thing he's thrown away?

Be you, in truth, this dull, slight, cloudy naught,
　　The more fool I, so great a fool to adore;
But if you're that high goddess once I thought,
　　The more your godhead is, I lose the more.

Dear fool, pity the fool who thought you clever!
　　Dear wisdom, do not mock the fool that missed you!
Most fair, – the blind has lost your face for ever!
　　Most foul, – how could I see you while I kissed you?

So... the poor love of fools and blind I've proved you,
For, foul or lovely, 'twas a fool that loved you.

If Frost had assumed this poem was written with Phyllis in mind, there is no reason to think she had not come to the same conclusion, both about this and other poems written in a similar vein by Brooke at this time. In fact there is little doubt it was Ka, and the feelings of anger and love she had inspired in him, that had acted as the catalyst for the works.

Her misapprehension must have given Phyllis a less than accurate impression of how strongly Brooke felt about her, in both a positive and negative sense. Ultimately it gave her hope that she seemed frequently to inhabit his thoughts, and still rouse passion in him of one form or another.

Farm Corner,
Tadworth,
Surrey.

Dear Rupert,

I am most pleased to have heard from you. For your letter has given me the handle I required before stating what I feel about it all. And your confession or apology has opened the way for mine. I am sorry that I was silly. I did'nt know, honestly, that I was an all-or-nothing person. I had so little experience. And even if I had known of it, it would have been very difficult for me to draw back earlier than I did. – And I also did'nt realise you any more than I did myself. I'm sorry to have been so violent and sudden, and must ask your forgiveness for my rough unskilful handling of a very difficult problem.

I don't know who told anybody anything about what happened. So few people (that I know of) knew anything. I would'nt have let any body know at all if I'd been able not to: only Mamma and Daddy could'nt help noticing that I never saw you; and I am a poor liar. Only some people are so clever at inference. I suspect del Re to be traitor.

My people would'nt tell anyone. I'm much obliged to whoever it was. It was no affair of his, or hers.

You need'nt tell me to give myself up to work. I have vain hopes that I may succeed. I have sold a picture out of the New English and got a commission for a decorating job. I am not in London, as a rule, more than I can help. I am not keen on much human society. I can live very happily in my studio among my drawings in the knowledge that I am improving in the quality of my work. And I have made expeditions within the United Kingdom, which suffice as a change, though they reach no Southern Ocean. A place is none the worse for being near – as near as the islands of Scotland, or the hills of Wales – if one has'nt seen the like before.

I could see you without being hurt. I know it. All the more, I suppose, will this be the case after a further lapse of time. By all means let us keep acquaintanceship. I was afraid that by my roughness of method it was destroyed. I am glad to think you can still keep the wish for it. I ask no better. It is beautiful, therefore let us not lose it. So I would take it kindly if you would occasionally write and let me know that you're alive. Don't get swallowed by a shark: I should imagine it was a somewhat painful and piecemeal ending.

– I was thrown from a horse into a Welsh river and had to swim for my life the other day. I consider my life very well worth saving from my own point of view. – Do not be afraid I shall make rash, or indeed any, generalisations about the male human being. My acquaintances among men do not offer enough similarities. And I don't know that my trust or mistrust of mankind in general has either increased or diminished through my dealings with you. I have men friends that I could trust utterly. (And in dealing with these the fact of sex is by no means all-important. I know it is an obsession with some people: the same, I think, who are given to very rash generalisation, as are other monomaniacs.)

I think there is a place for pride, and do not consider the pride that kept me from writing "out of turn" misplaced. Why should I shove myself upon a person who, not having written, has no further use for my communications? That's the point of view.

Well, it was very nice of you to write. And I don't seem to mind mileage. (If the earth's inside out, as the hypothesis you told me could have it, you should be telescopically visible somewhere overhead!) I hope this'll reach you sooner or later. Good luck go with you.

Phyllis.

I wrote that other sheetful and now think I'll add to it a bit.

I wish you understood my point of view more easily, because I think it's quite a good one. I mean not so much that I am able to bring convincing arguments in its favour as that I feel it to be all right. And most arguments used are only dictated by some feeling or other.

I want to spoil no one's liberty: I am not precisely keen on spoiling my own by giving it up to anyone else at all, but there are circumstances in which I would be prepared to do so: and enjoy doing so. And I have'nt the slightest wish to incur obligations unwillingly paid. I would a deal sooner they were'nt paid. But I like a sense of fair exchange – in love as in all other things. That is, moderately fair. (What the futurists call "semi-equality"?) I make no unconditional surrender. I'm afraid I am not explaining my meaning at all.

But at the start of things I thought of none of this. I did'nt weigh out causes and effects, rights and wrongs.

I enjoyed. But that incident is closed. And my memory has a happy faculty of retaining what is beautiful and rejecting what is not.

Can you understand that I can see you exactly in the light in which I saw you before and yet feelings towards you can be free of all desire?

There we have a basis for "acquaintanceship". – And should you come back, I would like such to continue. I would like to see you – preferably in no underhand manner. If necessary, I suppose I should bear the wrath of certain relations. None of their affair. But sufficient unto the day ... I would fight over a less matter. I have the say over my own actions. (I'm jolly glad I don't live in Cambridge.)

The trouble is, life is'nt long enough to fit in everything. I want to get away out of this and see the world, but even more I want to stick here and work as hard as I can. Which involves a good deal of doing nothing.

I have not succeeded in saying what I meant. Expression dodged me. It generally does. Anyhow, consider yourself in no way bound by, or responsible for, me. Don't worry about me at all. I am getting lots out of life. The joy of living is what matters. You have it: I have it.

There is much beauty all around us. As for what is'nt beautiful – God knows. I don't know a satisfactory philosophy. Since I last heard from you I have seen a live thing die. Our puppy was run over by a motor. It set me thinking about death more than any second-hand accounts could have done: because it was simple, incredible and utterly horrible. And I was awful fond of that little beast. That it was a dumb beast makes not much difference.

I suppose you do grow wiser by experience. It's the one consolation. Except that irrepressible feeling

"We'd rather be alive than not."

Here, I've written enough. Goodbye.

Eppwoo.[10] God bless you.

A third thought. Your "Pacific"[11] poem has excited many favourable comments.

(Personally I also am among those favourable to it.)

Whack the water! vide Masefield, "Lost Endeavour "

ΕΓΡΑΦΟΝ[12]

On the last day of 1913. de mortuis[13] ... but a good riddance, on the whole.

Mataiea
Tahiti

– March 1914

My dear Phyllis,

You may be dead, or paralytic, or married to a peer, or anything. So may everyone I know. I haven't had any mail since October. It's all waiting for me – news of death + sickness + joy + evil – in America. I've been rather out of reach of posts, for five or six months, roaming through the Hawaian Islands, Fiji, Samoa, New Zealand, + Tahiti, never knowing exactly where I was going to be a week or a month later. I just escaped falling over a precipice in Fiji, and somehow I evaded the various tropical diseases here and in Samoa, and shipwreck every where, so I'm beginning to think I'm fated to be hanged, to drift back to England. Surprising thought! – And disturbing. For unless the hanging takes place immediately, I shall have to <u>Work</u> to pay my debts, contracted in this unproductive occupation of travelling. And that I feel, I could never do...

Do not ever wander, Phyllis. Or not for too long. It becomes a habit – landing in a fresh port with a light heart, a full bag, and an empty stomach. You stay there a few days or weeks or months, make some friends, see some queer things; and then, one gay morning, a boat blows in, and the rumour gets round that she's bound for the Islands of the Blest. And you jump in with your bag, heavier by a few memories, and the anchor's up and the folk on shore sing "Goodbye, my flenni!" or "Aloh oe!" – and out and on you go again.

But now I'm frightened I may never be able to settle down to other desirable – more desirable – things – living in an English cottage and writing immortal plays. And oh! Lord, if I <u>do</u> settle, it'ld be so much easier to settle here than any where else. The South Seas have got into my blood: the lovely and gentle brown people, the flowers and the lagoons, and the moonlight. If only I <u>could</u> [double underlined] – I'd like to hire a small boat and spend five years cruising about these parts. – But five years would be too long. One could never go back to bowler hats and the Strand and the <u>Daily Mail</u> and teaparties after that – and through America too! Even now the thought of landing in that harsh hysterical hell twelve days after I leave this Elysium appals me. And I'll get back to talk about Shaw and Matisse and Schonberg and the Russians and all the things I'm interested in, and away from all the things that make up life here the things I only like – damn!

Et tu, Phyllis? (we speak bad French here – though it might be Latin for the matter of that.) It may be I shall find a letter from you when I reach America. It may be not. In any case I hope you're flourishing, working hard and happy. For myself, I may drift into England again soon, or I may not. I seem to have given up writing with any enthusiasm. I do just a little, as I knock about. But it seems, somehow, more amusing just to live. What a fate for a poet!

I have still some shadowy remembrance of a place called England. I suppose I will see it again soon. May it, and all the good things in it, flourish. And may you be happy and prosperous

Your friend, some 20 degrees S,

Rupert

My regards to your mother.

                                                          Farm Corner,
                                                          Tadworth,
                                                          Surrey.

End of April 1914

Dear Rupert,

I have got a letter from you from Tahiti. Apparently there's some chance of this reaching you at the same time as its predecessor which is probably waiting in America.

I'm glad the South Seas are like that. I wonder at your thinking of coming back. And yet I suppose beach-combing is'nt much of an existence really.

Did they let you wear a wreath of scarlet flowers and become a beautiful tan colour all over like the man you told me about once?

And are you sure that the whole South-Sea milieu which you say you only like is really any degree worse, or lesser, than those products of modern civilisation in which you state yourself to be interested?

I would like to see the South Seas. They say that some of the people there are but a poor remnant; How to be Gentle Though Decadent; does that show on the surface?

I went with Mamma the other day to see Frost, and to get at where he was ensconced we had to pass through the Poetry Bookshop; and the figurative or spiritual atmosphere thereof was little short of suffocating: I could'nt exactly say why: I don't wonder at your not wanting to come back to that! (Why do they keep a photograph of you in the back shop? Is it for the admiring female to stretch her intense chin at?)

– If you do work, what manner of work? The Muse should be harnessed so to hard cash; would you choose an occupation involving a bowler hat, a stiff collar, an early morning hour? And then you could do the immortal writing in your off-time, if any. Or would you be like our friend Guy Keeling, who, when he ran out of funds on his round-the-world trip, set his hand to whatever manual labour was there to do – he did'nt go to the tropics, though, – and is now manually labouring on a small holding? (The hours of his occupation are excessively early at times.) – Could'nt one pick up a living somehow in the Pacific – and if there were anything about it that had to be said, in verse or otherwise, say it and send it home for publication?

It came to me the other day that any art that was only a sort of patina upon the decomposition of the surface of civilisation, and was only called into existence by the mere easiness of its production under certain conditions, was not really good or shall I say great? Art. I think the writings of Oscar Wilde are a good example of what I mean. They have the same sort of richness of surface, and a very fine gradation of expression, as – I don't quite know what to adduce in comparison, really. But I feel as if writing with him were an affectation. The whole does'nt bear looking into really, though, because if I call one art a mere patina I am similarly indicting all art. And supposing it went? Work or idleness for the artist. Who else cares?

But in getting a long way away I should think you'd have got things more or less into true proportions, and have found out roughly what really is and what is really not worth while. The only thing is I fear that among the old surroundings you may forget it. I suppose the whole bother is there are too many people in England. At least in south-east England.

Me? Oh yes, I'm working. The buyer of my last New England picture is still unknown to me. I'm going to have another shot at the N[ew].E[nglish]. I tried the R[oyal].A[cademy]. with some animals which they would'nt have – but nobody minds them. I also have a vague chance of a decorating job in the East End. – No I have'nt married a peer: (I never dance in choruses, nor have I been in America.) By the way, Delphis and Christopher, who both collect stamps, collected one each off your last 2 letters with avidity, as being unusual places.

I shan't wander just at present. I think I'm getting on with my painting, so I shall sit tight and stick to it. If I was to up-camp it would be I think the islands off the West of Scotland I'd go to: for the sheer beauty of the scenery. There are too many moneyed folk and too few inhabitants, though … Where I'd go for company I have'nt seen enough of the world to know. – Oh yes, and I'm going to illustrate some abbreviated Scandinavian sagas. I mean, to be precise Icelandic. Going to come out as a children's book. Only the author, translator or abbreviator can't or won't hurry, so I've no material to start on.

Well, tell me when you're going to come back. Annoying thing to have to do when you're in such a good place. This of course omitting to notice the fact that you'll probably have left it by the time you get this – and be in some beastly hole or other where they keep letters. Have you grown any beards with crimson streaks or anything, or shall I know you again if I meet you in the street?

Meanwhile, good fortune go with you.

ΦΥΛΛΙΣ

All the same, don't give up writing – Because you have a wonderful command both of verse – I mean word – music – and of graphic description. I've been sorry not to see more of yours come out of late.

In all the letters he wrote to me about this time, there is a gradual finding of himself, a sloughing of the exterior left upon him by contact with the unwholesome set into which he had fallen, a return, through the influence of great open spaces and kindly primitive people and sunshine and sea-waves, to sanity and naturalness. I felt in a way that my violent silly protest against his whole attitude had not been wasted; that, even though I had lost him personally, I had not misused my life utterly so long as I had been able to help him, be it ever so little, to find his true self.

This time in the South Seas had been good for Brooke; he had at last found the freedom and opportunity to be truly himself, not having to play the part of poet, intellectual or English gentleman for anyone.

Being an artist, Phyllis should have realised that this part of the world had seduced and inspired Gauguin, for whom the Tahitian women, with their relaxed attitude to sex, had been at the centre of its appeal. The same was true for Brooke. In this tropical heaven, none of the rules of propriety that tormented him back in England existed; discretion, chastity and monogamy were not an issue and the women were freely available.

Brooke was staying at the Hotel Lorina, Papeete, Tahiti, when he wrote to Marsh of the 'beastly coral-poisoning ... and a local microbe on top of that'[14] which had infected his legs while swimming. He complained, 'I've been lying on my back for eight or nine days suffering intensely while I swab my skinless flesh with boiling disinfectant. However, I've got over it now, and have started hobbling about'.[15] All his life, Rupert had battled with a weak immune system. Ever since his childhood he had suffered from eye infections and colds, and would be laid up for weeks if kicked in a rugby game. As a man, his healthy appearance, with his glowing complexion and strong, tall build, belied this.

His time of illness led to an intimate relationship between Brooke and Taatamata,[16] the native woman who cared for him:

> I have been nursed and waited on by a girl with wonderful eyes, the walk of a goddess, and the heart of an angel, who is, luckily, devoted to me. She gives her time to ministering to me, I mine to probing her queer mind. I think I shall write a book about her – Only I fear I'm too fond of her.[17]

Phyllis didn't have the alluring Taatamata in mind when she imagined Brooke benefiting from being among the 'kindly primitive people' of the South Seas. He hinted at the reality of the situation when he wrote to Dudley Ward, 'The South Seas are heaven, but I no angel'.[18] Taatamata was arguably the only lover in Brooke's life with whom he found fulfilment and happiness, but this was helped along by the fact he knew from the very beginning of their affair that he would have to leave her; the issues of marriage and her suitability (or otherwise) to fit in to his life and place in society would never arise.

This time away from England had given Brooke a chance to distance himself from some of his emotional turmoil – the embarrassment and discomfort now associated with Phyllis, and his mixed feelings for Ka, which he was now finally able to lay to rest.[19] His relationship with Taatamata had temporarily quenched his sexual thirst and fed his realisation that such physical freedom had worked wonderfully well for him and enhanced his creative powers, leading to him produce some of his best poems, including 'Heaven', 'Clouds', 'Retrospect', 'The Great Lover' and 'Tiare Tahiti'.[20]

Writing to Marsh, Brooke declared:

> The game is up Eddie. If I've gained facts by knocking about with Conrad characters in a Gauguin <u>entourage</u> – I've lost a dream or two. I tried to be a poet. And because I'm a clever writer and because I was forty times as sensitive as anybody else – I succeeded a little. I am what I came out here to be – Hard. Quite, quite hard.[21]

Brooke stayed in Tahiti for just under three months, until he had completely run out of money and had to borrow his fare home from a friend.[22] In early April he sailed for San Francisco, then travelled on to Arizona (where he visited the Grand Canyon), Chicago,[23] Pittsburgh, Washington, Boston. Finally, on 21 May, he returned to New York.

The contentment Brooke had felt in the South Seas soon evaporated, something he touched upon when writing about the Grand Canyon: 'It is very large and very untidy, like my soul. But unlike my soul, it has peace in it.'[24]

[Postmarked: New York, 25 May, 3 a.m., 1914.]

Hotel McAlpine
Greeley Square
New York City

May 22 1914

My dear Mrs Gardner,

You must have thought me very slow in answering your letter of last Christmas. The truth is – as I hope you may have gathered, for I think I wrote a letter to Phyllis from Fiji – I have been away in the South Seas, beyond the reach of all letters, for some time. I only got back to San Francisco, and found all my mail, at the end of last month.

It was good of you to write. You seemed to think I was feeling lonely. I don't remember if I was. I think Canada depressed me. And it is always difficult to work, when one's travelling.

It is good of you, too, to recognise that we're different sorts of people, and leave it at that. That is about as far as the ages have led any-one. Whether it's true and a good conclusion, or not, I don't pretend to know. As long as Phyllis is all right – and I'm glad to hear that she is, – all seems to have ended well.

I expect to be in England this summer, working.

Yours
Rupert Brooke

On 29 May 1914 Brooke set sail for England on board the *Philadelphia*, with Maurice Browne and his wife as travelling companions. By now he was longing to see England again, but he was rather more hesitant about meeting its people. He wanted his arrival to be a low-key affair; of necessity he alerted only Marsh – 'to make sure of a bed.'[25]

Brooke's ship docked in Plymouth, on 5 June. From here he caught a train to Euston station: the very one he had said his farewells from before setting out on his travels just over a year earlier. His train was very late, eventually arriving in the early hours of Saturday 6 June. He spent the night at Raymond Buildings with Marsh, and the next day set off for Rugby to stay with his mother.

SEVEN

'FAR-OFF CATACLYSMS'

Good news awaited Brooke on his return to England: *New Numbers*, the venture in which he and fellow poet friends Lascelles Abercrombie, Wilfrid Gibson and John Drinkwater had invested so much time and enthusiasm, had been a great success since it was published in March (although the first issue was dated February). They had already printed two issues and more were on the way. It was a hot golden summer, and despite Brooke writing to Jacques Raverat that 'I'm rejuvenated and beachcomberish and all that, and hard as nails, but I have not got back to the point where I can enjoy gaiety',[1] he could not help being infected by it:

> I find England very lovely and quite unchanged – except that the upper classes are a little more anarchic. The last few days here have been glorious, and the air is so heavy (but not sleepy) with the scent of hay and mown grass and roses and dews and a thousand wild flowers, that I'm beginning to think of my South Sea wind pale and scentless by comparison![2]

On 28 June a shot was fired in distant Sarajevo, Bosnia, killing the Archduke Franz Ferdinand, heir to the Austro-Hungarian Empire. It must have seemed like a world away, yet with this single act a long shadow began to cast itself across that seemingly perfect summer.

Restlessness seemed always to haunt Brooke these days. He complained, 'I am leading a fragmentary life – as soon as I get to London I want to be out in the country, rolling in a meadow, and when I'm there, I'm looking up the next train to London to lunch with some friends I haven't seen for eighteen months'.[3] A large part of this restlessness appears to have been fuelled by an ongoing gnawing frustration. He touches upon this in a letter to Jacques, in whom Rupert increasingly seemed to confide:

> It's so BLOODY being celibate. One hangs hopelessly round young women one doesn't care for a scrap, and – at this date – sees through entirely. And if one <u>doesn't</u> do that: one's too bally restless to work. All very dull. Wish to God I was married. I don't see any fun or any profit in this cunt-sniffing business (I say, you mustn't let Gwen see this letter) … I want to be married: + I can't find anybody worth marrying.[4]

Having seen friends marry and settle down, some now with children, Brooke always returned to the idea that if he too were to marry he would find peace and could settle and work. At odds with this, however, was his own self-knowledge. The very thought of being trapped with one woman for life, with an inevitable loss of freedom and ensuing responsibilities, set alarm bells ringing. In his next letter to Jacques Brooke defends and illustrates his position further:

> I have no respect for young women. I have as little as a sick man has for that gruel which he has to take to keep him alive. I know <u>all</u> about them. And I hate them … I'm sorry you'll miss Cathleen. I should like her to see you. I should, even, like you to see her. I enjoy watching my friends dislike her. Perhaps, though, you'd have seen through her manner. The London manner is even worse than the Cambridge – though blessedly different. She has considerably less chance than the young woman I used to know,[5] + <u>far</u> less 'intelligence': but, thank God, a rather better nose. Which is the important thing.
>
> I desire to consult you about marriage. I <u>must</u> marry soon. And I can't find anyone to marry: – oh, I suppose one <u>could</u> marry anyone: but, I mean, I can't decide whom to marry. It seems such an important step. Perhaps there's a better choice in Samoa. … You'll be relieved to know that I pray continually. Twelve hours a day, that I may, sometime, fall in love with somebody. Twelve hours a day that I may <u>never</u> fall in love with anybody. Either alternative seems too Hellish to bear.[6]

As insulting as his tone is, it would seem that Phyllis was the intelligent 'young woman' for whom Brooke had much higher regard
than for Cathleen Nesbitt. Despite Brooke's callous tone and apparent
lack of feeling for Cathleen Nesbitt, in a letter he wrote to her at the
same time, it is all too evident that he was wrestling with conflicting
emotions:

> I <u>daren't</u> go wandering. You don't know what a helpless poor fool I am.
> It's only in love and marriage I can find peace. The rest is Hell. I want
> to love and to work. I don't want to be washed about on these doubtful
> currents and black waves or drift into some dingy corner of the tide …
> And the wandering is so grey and helpless: things get washed out of
> one.[7]

A statement such as this would have given Phyllis hope, if only it had
been written with her in mind.

> All the time, I hoped against hope that we might be lovers again.
> It may have been pride that kept me from acknowledging this to
> him: the wound in my spirit was not yet healed, but only so much
> recovered as to let me be sure it had not altogether destroyed life
> for me. A very little more of seeing him, or even of writing to
> him, would have brought me crawling to his feet like a beaten dog.
> But things did not give us time.
>   He wrote that he was coming to England. He wrote, later, from
> London, while we were away in Arran, asking me to meet him;
> I would have, but could not at once owing to our distance away
> from London.

[Postmarked: Rugby Station, 1 am, 15 July 1914.]

24, Bilton Road,
Rugby
Tel. 50 Rugby

June 13 1914

Dear Mrs Gardner,
    I'm so much decided in my own mind that I'm not born to be
drowned, that I forget that other people may not share my view.
Anyhow, I can swim. But I didn't have to, this time. I took the boat; –
which got me in a week ago. And now I'm busy trying to sort papers and
write and in general make up for a year's idleness.

I hope Phyllis is doing good work. I've seen no picture shows yet. England's extraordinarily lovely.

Yours

Rupert Brooke

24 Bilton Road
Rugby

August 3 1914[8]

My dear Phyllis,

I've been in England for some time without hearing anything of, or from, you; and it has from time to time occurred to me that there might be some question of 'pride', or the proper ceremonial, hindering communication. It's recognised that I don't understand about "pride", isn't it?

Anyhow I wanted to write, now that I'm freed for a time from that ghastly rush of London, to ask how you are, and to send you good wishes. Are you still illustrating Icelandic Sagas? Or have you started on allegorical pictures? Or turned poet?

I hope you're flourishing, anyway.

For myself, I've done nothing but rush about to theatres and parties since I returned. I've not done a stroke of work. Now I'm going to be in the country a bit: but I don't know if I shall be able to work even so. This damned war weighs one down, so. I wish I were a war correspondent, or a soldier.

I don't know what'll happen to the world.

Rupert

Since the fateful day in June when Archduke Franz Ferdinand was assassinated, the repercussions had been spreading far and wide. With terrible inevitability the fragile structure of the European alliances, which had maintained the balance of power for over 70 years crumbled. Within a month Austria–Hungary had declared war on Serbia. Germany then took the situation to the very brink by invading France, via neutral Belgium. Sensing the way things were going, Brooke prophetically wrote to Edward Marsh: 'Do you have a Brussels-before-Waterloo feeling? That we'll all – or some – meet with other eyes in 1915?'[9]

On 4 August Britain declared war on Germany. Brooke was staying with the Cornfords in their holiday cottage in Cley-next-the-Sea, Norfolk; on learning the news he was rendered speechless all day. Only in the evening, when Frances, thinking that only 'soldiers' fought wars, not poets and artists, assured him, 'But Rupert, you won't have to fight', did he gravely reply 'We shall all have to fight'.[10]

One did not foresee how things would go. While we were still in Arran the war broke out. We did not realise – no one did, then, – what kind of a thing it was.

Cromla
Corrie
Arran.

Aug. 7. [1914]

Dear Rupert

Pride is like this: that sooner than shove myself an inch further than I was wanted I'd go and drown. That's why I don't write out of turn. I said if you never wanted to hear of me again you'd only not to write. See? – You might let me know if you're going to see any active service.

This place is remote and secluded. At noon the entire population, men, women, children and dogs, gather by the boat-pier. The mail-coach arrives with papers and the population remains to read them. This morning began with rumours concerning the North Sea battle – they came early and continued with the dozen soldiers to guard the telegraph cable. They were put off the steamer in a boat.

Otherwise all here is perfect peace. The village is a little disturbed perhaps by these far-off cataclysms but go a hundred yards up the mountain behind and it is all gone. It looks as it must have looked before the arrival of Ossian: sheep, and empty spaces, and white waterfalls.

We may have to leave it all earlier than we meant, because our summer tenant at Tadworth is suffering from blue funk and wants to go home. He has a German name.

I don't think you need have waited so carefully till we were out of reach of one another to write. I would'nt have bothered you. After all we might easily have run into one another somewhere in London during last month – I have been there now and then, not very often – but I suppose you do occasionally walk about, or go in conveyances –

I went and saw the Frosts in the Nest of Singing Birds down Ledbury and Dymock way. I saw no other members of the poet community, though I rode on the bicycle of Mrs Abercrombie. That is remote too: very idyllic, and the inhabitants talk beautiful peasant English, but I don't care for that sort of country: it's over vegetated and you can't see out.

What are you going to work at?

Yes, I wonder what will happen to the world. I also wonder what will happen to individuals of my acquaintance and friendship who are helping it to happen. I suppose there is no one in the country who has no friends in it. If I were a man I'd volunteer: I want to see the Germans licked. As it is I am only competent to do first aid, or possibly drive a motor lorry. We have a little motor now. Mamma and I drive it, with all running repairs. But not here.

Facts as they are are most difficult to realise. I never know what's up till it's all over. – This minute I'm having my name put down as willing to do something or other, I'm not quite sure what. I don't believe it a bit.

Life is so unlikely. I gave up being surprised some years ago.

Here I take the opportunity to apologise once for all for any nasty or spiteful things I may have said to you, or may be going to say to you – Make allowances – I never mean them more than superficially, and I partly say them on purpose, to show you what I don't like. I am the more ashamed of them that you have not often, I won't say never, said anything that you meant to hurt my feelings. Certainly not since I last saw you. But I find it most difficult to make my point clear to you: almost impossible in fact: and you must understand that I am not trying to be nasty for nothing, but standing for this point of view which I am so keen on.

Don't get killed without letting me know.

Phyllis.

Despite the distractions of war, it is evident that the 'secret' liaison between Rupert and Phyllis was promoting curiosity. In a letter to Robert Frost, Edward Thomas[11] makes references to 'Mrs Gardner', concluding with the remark: 'I want to see her daughter, by the way.'[12]

Brooke had been hoping to take part in a war; now it had come to him. His first response was to write a lightly disguised autobiographical article entitled 'An Unusual Young Man' which was published in the *New Statesman*. It gives us a unique insight into his own thoughts and feelings at this time, many of which must have been shared by the whole nation:

Some say the Declaration of War threw us into a primitive abyss of hatred and the lust for blood. Others declare that we behaved very well. I do not know. I only know the thoughts that flowed through the mind of a friend of mine when he heard the news ... A youth ran down to them with a telegram: 'We're at war with Germany. We've joined France and Russia.'

My friend ate and drank, and then climbed a hill of gorse, and sat alone, looking at the sea. His mind full of confused images, and the sense of strain. In answer to the word 'Germany' a train of vague thoughts dragged across his brain. The pompous middle-class vulgarity of the buildings of Berlin; the wide and restful beauty of Munich; the taste of beer; innumerable quiet, glittering cafes; the Ring; the swish of evening air in the face, as one skis down past the pines; a certain angle of the eyes in the face; long nights of drinking, and singing, and laughter; the admirable beauty of German wives and mothers; certain friends; some tunes; the quiet length of evening over the Starnberger-See ...

A thousand little figures tumbled through his mind. But they no longer brought with them that air of comfortable kindliness which Germany had always signified for him. Something in him kept urging, 'You must hate these things, find evil in them.' There was that half-conscious agony of breaking a mental habit, painting out a mass of associations, which he had felt in ceasing to believe in a religion, or, more acutely, after quarrelling with a friend ... He vaguely imagined a series of heroic feats, vast enterprise, and the applause of crowds.

From that egotism he was awakened to a different one, by the thought that this day meant war and the change of all things he knew. He realized, with increasing resentment, that music would be neglected. And he wouldn't be able, for example, to camp out. He might have to volunteer for military training and service. Some of his friends would be killed. The Russian ballet wouldn't return. His own relationship with A–, a girl he intermittently adored, would be changed. Absurd, but inevitable; because – he scarcely worded it to himself – he and she and everyone else were going to be different. His mind fluttered irascibly to escape from this thought, but still came back to it, like a tethered bird ... Something was growing in his heart, and he couldn't tell what. But as he thought 'England and Germany' the word 'England' seemed to flash like a line of foam. With a sudden tightening of his heart, he realized that there might be a raid on the English coast. He didn't imagine any possibility of it succeeding, but only of enemies and warfare on English soil. The idea sickened him. He was immensely surprised to perceive that the actual earth of England held for him a quality which he found in A–, and in a friend's honour, and scarcely anywhere else, a quality which, if he'd ever been sentimental enough to use the word, he'd have called 'holiness'. His astonishment grew as the full flood of 'England' swept over him on from thought to thought. He felt the triumphant helplessness of a lover. Grey, uneven little fields, and small, ancient hedges rushed before him, wild flowers, elms and beeches, gentleness, sedate houses of red brick, proudly unassuming, a countryside of rambling hills and friendly copses. He seemed to be raised high, looking down on a landscape compounded of the western view from the Cotswolds and Weald, and the high land in Wiltshire, and the Midlands seen from the hills above Prince's Risborough ... At one moment he was on an Atlantic liner, sick for home, making Plymouth at nightfall; and at another, diving into a little rocky pool through which the Teign flows, north of Bovey; and again, waking, stiff with dew, to see the dawn come up over Royston plain. And continually he seemed to see the set of a mouth he knew to be his mother's, and A—'s face, and, inexplicably, the face of an old man he had once passed in a Warwickshire village. To his great disgust, the most commonplace sentiments found utterance in him. At the same time he was extraordinarily happy.[13]

Much to his surprise, Brooke found that all his initial attempts 'to get to the 'front''[14] were rejected as he had no military training. He also had no success in becoming a war correspondent; all posts were filled until journalists began being killed in action. It did not take Brooke long to realise that being a journalist would not fulfil the role he saw for himself anyway. He didn't want to find himself serving his country behind a desk or 'guarding a footbridge in Glamorgan'.[15] Maitland Radford, a mutual friend of Phyllis and Brooke, was by this time a qualified doctor;[16] his skills were immediately required in the field so he had no trouble enlisting.

In a letter Phyllis wrote to Maitland at this time, she tells him of how 'The Epsom Grand Stand is being used as a hospital', how she was raising 'quite a bit of money for the Prince of Wales' Fund by selling water-colours' she'd painted of Arran, and how her mother was 'going to offer herself as interpreter in the languages she knows', but most revealing is her annoyed, refreshingly frank comment:

> – I wonder why Rupert continues to write unconcerned little articles in the *New Statesman*.[17] I think he thinks he's being a great thinker, but I think he's being a perfect rotter. Though, as I have'nt any knowledge of what he's doing at present, I suppose I've no right to criticise.[18]

Brooke had just found himself a commission with the newly formed Royal Naval Division. It had been hastily put together at the outbreak of the war by Winston Churchill, then First Lord of the Admiralty, when he realised there were far more reserves of the Royal Navy than were needed for manning all the ships. From this overflow of men two naval brigades were formed and one brigade of marines, which was named the Royal Marine Brigade. They were organised into army-type units, but were under the command of the Admiralty.

In September 1914 the marines were sent to Dunkirk with orders to assist the defence of Antwerp, while the two naval brigades set up camp in Kent. They began training the somewhat depressed and bemused naval recruits, who were not very happy with the prospect of being used for land rather than sea service.

Edward Marsh used all his influence as Private Secretary to Winston Churchill to get Brooke and Denis Browne a place. 'I can make play with Winston having promised you an appointment,' Marsh wrote to Brooke, but it was apparent he could not share Brooke's pleasure in it, nor Phyllis's desire to see it come about. Instead he commented with worldliness and foresight in a letter to Denis Browne, 'I'll do my best, tho' I <u>hate</u> you both going, as this force is sure to be put in the field pretty soon and I'd <u>so</u> much rather you were "just behind the battle, mother"'.[19] It was not long before Marsh wrote with the news he had just succeeded in securing both Brooke and Denis Browne a place in the RND. 'I'm glad I could do it for you, since you wanted it, but I feel I'm "giving of my dearest", as the newspapers say.'[20]

And then he joined the R[oyal].N[aval].D[ivision]., and before I had a chance of meeting him again he was off to the defence of Antwerp. I did not know he was gone; I only knew that a short time before he had been in camp in training. I went to Cambridge for a while to stay with my Aunt. And as an example of the kind of half second-sight which has been vouchsafed to me throughout this affair, while there I wrote that poem beginning "Quiet is my house".[21]

C/C E. Marsh
5. Raymond Buildings,
Gray's Inn.

Monday 21 September [1914]

Dear Mrs Gardner,

I'm very glad you liked my New Statesman article. It was rather hurriedly written, I'm afraid. I've been rushing about a good deal, and, in the intervals, Drilling. Now I've got appointed to a Commission in the Naval Division (for land service.). I'm in London getting my kit, very busily. I go down to camp, on Wednesday evening or Thursday.

You say you'd like to see me. I'm pretty busy tomorrow in the day time. But tomorrow evening: or Wednesday: I might have an unoccupied bit. Of course, I shall be in London again – at intervals – or leave for a day or a few hours. It's queer entering on a new life like this.

Yours

Rupert Brooke

Phyllis surprisingly fails to mention in her memoir a meeting she had with Brooke, even though it was their first since his return from America and the South Seas. One can only assume that it was eclipsed in her memory by their subsequent meeting and the feverish atmosphere at the time. Instead it is recorded in a letter she wrote to Maitland Radford:

> Also is'nt it a funny thing that every time I grumble to you about Rupert he turns up trumps the next day?
>
> Mamma and I had tea with him in town the other day, and we all pretended it had'nt happened and were friendly; and now he's gone off into camp to do military training and expects to be sent out in January.[22]

'NOTHING TO FORGIVE AND SOMETHING TO FORGET'

On 1 October Brooke travelled down to Kent to join the Anson Battalion of the Royal Naval Division. By this time most of the trained, experienced men had already been sent out to strategic positions, leaving the responsibility of training naval recruits to officers who hadn't 'the slightest idea of army drill'[1] and who, only a month before, had been reliant on reading the commands from manuals. The men had been given mildewed leather equipment left over from the Boer War;[2] it was 'hard as iron' and of little use. Brooke was somewhat immune to this; coming as he did from a more privileged position than the men serving under him, he could afford to buy his own kit. For him the war and joining up with the Anson Battalion was an exciting new adventure; he enjoyed the sense of camaraderie and purpose, and was largely distracted from the issues that had been troubling him.

> Anson Battalion
> Second Brigade R.N.D
> Betteshanger Park
> Eastry, Kent

Friday October 2 [1914]

My dear Phyllis,

Many thanks for the socks. (They came about a week ago, but I've only just found time to acknowledge them.) They are admirably warm, and seem to me to fit perfectly. (Please tell your mother all this.)

I'm having a great time. Last night I was out all night in a night attack. I got about an hour's sleep from four to five a.m in a dewy field, till I was woken by a messenger to say the enemy were hard at hand again – it's queer, fighting all night, under a full moon, across miles of the loveliest Kent country. I slept between breakfast and lunch, and have been drilling since. Next week we march to Sheerness. Tonight I must read up on musketry. What a life! It's great fun being busy. No one knows when we go out or where.

It was nice to see you both. It seems a million years ago, now. I've changed my life so completely in seven days, and done such a lot.

Good luck to you

Rupert

Once again in a letter to Maitland Radford, Phyllis touches upon her true feelings regarding Brooke and her increasingly sober thoughts on the war:

National things can't quite evaluate personal ones. Though for sure it was national things that brought Rupert back to come-to-tea terms with us. Wish I knew what to think about him. Forgive-and-forget, of course; one can almost forget. But supposing we pretend it has'nt happened, and make acquaintances over again, what then? Is it a vicious circle? By the way, I heard again from him, in camp in Kent, practising night attacks and c with the Naval Division (for Land Service,) and not knowing when or where they were expected to go. Wish I had something to do – "fly on the 5th wheel". "They also serve who only stand and wait." I am a background. But I am also glad that it's not my job to slay people. I wish that this will be the last war there ever is. It's survival of the unfit, because so many of the best must be dead or maimed: it does'nt bear too much thinking.[3]

Since September the strategic Belgian fortresses at Antwerp had been at risk from the advancing German army. Only four days after Brooke had begun his training at the beginning of October, Churchill sent urgent orders that both the First and Second Naval Brigade must depart to help defend Antwerp. Prime Minister Asquith was acutely aware that if this highly important port fell into German hands, it would present a serious threat to French Channel ports – themselves vital for maintaining the British Expeditionary Force. The Belgian government were really feeling the pressure and had decided they must withdraw from Antwerp. Churchill, with Kitchener's full backing, managed to convince Belgium to hold its ground, promising that the Royal Naval Division would be sent out to help defend Antwerp.

The two naval brigades, of which Brooke was part, were alarmingly under-resourced: 80 per cent of the men went without even basic equipment such as water bottles, packs or mess tins. No khaki uniforms had been issued, and the men were given ancient, charger-loading rifles three days before embarking.

By the time Brooke and his brigade marched to Vieux-Dieu the battle was already as good as lost. Wagons of dead and wounded filed past, retreating from conflict in the adjacent province town of Lier. For a day and a half the Second Brigade held the trenches just outside the city. At last it was reluctantly acknowledged that the German forces were too strong for the exhausted Belgian army and the outnumbered Royal Naval Division, so a retreat was ordered around 17.00 hours on 8 October.

Under pressure of bombardment the city of Antwerp, now in tatters, and its fortress were surrendered to the Germans by the civil authorities on 9 October 1914. German troops then entered the city. The civil surrender was only endorsed by the military command on 10 October 1914. Brooke was met by a grim scene as he and his men pulled out:

> I marched through Antwerp, deserted, shelled, and burning, one night, and saw ruined houses, dead men and horses: and railway-trains with their lines taken up and twisted and flung down as if a child had been playing with a toy. And the whole heaven and earth was lit up by the glare from the great lakes and rivers of burning petrol, hills and spires of flame. That was like Hell, a Dantesque Hell, terrible. But there – and later – I saw what was a truer Hell. Hundreds of thousands of refugees, their goods on barrows and hand-carts and perambulators and wagons, moving with infinite slowness out into the night, two unending lines of them, the old men mostly weeping, the women with hard drawn faces, the children playing or crying or sleeping. That's what Belgium is now: the country where three civilians have been killed to every one soldier … it's queer to think one has been a witness of one of the greatest crimes of history. Has ever a nation been treated like that? And how can such a stain be wiped out?[4]

Churchill argued that his Royal Naval Division had delayed the German army long enough to secure the vital French Channel ports of Dunkirk and Calais. He maintained it had also given the Belgian army a chance to withdraw and destroy their ammunition and other resources that the enemy would have found useful. However, other figures in authority considered the whole exercise a costly failure that had misused the largely untrained men of the Royal Naval Division. Some 1,500 men from the First Brigade had become victims of bad communication. Left behind in the devastated city, the men were forced to seek refuge in the Netherlands, where, as the Dutch were neutral, they were interned – an outcome considered preferable to surrendering to the Germans.

Early on 11 October Brooke arrived back in Dover. He had lost all of his luggage and a number of unfinished manuscripts, which had been on a train that was bombed.

> I knew, somehow, then that he would be killed in the war. I knew
> that he had come to his full strength, that all his wrongnesses
> and foolishnesses were wiped out, and that he had therefore
> fulfilled his appointed task in life. I remember thinking, then that
> I should be neither surprised nor indignant if I were to hear of
> his death, – and that I should be both surprised and enraged to
> hear of the death of various of my other acquaintances who had
> gone to war, and about whom I did not care two straws. All the
> same, I was mightily pleased to get a telegram from my mother
> to say he had arrived safely in England. This telegram followed
> closely on a newspaper-cutting containing the information that the
> R[oyal].N[aval].D[ivision]. had gone to the defence of Antwerp,
> and that one battalion (not his: he was at this time in the Anson
> Battalion) had got interned in Holland.

Farm Corner   c/o Aunty. 1 Clare Road
Tadworth.   Cambridge.
Barton Surrey   (only for a short while)

Dear Rupert,
    O this queer Cambridge! One hardly knows it. King's playing fields a
barrack yard of temporary hospitals, and everything's different.
    The Cambridge Mag[5] says in a 2 line note with 91 against it that
you, who were to have lectured in English this term, have applied for

a commission. Aren't they behind? This will have been before Eddie obliged with an R[oyal].N[aval].D[ivision]. whatever it is.

Glad you got the lectureship. My father was asked about you. (Strictly confidential, and don't say I told you.)

Oliffe Richmond was'nt to be seen in chapel to-day. I heard he'd offered to decipher code messages and they would'nt have him. Wonder where he is. It was some time ago I heard that.

    Oct. 12. I see you've been defending Antwerp. I'm glad it was'nt your brigade that was cut off. I hope to goodness you're safe. Write and tell me you are. I wonder if this is addressed right.

    Phyllis

When I got back home from Cambridge my mother told me she had telephoned to Eddie's as soon as she heard any of the R[oyal].N[aval].D[ivision]. were back in England, to know if he were safe, and he had answered the telephone himself, and she had been overjoyed to hear his voice again after so long, and had arranged for her and me to meet him at tea on a certain day at Gatti's under Charing Cross.

Accordingly we went to town on this day, and I think we were going up to Charing Cross bookstall before going down to Gatti's, when we met him in the street. This was the first time I had seen him in uniform: it was also the last time I ever saw him, but I did not of course know this at the time. The uniform did not change him much. He was tanned a little with the South Sea sun, but his colour came and went as it had always done. His hair was a trifle shorter than I had last seen it; also he was looking serious, ill and very tired.

We went into Gatti's and sat down. He leaned his head on his hand, and told us how his division had taken over trenches from the Belgians, – how they had hurried there, – how there had been 'buses fresh from London with advertisements of plays and soaps still flaunting on their sides. He told us of a thirty-hour march without food or rest, – of the civilian population leaving their homes, – of officers taking to carrying packs because otherwise the Germans saw they were officers and picked them off. He told us he had caught pink-eye in one eye, and when the battalion arrived in England he had it bound up with a bandage, with the result that the onlookers cheered him to the echo as a wounded hero, and he felt a horrible fraud. Also he said the pink-eye has spread to the other eye and he thought he had a temperature. We thought he should be at home in bed. We felt sorry for him.

Then my mother remembered some messages she had to give in the telephone, and went and left us. We had a great deal to say to one another, but somehow we could not say any of it then and there. It might have been different if we had known this would be the last time we should see one another. But I felt all crumpled up with sorrow to see him so tired and ill, and could not bring myself to mention anything to him that would remind him of any past troubles or difficulties. I would have dearly liked to take him in my arms and say: – "Poor boy, I'm so sorry for you." And this again I might have done, no, certainly should have done, had I known that I would never see him again.

As it was we talked of indifferent matters till mother came back.

Phyllis enlarged on Brooke's return from Antwerp in another of her letters to Maitland Radford:

> Rupert got back all right from Antwerp, but he'd caught pink-eye and seemed rather a wreck. However, he went back into camp and promptly recovered. They seem to have had rather a beastly time there, and they lost all their things but what they stood up in, and apparently had to do a 30 hour march with nothing to eat. And here are we sitting comfortably in our houses.[6]

On 18 October Brooke was back at Betteshanger camp, Kent. Within days it was decided that the camp would be moved, and the various battalions of the Royal Naval Division were sent to different barracks around the south of England as a temporary measure. Anson, Brooke's battalion, was sent to Chatham at the end of October.

Ever since his return from Belgium, Brooke had been doing his utmost to gather together items of clothing, both for himself and, primarily, for his men, trying to replace what had been lost to the bombs of Antwerp. Before long he had enlisted the help of Phyllis and her family, who busied themselves knitting pairs of socks and arranging for sweaters to be sent on to Brooke.

Lack of clothing was not the only problem the returning men faced. Many of them were suffering from the effects of inhaling fumes from the coke stoves used for warmth at Blandford. Brooke had a bad reaction to his second dose of typhoid inoculation early in December and ran a fever. In spite of all this, it was at about this time he began composing his now famous war sonnets: 'I. Peace', 'II. Safety', 'III. The Dead', 'IV. The Dead' and 'V. The Soldier', fuelled not only by the public mood of the time, but also, probably more intensely, by emotions roused within him following Antwerp and news of killed or missing friends. He touched upon the latter in a letter to Mrs Arnold Toynbee, née Rosalind Murray, written on 20 November from Portsmouth: 'Just now I am rather miserable: because most of my school-friends are wounded, or "wounded and missing" or dead. Perhaps our sons will live the better for it all.'[7]

> Barn, Chatham. Anson Battalion
> Nat. Tel: No 87 Gillingham. R.N.D
> Royal Naval Barracks
> Chatham

2 November [1914] .

Dear Mrs Gardner,

 – No parade this morning: for a quarter of the battalion have drafted to sea, a quarter gone to Sheerness for musketry, and a quarter not yet returned from Sheerness. So I get a few moments for letter writing.

Many thanks for everything you have sent me. The French decoction I've not tasted yet: for I'm quite well: (Also, my eyes are perfectly all right; they recovered very swiftly.) –

If you know of stores of socks etc. made by charitable people I can manage with any amount for the attractive but ill-clad privates under my command.

We're here for a week or two. Then somewhere in Dorset.

The Barracks are the haunt of all officers saved from sinking ships, while they wait for new jobs; also of submarine officers taking five days rest. So there is a good deal of good talk going on. It's very luxurious, after camp –

Love to all –
    RB

Farm Corner,
Tadworth,
Surrey.

Dear Rupert

This is a detachment. We've been a-begging, with what result I don't
quite know, except that J. Penoyre, who is a friend of ours and has been
collecting sweaters, is going to send you some. I hope the shipwrecked
and others are getting along all right. Delphis and Christopher are
co-operating some knitting – (Don't be scandalized at a boy knowing
how to knit – lots of Scotchmen can) which they intend to be a jersey for
a shipwrecked sailor, but I don't think it'll be in time for your friends.
Still, the intention is there.

There are more things to follow, obtained from a local working party.

Daddy has joined the artillery branch of London university O.T.C.
which does'nt have an age limit. He's every bit as fit as lots of younger
men, and is delighted to have found they'll have him.

I don't seem to be doing any more than I was. I am made wagon
orderly to an ambulance corps but that only seems to mean that I go and
look on at stretcher drills, besides standing by to run errands.

I am doing a window design for the Toy Shop, 21a Old Bond Street.[8]
Possibly you'll see it when it's there, which won't be quite yet.

When are you going to have some leave and come and see us? This
place is looking very nice, and I want to show you Chuffy, and how well
we drive her.

Good luck to you.
    Phyllis.

Farm Corner,
Tadworth,
Surrey.

Dear Rupert

Are these the sort of thing? Hand knitted ones follow when they
are made, but it takes time. We are all very busy trying to track down
signalling to the coast. We have chased several quite unoffending wild
geese, including a firework factory and a hurricane lamp swinging inside
a door that had a crack in it.

Yours
    Phyllis.

Farm Corner,
Tadworth,
Surrey

Dear Rupert

In case the other pair did'nt arrive. Also will you consider this offer.
If you have holes that want darning send them here. With their context
of course. They shall be competently darned, or if they're socks and

are very far gone, knitted new feet into, and returned. If we must be knitting, and c. for the defenders of our country, why not for you in particular? Mamma is making progress with that belt thing. It'll very soon be done now. I see of course you'd want to go back into camp if you were only half well, only one should'nt knock up. It's wasteful.

– The man with a cold whom we were expecting the other day stayed one night and said he was cured. But that Epsom camp is disbanded now – "Harrods' own". We had our nursing exam yesterday. I hope we've passed. If they don't pass Mamma they're prize asses, as she is an awful good nurse in practice. But we were amazed at mothers of families, presumably educated, who could'nt read a clinical thermometer.

Good luck.
   Phyllis.

> Farm Corner,
> Tadworth,
> Surrey.

Dear Rupert

I hope we are'nt overdoing it – Let us know if we are – I daresay it won't be much good sending things after you move on. When do you? People are all so willing to give things, whether they have or have'nt them –

Phyllis

> Farm Corner,
> Tadworth,
> Surrey.

25 November [1914]

Dear Rupert

Mr Penoyre is naturally extremely fussy. I'm very sorry, I can't do anything about it. He has written me a somewhat agitated note complaining that you have'nt acknowledged a certain parcel of sweaters he sent to you at Chatham.

I think my writing is not usually very illegible, but he or his minions put you down in the note to me as E. Brook. He says he sent that person an acknowledgement form with the sweaters, and another afterwards separately; which is of a piece with his aforementioned natural fussiness; and he seems distressed at not having received either form back again. Do have pity on him, and look for his notes. He thinks his sweaters have gone astray, to the number of 20.

Sorry to bother you.
   Phyllis.

A rather less patient account of this saga appears in a letter Phyllis wrote to Maitland Radford:

[I heard] again from Rupert. He is'nt [one of tho]se people who speak twice before [think]ing, and write three times. He is [without] exception the worst correspondent [I know], and when one gets people to send him things for his half-dressed battalion who lost all their things he won't acknowledge them, [w]hich is a nu[isance]…"[9]

Farm Corner,
Tadworth,
Surrey.

Nov [In Brooke's handwriting.]

Dear Rupert

I've been wondering for a long time whether I would'nt write to you – only it's so difficult. I want neither to rake up the past nor to suppress what in it does'nt want suppressing: therefore it would be rather better to leave it unmentioned. Take it as read and go on to the present and future.

There is this. At the moment I don't suppose you're in any particular danger. But you will be.

Therefore don't let's have misapprehensions. Please forgive me for being a blunderheaded clumsy ass and saying beastly things I did'nt mean. I will try never to do so again. I don't want to shove myself on you, but I should like to be just decently friendly.

It's awfully difficult writing. I wish I could see you for a bit. I might have tried to say something in the way of an apology when we were at tea in London and Mamma went off to telephone; only I was so sorry for you and your eye that it sort of did'nt seem fair: and you straight back from some hell of a job and I having come fresh from a comfortable home – Besides, that was only a minute at the best.

I think that's all. Unless I were to go on and say a whole heap. But that would be no manner of good as I never seem to succeed in saying what I mean and you probably would'nt have time to read it.

I wonder if you've gone from Chatham.

God bless you.

Phyllis.

On the last day of November Brooke took an opportunity to transfer to 'A' Company of the Hood Battalion, under Colonel Quilter, based at Blandford, Dorset. Arthur, universally known as 'Oc', Asquith,[10] was already in this battalion; before long Denis Browne managed to get himself transferred to their company too, and Patrick Shaw-Stewart, an old acquaintance of Brooke's, also joined them. Brooke also formed new friendships with Cleg Kelly,[11] Charles Lister[12] and their company commander Bernard Freyberg.[13]

Hood Battalion
RND
Naval Camp
Blandford
Dorset

Excuse pencil + paper
1 December [1914]

Dear Phyllis,

I've been rushing wildly about England for some time. Now I am settled (D.V.) for a bit, though in mud. That rushing's the reason why I didn't answer the Penoyre, nor you, I'm very sorry! As a matter of fact, – I did tell a man Lucas, who said he was helping P.dye, to tell him how grateful I was. It didn't get through. Nor did the P's second note. But I've written now.

My dear Phyllis, of course let's be "friendly"; as far as one can be anyhow in this turmoil. That's what I want. Only remember that you're being friendly with a wandering and selfish person. (Don't, however, put down any silence and inaccessibility at this time to that. I really am rushed!) – I have nothing to forgive and something to forget: you have a deal of both. But that's all before the war – anti dileuvian.[14] I have this job. I don't know when or how it will end. God be with you.

Thanks to you all for all the various clothes. The woollen things are highly appreciated. Some of the shirts and pyjamas, don't fit so well with the men's service needs. I think they'd be better for the wounded. I shall send them back to you for that purpose, my men can't wear pyjamas. They're very much limited by regulations and by weight, in what we take. Gloves socks and helmets – –

Love to you all.

Excuse these jagged sentences I write in a hut, by a flickering taper, couched on the floor.

But I get fun as well as woe out of this distracting time. Most people can only get woe. It's a bad year. Keep well and be happy.

Rupert.

Farm Corner,
Tadworth,
Surrey.

15 December [1914]

Dear Rupert

I think it was jolly nice of you to write at all considering the unfavouring circumstances.

I find letters hard enough in all conscience, though I'm not doing military exercises all day, nor am I obliged to write in some odd corner by the uncertain light of a candle. And it was particularly nice of you to say you have nothing to forgive. I doubt if that's strictly true, but we'll let it pass. It's probably about as true as if I said I had nothing to forgive. So now we're quits. – I'm glad you're getting some fun out of all this. You're certainly getting some new experiences. So are we all. I hope you're not flooded out.

Mamma and I have been asked to serve our country by recruiting in a caravan in Sussex. We mean to go. We are to start on Jan. 2nd, and catch the country yokels as they make their New Year resolutions. I wonder if we'll have any success. Wish us luck.

I say, it would be a good idea to see you some time soon. Can you come down here? Or if you have'nt time for that, could you state a date in town? / Just close to Christmas I expect we shall have rather a houseful: but could doubtless fit you in somewhere for a night if you came. My grandparents will be here.* Wonder what my grandfather thinks of all this: he's an old Scots Greys man.

We shall be away a week on our Sussex tour: so unless you're going to be where our caravan will be likely to discover you this possible meeting with you must be before the 2nd or after the 9th of January.

I have been several sorts of ass about my painting: I was so taken up with one thing and another that I not only forgot to send up for the International, but also for the New English. However, it does'nt make much odds to anybody, as nothing seems to be doing, commercially or otherwise, in the art line – All the shows seem deadly. The only chance these days for a painter to attract either notice or buyers is to be a Belgian, unless he descends to fancy pictures of "Unparalleled Charge of the Blanks of Blanks" for the illustrateds – if the job's available. I said to an artist I know who does things for the illustrateds, "How does one get these jobs?" He said "The thing to do is to see the editor. I went into his office and took him to have a drink." Wonder what an editor would say if I tried that on.

That's good advice of yours, to be happy. The way to do it is to be doing something one think's worth doing, for its own sake or otherwise. I shall be very happy in our caravan, because it's worth going simply for the fun, and if a grateful country (or whoever it is – I'm not quite clear) thinks it sufficiently worth while to stand one's expenses, well and good. I only hope we shall get some recruits. I hear the district is slightly unpromising.

Well, I hope to see you soon. It will be rather disappointing of you if you don't manage just a while – here if you can. Meanwhile, good luck.

Phyllis.

* They won't: not when I thought: they're only going to come for Christmas Day, so we will put you in the spare room if you come. The post came in while I was writing – Any time will do. Do manage to come. We only had you for such a little while when we met in town.

NINE

'TOO BRIEF THE SONG'

B rooke spent Christmas at Blandford Camp tending the stokers under his command. He took it upon himself to get his mother to send mince pies for 150 men, plus three bottles of his 1887 vintage port, while his uncle sent money to buy playing cards, draughts, and hoops and pegs. The intention was to try and keep his men entertained and hopefully sober, but this largely failed as they ended up being drunk throughout the festive period. Brooke was given six days' leave of absence from 29 December, which he spent with his mother in Rugby. Although the fourth, and ultimately final, issue of *New Numbers* was due to go to print in December, and this was the date given on its cover, Wilfrid Gibson and Lascelles Abercrombie actually delayed publication until February so Brooke's war sonnets could be included. When Brooke received the proofs, he wrote to Edward Marsh from Canford Manor near Blandford camp on 24 January: 'God, they're in the rough, these five camp-children – 4 and 5 [IV. 'The Dead' and V. 'The Soldier'] are good enough, and there are phrases in the rest.'

[Postmarked: Blandford.]

[Hood Badge] The Hood Battalion,
The Royal Naval Division.

10 January [1915]

Dear Mrs Gardner,

I <u>hadn't</u> gone on leave when you wrote, a fortnight ago. I took my leave late, at New Year. But I spent it all but a few hours at home. My brother got no leave: and my mother was left alone, – and she'd not been well.

I got back to find a shortbread cake waiting. Thanks very much. It brightened our tea for two or three days.

We've begun to work fairly hard again. But I'm rather depressed by the news, that – though we're almost ready – we've got to wait for the rest of the Division: till April. However, one must use one's patience at this game.

Thanks to various generosities we're getting comfortably fitted out. Long thick warm mufflers – very long – are the only thing we badly need now. Also, if you know of people who take in such things as the Tatler Sphere etc., and don't (who would) want to keep them: I (for my platoon) am a very willing recipient, four days or so after issue – forgive this practicality.

Love to all: and a Happy New Year to all: one can wish it, even in all this.

    Ever
      Rupert Brooke

Farm Corner,
Tadworth,
Surrey.

30 January [1915]

Dear Rupert

It seems a goodish while since I wrote to you, although I've assisted in the despatch to you of various objects. I've just been to Cambridge, which is looking even more unlike its usual self than other places. The streets are full of khaki men and blue men and guns and transports and ambulances and cavalry mounts: and you can't show a peep of light anywhere after dark, and all the early milk-carts are searched when they come in. And all the people I came across knew exactly what they were going to do when the raid came. I think there was a special burst of caution when I was there because it was the Kaiser's birthday. – What price cultured ease? I see the Cambridge Review is very apprehensive: Learning will no longer be the privilege of the Chosen Few: I can't see the sequence personally, and anyhow rather like the notion, but that's how it seems to the writer of the article.

I wonder what you are doing now, and if you're up to the neck in mud. The field where they camped the horses up the Barton road was a deep bog, and they had to move on.

I wonder what manner of mental or spiritual atmosphere one gets in a collection of men, probably nearly as haphazard as one I heard of: A teacher in the Goldsmith's College, a poacher, three miners, two corner boys and two indescribables, all in one tent: and if the said atmosphere is more to your liking than the scholarly seclusion that was Cambridge.

I have just flown out on a bicycle to deliver an urgent telephone message to an inspector of special constables, in a motor, who had gone to cross examine some Belgian refugees about flash-signals. I wonder if they have caught a spy. I caught the inspector all right. He'd taken Daddy with him.

Well, goodbye.

Phyllis.

By the beginning of February a cold with which Brooke had been battling with for weeks turned to severe influenza. He was given sick leave and went to Gray's Inn to recover. However, he became so ill that Marsh's housekeeper, Mrs Elgy, felt unable to provide the medical attention he needed, so Brooke was moved to 10 Downing Street. Here Violet Asquith tended to him for the next nine days. After a short visit to Walmer Castle, he returned to London on 14 February to have dinner with Marsh and Winston Churchill at the Admiralty; by that evening he was back at Blandford [1].

[Hood Badge]
The Hood Battalion,
Royal Naval Division.
Blandford

14 February 1915

My dear Delphis,

I'm afraid I've taken a long time to acknowledge or answer your letter – to say nothing of subsequent communications from your family. To tell the truth, I've been having influenza, for two weeks and a bit more, and I've only just come back into Camp. I lay in bed and felt half too sleepy and half too depressed even to write a letter.

But now I'm back here, and well again: and even the weather is a bit better: and we're most of us a little more reconciled to the boredom of training. Though when we shall get out to the front – to any front – we still don't know.

Do you know, your handwriting is exactly like Lascelles Abercrombie's – if that conveys anything – honour or the reverse – to you. I should think it an honour.

I wonder what the rest of the world's doing. Everything passes by here, unnoticing us, and unnoticed

Yours

Rupert Brooke

Many thanks for the French book. But my men haven't the wits to learn French, I'm afraid.

[Postmarked: London W. 3 pm. 22 Feb 15.]

[Hood Badge] The Hood Battalion,
Royal Naval Division.

19 February [1915]

Dear Mrs Gardner,

Many thanks for the scarves. They were very good. I should like some more, – only we're leaving here in three days, and England soon after. Only for a month or two, I fancy. Then back to pick up the rest of the Division, before going to Flanders. We're going to the Mediterranean. But please don't talk either of our movements, or of our destination. If you have another scarf or two <u>finished</u>, I could give them out before starting.

Best wishes to Phyllis and all of you –

Yours

Rupert Brooke

On learning that the Royal Naval Division was going to be part of a short sharp campaign, Rupert wrote to his mother: 'We are going to be part of a landing force to help the fleet break through the Hellespont and the Bosphorus and take Constantinople, and open the Black Sea.'[1] Brooke's reaction to this news was one of unsuppressed excitement, his schooling in Classics coming powerfully to the fore:

> It's too wonderful for belief. I had not imagined Fate could be so benign. I almost suspect her … I suddenly realise that the ambition of my life has been – since I was two – to go on a military expedition against Constantinople. And when I <u>thought</u> I was hungry, or sleepy, or falling in love, or aching to write a poem – <u>that</u> was what I really, blindly, wanted.[2]

After several days of great activity making preparations, checking their kit and inspections by Churchill and the King, on 28 February, the Royal Naval Division marched out of Blandford camp wearing pith helmets. In the pouring rain they marched ten miles to Skillingstone station, where they caught a train to Avonmouth Docks, Bristol.

On 1 March Brooke and his battalion boarded their ship, the *Grantully Castle*. Violet Asquith was the only person there to see off Brooke and her brother Oc. She later poignantly recalled in her diary that: 'Rupert walked with me along the narrow crowded decks – down the little plank stairs – then I said goodbye to him. I knew by his eyes that <u>he</u> felt sure we should never see each other again.'[3]

Before very long he was sent out to Gallipoli.

I was by now abjectly sorry for having been so brutal and silly before. I made a little wooden carving of a person sitting crumpled up in an attitude of despair: I thought he would perhaps understand that better than a written thing. I did it up in a little parcel and sent it to him.

Then, one Saturday night, I suddenly and without cause felt anxious about him. I seem to have entered in a diary: – "Is R[upert]. all right?" On the Sunday morning following this we went up to Lower Kingswood to church. The curate produced a book which he offered to lend my mother. She opened it at a picture of St. George and the Dragon. St. George was lying on the ground, exhausted, with his eyes closed.

"That isn't my idea of St. George and the Dragon," said my mother. "He looks as if he was dead – and he wasn't!" I saw her looking very seriously at the picture, and for a longer time than its nature warranted. I knew what she was thinking.

When we got home she wrote to Lascelles Abercrombie, asking him if he had any news of R[upert].

A day or two later, when I came down to breakfast, a letter in a queer shaky handwriting I did not know lay at my mother's place. I looked at it: somehow the shakiness of the writing frightened me. R[upert]. had once said Abercrombie's writing was a little like Delphis's. This was not like Delphis's, but there was enough likeness...

My mother came down. She picked up this letter and tore it open, and having read a little of it she rushed away upstairs. I rushed after her, saying: – "I insist on seeing that letter." She turned on the stairs and flung her arms round me, and said: – "I'm sorry for you."

I went down again and sat on the dining-room hearth. My father did not ask me what the matter was: he probably knew. After half an hour my mother reappeared with the letter and showed it to both of us. [4]

I sat down on the fireplace again, and I do not know exactly how long I had been there when there came a ring at the front door bell. An old lady, a neighbour of ours, was let in. She was full of indignation about the bad management of the supplies for the camp which was beginning to arise at Tadworth, and came to us to set forth a proposal for starting a canteen to help tide matters over for the present.

I welcomed the diversion. I did not at once want to think this thing out in all its ramifications. I flung myself wholly into the plan, and offered myself to be its executive. This meant a good deal of work, and from this moment on for several months I had but a few spare minutes [20].

5, Raymond Buildings,
Gray's Inn.

3 May 1915

Dear Mrs Gardner,

I wish I had anything to tell you. I suppose I must soon get news from one or other of the friends who were with him – but so far every day had been a blank. Letters as a rule take ten days at least to come.

I got one dated April 3rd from L. Ian Hamilton, telling us that he had seen Rupert and that he had a touch of the sun, but he'd be all right in a day or two, as he was otherwise perfectly fit – Soon after I heard from Denis Browne that R had diarrhoea – Still I was not anxious – And then on the 23rd came the telegram that he was in the French hospital ship with septicaemia – "condition very grave" – and then another the same evening saying all was over – That is all that is known.

All his friends must feel for each other – I am beginning to get over the first violence of the shock, but each day brings me more realization of what I have lost. I went this Saturday and Sunday to see his mother – she is very brave – though of course broken hearted – as I am.

Yours sincerely
E Marsh.

Tuesday

P.S. I send you what I wrote last night – but I got a letter from him this morning, undated, but also one from his comrade in arms, Denis Browne, of <u>April 15th</u>, saying that Rupert was quite fit again though rather thin – so his real illness must have been quite short. This is a great comfort. EM[5]

Farm Corner,
Tadworth,
Surrey.

11 May 1915

Dear Mr Marsh,

It was very kind of you to write in the midst of your own sorrow. The loss to poetry is irreparable. Personally what I feel is that I did not do all I should for him – I cared too much he should be on the same side in the great battle. His spirit was to me that of a great angel. In some ways he now seems nearer.

I still seem dazed, and can only say to myself "God's mercy is over all his works".

Again, thank you for your letter.
Yours sincerely
Mary Gardner.

P.S. if you thought of putting a memorial to Rupert at Lemnos I should like to know and to contribute – I think his friends would like it.[6]

RB
Had we been fit to hear thy voice
O Lord of all the whirling spheres
Thou would'st have spoken to rejoice
Our listening ears
Had we been fit to see thy face
O God of all serenest thought
Thou wouldst have smiled a little space
On what we wrought
Too brief the song, too swift the sight
Before thy angel took his flight.
[MARY GARDNER][7]

It was not one illness but a sequence of them that led to Brooke's death. Still not in the best of health following his recent bout of flu, after reaching Egypt and Port Said on 28 March, Brooke suffered from heat stroke, dysentery and a mosquito bite on his lip that swelled and throbbed. Colonel Quilter wanted him to go to a military hospital, but he was adamant that he would stay with his men.

It took the *Grantully Castle* a week to reach Trebuki Bay, Skyros, on 17 April; throughout this time Brooke remained in bed on sick leave. On 20 April, although very thin and tired, he took part in field exercises on Skyros, but by the following day he felt unwell and his upper lip had become very swollen again. Within hours his health had declined to such a point that he was falling in and out of consciousness. To try and establish how to treat Brooke, a swab was taken of his infected lip and studied under a microscope: pneumococcus, a relatively rare cause of septicaemia, was found to be present. Following consultations with doctors and a surgeon it was decided that Brooke should be moved to the French hospital ship, the *Duguay-Trouin*. Here he was anaesthetised, the infected area cauterised and attempts made to draw the poison off through a focal abscess on his thigh.

Nothing else could be done. Denis Browne and Oc Asquith looked on helplessly as Rupert became weaker and then, at 4.46 p.m. on 23 April, died from acute blood-poisoning. Denis Browne expressed his emotions in a letter to Marsh. 'It is all so near, so impossible. One can't realize that that spirit that knew and loved all the beautiful things of the world so strongly is cut off from them for ever.'[8] In the logbook of the *Duguay-Trouin* the ship's captain wrote:

> Never did face seem paler on the bed of death. Is it because of that black mark on the lip? Or is it that the Eastern lights beat more pitilessly on the skin of this man from the North? Then a voice says: "England has lost her greatest poet." ... O pale, pale, English face that no one will look on ever again! Face of passion, of dreams, and of torment! Poetry not of the world, but of beyond the world, dwelling so early on the other side.[9]

At this moment, the transition from man to myth began.

As the *Grantully Castle* had to sail for Gallipoli the following morning, Rupert's burial had to be carried out rapidly. His friends went ahead to dig the grave by moonlight in an olive tree grove covered with fragrant wild sage, which he had admired only three days earlier, while 12 petty officers of the Hood Battalion carried his body for a mile, by torchlight, and with great difficulty along a stony dried-up river bed.

The coffin was lowered into a grave lined with olive and sage. A service was held, and three volleys were fired into the air. Then, as most of the men made their way back to the ship, Freyberg, Kelly, Asquith, Lister and Browne stayed behind to cover his grave with lumps of pink and white marble, gathered from the surrounding area. A small cross, sent by Brooke's platoon, was placed at the foot of the grave, and a larger one bearing his name set at its head. On the back of the latter the battalion's interpreter wrote an inscription in Greek, which translated read:

Here lies
the servant of God
Sub-lieutenant in the
English Navy
Who died for the
deliverance of Constantinople
from the Turks

Three days later an obituary written by Winston Churchill appeared in *The Times*. Its rousingly emotive style, a precursor of his famous Second World War speeches, canonised Brooke:

Rupert Brooke is dead. A telegram from the Admiralty at Lemnos tells us that this life has closed at the moment when it seemed to have reached its springtime. A voice had become audible, a note had been struck, more true, more thrilling, more able to do justice to the nobility of our youth in arms engaged in this present war, than any other – more able to express their thoughts of self-surrender, and with a power to carry comfort to those who watched them so intently from afar… Joyous, fearless, versatile, deeply instructed, with classic symmetry of mind and body, he was all that one would wish England's noblest sons to be in days when no sacrifice but the most precious is acceptable, and the most precious is that which is most freely proffered.[10]

Once started, our canteen grew, and we had to employ more and more helpers, and I did all the shopping, a good deal of the organising, and some part of the sweeping, washing and other physical work, so that I had little time to worry during the day and when night came was tired enough to fall into bed and go straight to sleep.

But near the beginning of this time a wonderful thing happened. My mother and I were in town, and while we were walking in Regent Street near the Queen's Hall I saw a newsboy with a big placard: – "Heavy fighting in Gallipoli". The thought flashed across my mind like a streak of lightning: – "I know someone who's well out of that!"

I thought again: well out of it? And again the lightning flash came, without a shadow of uncertainty, "yes! And you are not to worry: he wanted to go: – he's better off where he is: you would be wrong and disloyal to worry." And somehow it seemed as if his presence were with me, reassuring me and comforting me. It stayed with me all the way home in the train, and gradually faded away in the evening, but it left me with a great sense of calm and of certainty that all was well with him.

While this feeling was still strong upon me, old Dr Freshfield[11] came in with a rough plan and some photographs of the ruins of the Church at Hierapolis. This was one of the very earliest of Christian churches; one is not sure but what it existed in the time of St. Paul (v. Colossians, IV, 13). On one of the lintels of doors there is a design of two interlaced squares in a circle, with a cross in the middle; and Dr Freshfield had a theory that the church was built with this form as a ground plan. He gave me some measurements he had taken on the spot (apparently at some personal risk, the country being infested with brigands), and some photographs, and I set to work to try and reconstruct the plan. The measurements fitted in like a puzzle; the thing worked out much better than either Dr Freshfield or I had hoped it would. I sent him the finished plan, and he was delighted, and gave me as a professional fee a sum far larger than I thought the work was worth. I devoted a part of this sum to having a little gold ornament made in the form of the plan for him, and another exactly like it for me; and as I imagined that the mystic significance of the pattern was somehow connected with my new certainty of the survival of the soul after death, I took to wearing the ornament as a kind of reminder in case I should ever lose faith.

[Phyllis to Maitland Radford.
Envelope addressed: Lieut. M .Radford, R.A.M.C,
No 3 General Hospital, British Expeditionary Force c/o G.P.O.]

Farm Corner,
Tadworth,
Surrey.

8 May [1915]

Dear Maitland

I wonder if you heard about Rupert. (Your mother wrote to me at once because she is an angel.) I hardly know what to say: except that I can't honestly say I was surprised – Some times one has queer flashes of foresight: I've had so many with regard to him.

I can't really tell you all about it, not in a letter.
It is difficult to write.

There is a red cross detachment just passing the fence, bugling and drumming. There are I don't know how many thousand men encamped close here. I said that when I last wrote, the day before I had news. It is all very noisy and unpeaceful: they bugle all day and night. We are working very hard at running a restaurant for them. I am glad to have something to work hard at.

I want very much to draw, but my ideas are wandering about so, and the things I think are totally undrawable. Tell me, you, what do you think becomes of the souls of the dead? Have you ever lost anyone you were on thought-reading terms with?

It seems to me that, for a little while at all events – longer times I know nothing of – one can get certain intuitions – I was for the first few days without any notion, except of the pity and waste and cruelty of it all, and then quite suddenly I was reproved and knew that I was wrong in being so sorry: I did'nt think it, I knew it, as though it were spoken aloud. (They're cheering down in camp – I am in the west end of the attic) I could enlarge on this and tell you exactly what I mean, but it would take a long time.

Do write and tell me how you're getting on: and for heaven's sake don't go and catch anything and die.

– When I last wrote I tried to be lively and all that but really at the bottom of my heart I knew about Rupert – I knew, and was sorry, and had'nt had that last message – I don't see that I can say any more just now. I sit with the paper in front of me, you know the way.

I had a funny little idea the other night: St Peter, at the gate of Heaven, in khaki; with a bayonet, saying "Pass friend all's well!" It made me laugh a lot although it is'nt really at all funny – It might be more so if I had a profound belief in St Peter guarding the heavenly gates.

Well – so long. Write some time.
Yours
Phyllis.[12]

[Mary Gardner to Maitland Radford, 7 July 1915.
Envelope address: Lieutenant Maitland Radford,
No. 3 General Hospital, Tréport B.E.7.]

…You might understand what an awful shock and horror Rupert's death is to me personally. I had and have a great and tender affection for him personally, quite away from my admiration of his personality as a poet. I don't know how to express myself, but I expect you would sympathise very understandingly. Perhaps Walt Whitman's "Come, lovely and soothing death"[13] expresses my feeling best. His was a soul that once it shook off its fetters we could not keep. And these last verses of his show that he was shaking them off. Death appears as the "Strong deliveress" for him. I simply could not answer your mother's kind letter at the time; and I don't think I could now. It is different with you because you are in some danger yourself ....

  Your affectionate friend
  Mary Gardner[14]

A little later there came to me a knowledge that if R[upert]. wanted me I must come, but by what method I know not: and the sign was to be if I actually saw a waking vision of him.

  One evening I had gone in and lain down on my mother's bed, and I suddenly began to shake with fear. The light cast by the by-pass of the gas on to the ceiling very nearly began to take his form ... I could not possibly explain then to her, but I did afterwards. However, the likeness took no further form, and I did not consider it definite enough to take for a sign. Therefore I am here to tell the tale.

  And after another day or two I was due to spend a day or two with my aunt in Cambridge. The others were all sitting round the table, and I came to join them, and my mother said: – "When are you going to Cambridge?"

  I was just sitting down in my place beside Delphis, but somehow the thought of going to Cambridge was altogether too much for me. I rose up again and fled into the drawing-room, calling out as I went: – "I don't want to go to Cambridge," in something as near a flood of tears as I have ever compassed within my own memory. I flung myself on the sofa and was shaken with silent sobs.

  After a while my mother came in. "Come and try to eat something," she said. "You needn't go to Cambridge."

  So presently I got up and came in again. I had command over myself by this time, and said: – "I'll go. I don't really mind."

Brooke had asked Edward Marsh to be his literary executor, something he touched upon in a letter written for Marsh in the event of his death:

> This is very odd. But I suppose I must imagine my non-existence, and make a few arrangements. ... If you go through my papers, Dudley Ward'll give you a hand. ... You must decide everything about publication. Don't print much bad stuff.[15]

Marsh felt it part of his duty to write a memoir of Brooke, so he gathered together all the material he could. By the end of July 1915 he
had started to compose it, while staying with Wilfrid Gibson and his
wife. Marsh returned to their senders the collections of correspondence
Brooke had carefully stored, including those from Phyllis; it appears
that he also sought her permission to use Brooke's letters to her in his
memoir.

> Farm Corner,
> Tadworth,
> Surrey.

23 June [1915]

Dear Mr Marsh,
      Thank you very much for my letters.
      I hope you will understand my not liking my letters from him to be
published.[16] The most beautiful parts are often the least publishable.
      I have them all kept and do not know if I shall leave them to anybody
in my will.
      I wish this war was over.
            Yours sincerely
                  Phyllis Gardner
P.T.O
P.S. if you happen to know where a little wooden carving of mine of a
little man with his head between his knees is I would take it as a very
great favour if I could have that – It has a merely sentimental value – But
don't trouble about it. I don't know if he ever got it, it was the last thing
I ever sent.[17]

It is not known if Phyllis's little wooden man ever reached Brooke or
if it was later found and returned to her. Brooke's sudden and untimely
death left many questions and hopes unanswered for Phyllis, as was
the case for so many young women who lost the men they loved to
the war. In hindsight it could be argued that perhaps Brooke's death,
which catapulted him and his poetry to such national fame while he was
still young, handsome and possibly at his brightest, allowed Phyllis to
treasure and preserve the romance of Brooke's memory and her time
with him.

      Had he survived and things naturally petered out between them,
Phyllis probably would have witnessed him marrying, having a family
and perhaps his fame as a poet fading; none of her memories would

have remained so treasured, poignant and loaded with the eternal question: 'What if?' In turn she may never have written her memoir and therefore left a lasting record of a wonderful love story, with a rare insight into Rupert Brooke and an elite, innocent, Edwardian lifestyle that would so soon be smashed and changed forever. But arguably, our greatest loss might have been to have missed out on the privilege and pleasure of getting to know Phyllis Gardner through her own words. She emerges from these letters and memoir with such clarity, intelligence and strength, her voice is so strong and clear, yet vulnerable, sensitive and unforgettable: a fine example of the generation of women who through their daily actions fought for women's rights and the vote … and won.

EPILOGUE

'THE YEARS AFTER —
AFTER—'

On 14 June 1915 Alfred, Mrs Brooke's last surviving child and youngest son, was killed in the trenches of Loos by a direct mortar bomb strike.[1] Two days later Rupert's much anticipated posthumous collection of verse, *1914 and Other Poems*, was published. The first thousand printed sold rapidly, and numerous impressions were to follow.[2]

Ever since Dean Inge had read 'The Soldier' as part of his sermon in St Paul's on Easter Sunday, during the last weeks of Brooke's life, public interest in this virtually unknown poet had begun to swell. His War Sonnets, in particular 'The Soldier', struck a chord with the nation at that time, reflecting the public's patriotic mood and romanticised ideas of war, before the brutal realities of trench warfare hit home. Brooke's death, following so swiftly in 'some corner of a foreign field', as he had predicted, was intensely poignant for a country which had begun to mourn its lost men.

A media frenzy rapidly followed, headed by Churchill's obituary in *The Times*. It was mainly driven by journalists, but some of Brooke's friends and acquaintances also rushed to express their grief in print. The emotion of the moment made many lose their sense of proportion and judgement; Lascelles Abercrombie, for example, declared:

Not since Sir Philip Sidney's heroic death have we lost such a gallant and joyous type of the poet-soldier ... the history of literature, so full of Fate's exquisite ironies, has nothing more poignantly ironic, and nothing at the same time more beautifully appropriate, than the publication of Rupert Brooke's noble sonnet-sequence, "1914," a few swift weeks before the death they had imagined, and had already made lovely.[3]

Professor Gilbert Murray lamented:

Rupert Brooke dead! It seems incredible as well as cruel. He was such an incarnation of youth and the spring ... I cannot help thinking that Rupert Brooke will probably live in fame as an almost mythical figure. Among all who have been poets and died young, it is hard to think of one who, both in life and death, has so typified the ideal radiance of youth and poetry.[4]

Some wiser friends, such as Harold Monro, tried to address the extravagant outpourings:

I am glad that the obituary notices of Rupert Brooke are mostly written, so that I may come late into the field with something to write about his poetry, irrespective of the circumstances of his death. There is no doubt that these circumstances, in providing a sentimental basis, have drawn the attention of the English public to him more directly than could otherwise have been expected, and that his name, as soldier-poet, will be on the lips of thousands who will hardly care to read a verse of his poetry. ... Romance apart, one would rather have had him duly recognised as a poet than advertised as soldier-poet. One fears his memory being brought to the poster-grade. "He did his duty. Will you do yours?" is scarcely the moral to be drawn. There is no doubt that he took the duties brought upon him by the war very seriously, and his war sonnets in New Numbers, IV., are among the strongest and sincerest of his verses. Nevertheless, I believe that he himself would least have desired to be recognised principally in this aspect of soldier-poet. His whole poetry is full of the repudiation of sentimentalism. His death was not more lovely than his life. His death is a sinister and ironical episode in the annals of this melancholy war, another instance of its dreary and incomprehensible waste.[5]

Phyllis's war work for the next three years included driving a munitions lorry to Woolwich Arsenal, about which she wrote a series of articles for *The Motor* magazine.[6] She then went on to work alongside her father in the Geographic Section of the Admiralty Intelligence Department at the Wallace Collection. In 1916 a committee, including

Francis Cornford, Robert Whitelaw and Edward Marsh, was formed to organise a fund for a memorial plaque to be erected in Brooke's memory at Rugby School Chapel; a record was kept of those who donated money to the fund, and the name of Gardner features on this list.[7] Phyllis's old Slade tutor Harvard Thomas was chosen to carve the bas-relief medallion based on the now famous Sherril Schell profile portrait photograph of Brooke, which had been used as the frontispiece of *1914 and Other Poems*, and Eric Gill, one of Brooke's favourite artists, cut the lettering of 'The Soldier' for the plaque.

Throughout 1918 Phyllis wrote her memoir. In a letter to Delphis she refers both to this project and to the wall painting in Farm House attic which Brooke had admired back in September 1912

> Hertford House
> 22 Feb.
> ...I have all sorts of projects in my mind; a) I am writing a (true) story, which you may have heard before, all about some things that happened to me, and it makes a very good but improbable yarn, the only disadvantage of which is that when it is done I shan't be able to show it to any-one; or nearly no-one – b) When this is done (I am doing it in my spare moments) I am going to do certain drawings, (one always is!) which any show ought to be proud to take. One of them will be a procession, which you shall see, founded upon a tune of Schubert's, and containing a knight on a black horse, a lady on a white one, an old magician in a black cloak on foot, and a lot of pages and torch-bearers on foot, and a sunset, – and so forth. I began it in the attic long ago. Also I am not sure I shan't do the triumphal entry of Andrew in to Valleia, perhaps instead of this other: it would be much the same sort of effect...[8]

Although only a small amount of Phyllis's art survives, it is evident from what remains that Brooke continued to haunt and inspire her for many years. An illuminated manuscript of Scottish ballads [30] in the form of a little book, painstakingly created by Phyllis in 1919, features among its finely decorated pages a naked, fair-haired man bearing a striking resemblance to Brooke. A pair of eyes, unmistakably his, gaze out at you from a capital letter motif.[9]

In 1920 Stanley Casson, an archaeologist and friend of the Gardner family who was working in Athens, agreed to undertake the job of constructing a formal tomb over Brooke's grave, following the instructions of his mother. This led to Casson writing an article entitled 'Rupert

Brooke's Grave'. It was published in *The London Mercury*[10] in 1920 and then reproduced in book form in 1921, under the title *Rupert Brooke and Skyros*.[11] The book also featured 11 woodcut illustrations by Phyllis; based upon photographs Casson had taken while working on Brooke's tomb, they depict the grave and views of the island [13].

Phyllis also produced a twelfth woodcut – not for general publication, but instead a very private, poignant and symbolic interpretation of her own grief. It shows Phyllis naked, curled up, head in hands in an attitude of grief, very much fitting the description of the carved figure she sent to Brooke, sitting on the shores of Skyros with the sun setting on the horizon.[12] She gave the woodcut the title 'So sinks the day-star' [12]. This line was taken from John Milton's 'Lycidas', a pastoral elegy dedicated to the memory of Milton's young Cambridge friend who drowned. The name Lycidas derives from a character who was a poet in the Greek *Idylls* by Theocritus. With Phyllis's desire that her art be multilayered in meaning, there can be little doubt that her quote was carefully chosen to unite diverse elements with a personal connection to both Rupert and herself.

> Weep no more, woeful shepherds, weep no more,
> For Lycidas your sorrow is not dead,
> Sunk though he be beneath the wat'ry floor.
> So sinks the day-star in the ocean bed,
> And yet anon repairs his drooping head,
> And tricks his beams, and with new-spangled ore
> Flames in the forehead of the morning sky:
> So Lycidas sunk low, but mounted high.

To the editor's knowledge, only two prints were made of this woodcut. Phyllis pasted one into her own copy of *Rupert Brooke and Skyros*. She gave the other to a friend who also stuck it into the front of their copy of this book.[13]

By the end of the war in 1918 the Gardners had moved from Farm Corner. They briefly resided in two different houses in Hampstead before removing themselves from London society, probably due to Christopher's autism becoming harder to hide or handle now he was 16. The family moved to a large house called Recess in Maidenhead, where they were to remain for the next 20 years. During this time Phyllis fully immersed herself in what was to become a great passion, the keeping of Irish wolfhounds [7 and 9].

Over the ensuing years she made a name for herself as a breeder, with the kennel name of Coolafin – a variation of Coolavin, her mother's Irish birthplace. In 1931 Phyllis wrote a history of the Irish wolfhound,[14] now regarded as a bible of the breed. Delphis had by this time also become very involved with the dogs, and she and Phyllis provided the numerous woodcuts used to illustrate the book. Both Gardner sisters were talented artists. They produced beautiful woodcuts and carvings, made their own silver jewellery and ran a printing press on which they created limited edition art books under the name of the Asphodel Press.

There is a definite sense that Phyllis had now become the backbone of the family, with her parents increasingly frail and in need of care, and Delphis shadowing her in all that she did. Being a very digni-fied, proud person – a quality once touched upon by Brooke – Phyllis took charge of Christopher, whom she obviously dearly loved. She involved him in all that they did, took photographs of him posed with the wolfhounds and in formal documents gave him the title of 'Irish wolfhound breeder'.

In 1934 Mary Gardner wrote to Ernest Rhys: 'Now-a-days I seem to read very little and go about very little. In fact we are almost hermits. So you must take pity on us and come over one day to see how long our hair and nails have grown.'[15] Close friends and family continued to visit the Gardners, especially those who moved within the same circles of Irish wolfhound enthusiasts and artists. Among the latter was Phyllis's good friend Mabel Alice Bovenschen, a fellow member of the Society of Women Artists. Her daughter Katharine often accompanied her mother on her visits to the Gardners during the 1920s and 1930s, and has very fond memories from that time:

> The Gardners house was gloriously untidy, large, specially made, dog baskets seemed to be in every room, occupied by Irish Wolfhounds … they [Phyllis and Delphis] both wore hand crafted (by themselves I think) silver pins to hold their hair in place. I believe the coat Phyllis wore when with the Wolfhounds was one she had at school·…There was a studio where both Phyllis and Delphis worked … Phyllis was dignified but fun.

Phyllis never mentioned Rupert Brooke in my hearing. It was when we were driving home one day, after a visit, that my mother told me about their love affair.[16]

Although Phyllis had other admirers, it would seem that her feelings for Brooke remained unrivalled. He was to remain the 'Alpha and Omega' in her life; or perhaps the sentiment that she had once expressed in a letter to Brooke, 'I am not precisely keen on spoiling my own [liberty] by giving it up to anyone else at all', came to the fore. In 1926 Phyllis wrote a poem in which, the editor believes, she describes meeting Brooke's spirit years after his death. The final line powerfully describes how she saw her enduring connection with him:

Sonnet[17]
Feb. 1926
The orchestral music dies upon our ears:
The curtain rises up: the players play.
O you beside me, new from far away,
Do we meet as strangers after all these years?
And will you laugh while I hold back my tears?
No: silent, motionless, I feel you stay:
You understand the things I need not say,
And from my soul are fled the unfaithful fears.

Dear, with heaven I not in vain have cried
In those old difficult days when, not in vain,
I strove with Fate that you should be my friend:
Though you face forth into Earth's uttermost end,
And though in Time we may not meet again,
Eternally we two fight side by side.

On 6 December 1936, after suffering from a heart condition for several years, Mary Gardner died at home. Eighteen months later Phyllis was diagnosed with breast cancer and underwent major surgery.[18] Sadly the cancer soon returned, and on 16 February 1939 Phyllis died at home, surrounded by her family and beloved wolfhounds. She was 48 years old.[19]

Nearly ten months later Professor Gardner also passed away.[20] Phyllis and her parents were buried in the graveyard of St James-the-Less at Stubbings in Maidenhead. Mary and Ernest Gardner shared a plot and headstone, but Phyllis's grave was regrettably left unmarked.

Although financially well provided for, Delphis, who had always depended on Phyllis, struggled to cope with taking care of Christopher. A Maidenhead resident recalled how as a child she saw Christopher going each morning to collect the newspaper, dressed in ragged pyjamas and accompanied by two wolfhounds. Such unusual behaviour apparently unnerved the local residents; parents would tell their children not to look at him as it was not fitting to see him in his nightwear. Matters came to a head in 1947, when Delphis was taken to court by the RSPCA for causing unnecessary suffering to the 11 dogs in her care. The scarcity of meat after the Second World War, due to continued rationing, combined with Delphis's inability to look after the dogs properly and an outbreak of distemper and mange, led to the animals being found in a 'pitiful' state of malnourishment with skin infections. It was acknowledged that Delphis was not a 'person of cruel disposition', but that she had failed to care for the dogs, and she was duly fined by the Borough Magistrates in Maidenhead.[21]

This public humiliation and damage to Delphis's reputation, both among the Maidenhead community and the wolfhound world, must undoubtedly have been the main impetus for her decision to sell up and move to Ireland sometime around 1949. This prompted her to donate Phyllis and Rupert's letters and memoir, which she probably discovered while clearing 'Recess', to the British Museum. She and Christopher bought a farm in Bently, Curracloe, in the County of Wexford. Here they continued to keep and breed their Irish wolfhounds, Welsh springer spaniels[22] and horses, while Delphis carried on Phyllis's work of documenting the history of the wolfhound. A journalist for the *Wexford Echo* recently recalled his childhood memories of Delphis:

> Small boys of curious minds and urban mischief no less than older folk were slightly nervous of her. Small boys thought she could put a spell on them or turn them into goats. Although utterly harmless, her appearance was not that of a 'normal' English eccentric who had discovered her personal nest. She resembled to me, at any rate, a lost, wild woman: tall, boney, gaunt, striding along in wellington boots, or boots, in a worn dirty showerproof mac.[23]

A fellow wolfhound fancier, Annette O'Flaherty, came to the Gardners as their housekeeper, and lived with her son in a separate dwelling on the farm; according to close friends of Delphis, O'Flaherty took advantage of her ingenuous nature.[24] It grieved Delphis's friends, who went to stay with her and Christopher, to discover that items were being taken from their house and sold to shops in the neighbourhood.

Anne Kirwan has very fond childhood memories of her time spend with O'Flaherty:

> I knew Christopher, and possibly Delphis, when my family took a caravan just outside their boundary in 1956–7. I was about 10 years old and Mrs. O'Flaherty took us for rides along the beach every day. Their house was called Bently, and a wonderful house it was. It wasn't til I was 16 years old that I took up riding regularly and was a constant visitor to Bently...
>
> We were never allowed into the house until latter days, and it was a revelation. There were dogs of all sorts, chickens, and a crow with a broken wing living on the beautiful spinnet! No electricity. Christopher lived in one wing and Annette lived with all the animals in the kitchen, with a little staircase up to some sort of bedroom above. In another wing, upstairs, there were quite a few chickens being kept. Only Sean and myself ever entered the house.
>
> One thing is clear. Christopher was certainly very withdrawn and communicated rarely... Himself and Delphis in earlier days would cycle into Wexford town to collect meat and offal for the wolfhounds. They were well known figures in the town at that time, known as eccentrics; as their circumstances worsened they, in turn, used to wear long trench coats, and were an uncommon sight! After Delphis's time Christopher used to wander off into the sand dunes, always with a book, and we would be sent out on the ponies to find him. Curracloe was a very quiet place then except in July and August, so he would be left in peace for hours. Annette would then decide it was time for him to come home. Some days he would be found in a tree. He became very forgetful and withdrawn and would forget to put on all his clothes at times! My memory is that Christopher was receiving some sort of pension from England and this arrived every so often, probably every month, and we would have to find him to have it signed, so that Annette could cash it and survive.
>
> ... The house is now virtually non-existent. It was ransacked after it was left vacant... There is no trace of the house, but the surrounding piece of land is the same and untouched. There is the remains of the stables.

Delphis died in Wexford County Hospital in 1959.[25] She had always made it known that she wished the Bently farmhouse and its land to be inherited by her godson who lived back in England, but within 14 days of her death Christopher was taken to a solicitor by O'Flaherty. She acted as witness to his will, which left 'all my property ... for her [O'Flaherty's] own use and benefit absolutely and I appoint her as sole Executrix of this my Will IN WITNESS'. Christopher passed away in 1968.[26] Both had funeral services in the Church of Ireland, Ardcolm, Castlebridge, and were buried in unmarked graves in Ardcolm Church graveyard.

These latter years of slow decline for the Gardner family offer a sad and sobering contrast to their heady pre-war days in London and Surrey, when they attended concerts and mixed with the top writers and poets of the time. Some of these lifestyle changes were chosen, while others, one suspects, were forced upon them as a response to Christopher's condition. Yet there is also a strong sense that for this family, as for many others, the First World War heralded an end to happier times. For the privileged, those golden, pre-1914 days were never to return. Yet thanks to the letters of Phyllis and Rupert being preserved, and their intense time together recorded so evocatively in Phyllis's memoir, both will remain to all who read their words forever young, vivid and full of hope.

NOTES

ABBREVIATIONS

LRB *The Letters of Rupert Brooke*, edited by Geoffrey Keynes (London: Faber & Faber, 1968)
CH *Rupert Brooke: A Biography* by Christopher Hassall (London: Faber & Faber, 1964)
SL *Song of Love: The Letters of Rupert Brooke and Noel Olivier*, edited by Pippa Harris (London: Bloomsbury, 1991)

PREFACE

1 Virginia Woolf, 'The New Crusade', a review for John Drinkwater's *Prose Papers*, *The Times Literary Supplement*, 27 December 1917, p. 647.
2. *The Diary of Virginia Woolf*, edited by Anne Olivier Bell (Hogarth Press, 1977), Vol.1, p. 171.
3. Mrs. Brooke appointed in her will J T Sheppard, Dudley Ward, Walter de la Mare and Geoffrey Keynes as Brooke's literary executors.
4. Keynes paid to keep *The Letters of Rupert Brooke* standing in type for 11 years while waiting to get permission to publish.
5. CH, p. 277.
6. Brooke to Cathleen Nesbitt, 24 August 1914, LRB, p. 611.
7. Siegfried Sassoon, *The Weald of Youth* (London: Faber & Faber, 1942), p. 231.
8. CH, p. 190.
9. *The Diary of Virginia Woolf*, edited by Anne Olivier Bell (Hogarth Press, 1977), Vol.1, p. 172.
10. Woolf to Raverat, 8 April 1925, *Virginia Woolf & the Raverats*, edited by William Pryor (Clear Books, 2003) pp. 170–1.
11. Forster to Malcolm Darling, 2 August 1915, P N Furbank, *E M Forster: A Life* (London: Secker and Warburg, 1977–8), Vol.II, pp. 18–19.
12. From 'Libido', later changed to Brooke's preferred title of 'Lust', 1909.
13. From 'A Channel Passage', 1909.
14. From 'Jealousy', 1909.
15. CH, p. 38.

INTRODUCTION

1. Ann Payne, head of manuscripts at the British Library. Quote taken from an article in *The Daily Telegraph* by Andrew Wilson, 11 March 2000.
2. When Delphis Gardner donated her sister's papers in November 1948, she was required to write a note giving the Museum Trustees permission to destroy the memoir if they thought 'it should not be made available to the public' when opened in November 1998. In the British Museum's minutes, written at the time Delphis Gardner donated the letters and memoir, their contents was described as being of 'very intimate character…'
3. LRB, p. 565.

4. CH, p. 435.

5. Percy Gardner, *Autobiographica* (Oxford: B. Blackwell, 1933), p. 4.

6. Dr E A Gardner's obituary in *The Times*, 29 November 1939.

7. Mrs Mary Gardner's obituary in the *Maidenhead Advertiser*, 16 December 1936.

8. Phyllis Gardner, *The Irish Wolfhound: A Short Historical Sketch* (Ireland: Dundalgan Press, 1931) p. 98.

9. The rose represents England, the thistle Scotland and the shamrock Ireland.

10. Mary Gardner Memoir held among the Gardner Family Papers at the British Library: Add MS 89076/5.

11. Held among the Kipling papers at Sussex University [ref no: 19/3].

12. *Studium* is the Latin word for study. In 1905 Alice Gardner published: *Theodore of Studium. His Life and Times*. Edward Arnold.

13. Alice Gardner, *Letters to a Godchild* (Edward Arnold, 1906).

14. 'Memories by Geoff Pushman', printed in *Lights Up!*, July 1949.

15. Ibid.

16. Samuel Gardner (18??–1931), Phyllis Gardner's uncle. He was a London stockbroker who had gained an external BA degree at London University in his spare time; he was also a member of the Managing Committee of the London Stock Exchange. Samuel Gardner acted as Chairman of St Felix School Council from 1900 until his death in 1932. Like a number of his siblings, he wrote several books including *A Guide to English Gothic Architecture* (Cambridge University Press, 1922) and *The Architectural History of Harrow Church* (J C Wilbe, 1895). He not only helped to establish St Felix School, but also Orley Farm School of Harrow, where he lived and owned land.

17. Who later acted alongside Brooke in *Comus*, 1908.

18. Bernard Keeling assisted by Nancy Pelling, *Saint Felix School Southwold and The Old Felicians* (Longmore Press), p. 1.

19. Florence Nightingale took the first women nurses to the battlefront; Elizabeth Fry, prison reformer; Millicent Fawcett, leader of the constitutional suffrage movement.

20. Katharine Cox, Evelyn Radford and Phyllis Gardner.

21. *The Felician*, No. 20, December 1907.

22. Phyllis left the Slade in 1913. During her time there she won three awards for Drawing, Fine Art Anatomy and Painting.

23. W Frank Calderon (1865–1943) was born in London, the third son of the artist Philip Calderon, RA. He was educated at University College London, and won a scholarship to the Slade School of Art from the age of 14. From the age of 16 he exhibited and sold work at the Royal Academy.
    In 1893 Calderon founded the School of Animal Painting at 46 Baker Street, London, and in 1899 he bought Headley Mill Farm, near Liphook, Hampshire. During the summer months, he ran a school in the countryside surrounding his farm, in which pupils painted and sketched animals in a natural setting. Calderon was a very successful painter, best known for his paintings featuring horses, dogs and hunting scenes; he numbered many of the twentieth century's leading animal artists among his students, including Lionel Edwards, Cecil Aldin, Frederick Whiting and Kathleen Wheeler.
    Calderon kept a variety of animals who acted as models for the students, with Patrick the Irish wolfhound a favourite among them. After Cecil Aldin drew Patrick he gained a lifelong love of the breed, and Phyllis's passion for them may well also have been kindled during her time at Calderon's school.
    In 1911 Calderon let the farm, moving his London school into an extension of his family home and studio in St. Mary Abbot's Place, Kensington. He also lectured on animal anatomy at the Royal Academy, and in 1936 published *Animal Painting and Anatomy*.

24. Mrs Mary Gardner in a letter to Maitland Radford, 26 May 1914.

25. Mrs Gardner's letters, at the time he was attending school, reveal an underlying tone of protectiveness towards Christopher, along with concern for his being treated differently. Ernest Rhys recalls that Christopher had a gift for music in later life, something touched on by Phyllis in a letter to Maitland Radford in January 1915, when she records the first signs of this burgeoning talent: 'Christopher since you were last here has blossomed out into quite a musician: he learns to play a piece by heart on the piano inside 3 days, and will sit down and play all he knows to a roomful of strangers if you ask him: little short of miraculous for such a shy person.'

26. Brian Rhys, born 4 October, 1891, was the eldest child and only son of Ernest and Grace Rhys. He went to Oxford and then served in the Navy during the First World War as a coding officer, devising a triple secret code in English, French and Italian. After the war he took charge of

Dent publishers in Paris, befriended French writers such as André Gide and translated texts for a number of books. Rhys married and had a son.

27. 'I wrote that poem beginning "Quiet is my house".'

28. Manuscript in editor's private collection.

29. Maitland Radford (1884–1944), son of Dollie and Ernest Radford, was educated at Abbotsholme and then studied medicine at University College Hospital, London, qualifying as a doctor in 1913. His desire was to work in the Public Health Service, so he obtained the post of Assistant Medical Officer to the North Eastern (Infectious Diseases) Hospital until the First World War broke out. Radford joined the RAMC and had been dispatched to France by August 1914, where he was in charge of the Medical Division of No. 3 General Hospital. Following the war Radford was appointed Medical Officer to Queen Mary's Hospital, Carshalton, where he obtained a DPH and MD in State Medicine. He finally achieved the position of Medical Officer of Health at St Pancras. A posthumous collection of his poems was published in 1945 (*Poems by Maitland Radford: with a memoir by some of his friends*, George Allen and Unwin Ltd, 1945).

30. *Poems by Maitland Radford: with a memoir by some of his friends* (London: George Allen and Unwin Ltd, 1945), p. 13.

31. Photographs in the Rupert Brooke Archive at King's College, Cambridge show both Maitland and Evelyn Radford on outings with Brooke in 1909–10.

32. Margaret Maitland Radford.

33. The Rhymers Club was a group of poets founded in 1890 by W B Yeats and Ernest Rhys. Members included Ernest Dowson, Lionel Johnson, Arthur Symons, Ernest Radford and Richard Le Gallienne.

34. University College London Archive, among the Gardner Papers [MS.Add.82/21].

35. George G Harrap and Co Ltd. Poem entitled 'A Miracle', p. 239.

36. Ernest Rhys, *Wales England Wed* (J M Dent and Sons Ltd, 1940), p. 181.

37. Hampstead Heath.

38. Ernest Rhys, *Wales England Wed* (J M Dent and Sons Ltd, 1940), p. 180. The chess sets referred to here were not made by Phyllis and Delphis until some years later.

39. Robert Frost to John T Bartlett, 30 August 1913, *Selected Letters of Robert Frost*, edited by Lawrance Thompson, (New York: Holt, Rinehart and Winston, 1964), p. 90. Frost repeatedly misspelt the name Gardner in this letter, perhaps reflecting his irritation with them at the time. Lawrance Thompson remarked in regard to this letter that it showed 'the expression of obsessive resentments, through letter-writing, as a way of "blowing off steam" quite typical of Frost'.

40. Quoted from CH, p. 363.

41. Brooke to Dudley Ward, 18 January 1910, LRB, p. 211.

42. *The Diary of Virginia Woolf*, edited by Anne Olivier Bell (Hogarth Press, 1977), Vol. 1, p. 172.

43. German to English translation: *highly poetic*.

44. Brooke to Ka Cox, April 1912, LRB, p. 375.

45. James Strachey (1887–1967) was the younger brother of Lytton Strachey, a central figure in the Bloomsbury Group. James Strachey became a notable psychoanalyst and primary translator of Sigmund Freud's work.

46. Geoffrey Langdon Keynes (1887–1982), surgeon, scholar and bibliophile, became one of Brooke's Trustees. His younger brother was the economist John Maynard Keynes.

47. William Denis Browne (1888–1915), composer, critic, pianist and organist, was killed in action at Gallipoli.

48. Sir Geoffrey Keynes, *The Gates of Memory* (The Clarendon Press, 1981), p. 40.

49. Meaning 'the coal burners', in tribute to an Italian nineteenth-century revolutionary group.

50. The University Amateur Dramatic Club.

51. LRB, p. 66.

52. Edward Marsh, *Memoir* (Sidgwick and Jackson, 1918), pp. 20–1.

53. Edward Marsh, *A Number of People: A Book of Reminiscences* (William Heinemann Ltd, 1939).

54. Ibid, p. 274.

55. Brooke's *Poems* was featured as 'The Book of the Month' and reviewed by Edward Marsh in *Poetry Review*, April 1912, pp. 178–81.

56. On 13 January 1907.

57. Brooke had entered poetry competitions run by the *Westminster Gazette* while still at Rugby, under the pseudonyms of 'Sandro', 'Teragram' and 'Mnemon'. Now, in February 1907, he at last allowed his work to be published under his actual name. In 1907 Brooke's poems also started to appear in King's College's own magazine, *Basileon*.

58. LBR, p. 116.

59. Students of the all-female Newnham College, Cambridge.

60. LRB, p. 117.

61. Ibid.

62. *The Times Literary Supplement*, 8 August 1918.

63. Brooke to Frederic Keeling, September 1910, LRB, p. 258.

64. Frances Cornford, *Poems* (Hampstead: The Priory Press, Cambridge: Bowes & Bowes, 1910), p. 15.

65. 'One of the few phrases in the whole masque which seem to have caught something of the fire and intensity of the great Elizabethans occurs in the splendid passage in which the Attendant Spirit describes how, as he was sitting in the wood, he heard the lady's song – *I was all ear, / And took in strains that might create a soul/ Under the ribs of Death*. That is not only beautiful, it is exciting; but, as it was enunciated by the actor, one felt the beauty of it and nothing more. However to have accomplished thus much is no small achievement. How infinitely rarely does one hear, in any theatre, the beauty that is blank verse! From this point of view, the performance at Cambridge was indeed memorable...The existence of such a body of able and enthusiastic lovers of poetry and drama must be welcomed as at least an augury of a better state of things.' CH, p. 165.

66. LRB, p. 163.

67. My dear young lady.

68. SL, p. 230.

69. Brooke to James Strachey, 14 June 1912, *Friends and Apostles* edited by Keith Hale (Yale University Press, 1998), p. 246.

70. Brooke to Hugh Dalton, CH, p. 186.

71. Brooke to Erica Cotterill, July 1909, LRB, p. 172.

72. The *Granta*, 5 February 1910.

73. Brooke to Dudley Ward, May 1910, CH, p. 238.

74. LRB, May 1911, p. 304.

75. Produced later as a book with preface by Geoffrey Keynes. *Democracy and the Arts*, Rupert Hart-Davis, 1946.

76. Brooke to Lytton Strachey, September 1909, LRB, p. 185.

77. Brooke to Erica Cotterill, September 1911, LRB, p. 314.

78. Perhaps a misprint in the original text. The editor believes it should read 'his' instead of 'our'.

79. Helen Bailey, 'I Remember Rupert Brooke', *The Queen*, 2 October 1956.

80. Clara Ewald (1859–1948), portrait painter, was born in Dusseldorf, Germany. After the death of her husband, an art historian, in 1909, she moved with her son Peter to the village of Holzhausen, an artists' colony on the Ammersee, a lake near Munich. There in 1911 she painted the portrait of Brooke that now hangs in the National Portrait Gallery, London (she later painted a copy for King's College, Cambridge). It was to become Ewald's best known work. At the time Brooke posed for her he was on a European tour, and had made the acquaintance of Peter Ewald, then a student at Munich University; the broad-brimmed hat that is such a feature of the picture actually belonged to Peter.

81. Elizabeth van Rysselberghe (1890–1980), a sculptress and daughter of the Belgian neo-Impressionist painter Théo van Rysselberghe, for whom she often posed. She was a friend of Clara Ewald and spoke fluent English. Just before his death, Brooke wrote a letter to Dudley Ward instructing him to burn all the letters van Rysselberghe had written to him; she was to treasure his for the rest of her life, and apparently always regretted not having a child with him. In 1923 she had a daughter with the French writer André Gide.

ONE

1. Original title given by Phyllis Gardner to her memoir.

2. 'Uncle Stanley' was Stanley Price Morgan Bligh (1870–1949), landowner and author, husband to Mary Gardner's sister, Matilda Agnes Wilson. Educated at Eton and Trinity College, Oxford, and member of the Inner Temple, he was called to the Bar in 1895, subsequently taking over the management of Cilmeri, his family's estate. Bligh had an interest in the theories of Sigmund Freud, which inspired him to write three books on psychology. It is interesting to note that Brooke owned a presentation copy of Bligh's first book, *The Direction Of Desire – Suggestions For The Application Of Psychology To Everyday Life* (Oxford: Horace Hart, 1910), on the subject of 'directive psychology' – studying one's own personality so weaknesses can be corrected and strengths utilised.

3. It was before this date, probably 10 November, that Phyllis first saw Brooke at the train station: she sent the 11-11-11 postcard to her mother at least a day after she arrived in Cambridge.

4. Very likely Alix Sargant-Florence (1892–1973), who had recently left the Slade and was at this time studying at Newnham College, Cambridge. She had attended the Fabian camp in Lianbedr alongside her brother Philip in the summer of 1910, which is when she would have met Brooke. Later she married James Strachey.

5. Fanny Foster (1891–1975) had also been a pupil at St Felix School; her mother, Gertrude Foster, had been involved in the school's establishment and acted as one of its governors. In 1910 Fanny went up to Newnham College, Cambridge. She was a very able violin player and later returned to live out the rest of her life in Southwold, Suffolk, where she became mayor.

6. See note 49 above.

7. Annette Reid was the daughter of James Smith Reid (1846–1926), who was married to Ernest Arthur Gardner's sister Ruth. James Reid ceased to be a Fellow of Christ's College, Cambridge, following his marriage in 1872, but he was elected to a Fellowship at Gonville and Caius College in 1878, where he remained for 44 years. Between 1873 and 1885 Reid was lecturer in Classics at Pembroke College, Cambridge. In 1910 he played a large part in founding the Society for the Promotion of Roman Studies, succeeding F J Haverfield as president in 1916. Reid received the honorary degrees of LittD of Dublin University and LLD of St Andrews University, and in 1917 he was elected a Fellow of the British Academy.

8. Hugh Gardner, son of Samuel Gardner.

9. Oliffe Legh Richmond (1881–1977) was educated at Eton and King's College, Cambridge. He was elected a Fellow of the College in 1905 and a College lecturer in 1909. In 1914 he became Professor of Latin at University College, Cardiff. During the First World War Richmond served in the Artists' Rifles, and as an Intelligence Officer at the War Office and the Italian Headquarters. In 1919 he was appointed Professor of Humanities at Edinburgh University. His publications include classical works and verse.

10. Guy W Keeling.

11. Florence Kate Kingsford Cockerell (1871–1949) was a very talented artist and calligrapher who trained under Edward Johnson, the eminent scribe and designer. She illuminated many books including *The Song of Songs* printed by the Ashendene Press (1902, 1904). Her husband was Sydney Carlyle Cockerell (1867–1962), one-time librarian to William Morris and secretary to the Kelmscott Press. Appointed director of the Fitzwilliam Museum, Cambridge in 1908, he transformed the museum's appearance and standing forever. Florence Kate Kingsford Cockerell's work appears to have been a source of inspiration to Phyllis; she also produced some beautiful illuminated books similar in style to those by Cockerell.

12. Unbeknown to Phyllis, Brooke was playing a walk-on part as a Slave in this production of *The Magic Flute*; he was busy rehearsing his part at this time ready for the opening on 1 December.

13. Margaret Maitland Radford.

14. The Olivier family had only just moved into this house at 12 Loudoun Road in St John's Wood.

15. In English, 'shy'.

16. In English, 'It is all very simple, is it not?'

17. Brooke to Katharine Cox, 20 January, 1912, Rupert Brooke Archive, King's College, Cambridge. Brooke has marked the last sentence with a cross and written the additional comment at the bottom of the letter page. Geoffrey Keynes omitted this comment when he published the letter in LRB, p. 340.

18. Robert Frost was later to write to John T Bartlett, 30 August 1913: 'These Gardiners [sic] are the kind that hunt lions and they picked me up cheap as a sort of bargain before I was as yet made … and at the present moment they are particularly keen on lions as creatures who may be put under obligations to review them in the papers … The Missus Gardiner is the worst.' *Selected Letters of Robert Frost*, edited by Lawrance Thompson (USA: Holt, Rinehart and Winston, 1964), p. 90.

19. Throughout this whole affair Brooke had become obsessively and unfairly convinced that Lytton Strachey, who until this time he had considered a friend, had conspired to bring Ka and Lamb together. This would seem highly unlikely, as Lytton was infatuated with Lamb and wanted him for himself, but from this time on Brooke came to hate, with an irrational vigour, Lytton and his circle of friends, later to become known as the 'Bloomsbury Group'.

20. In Brooke's library, now held at Dartmouth College, Hanover, NH, USA, is a copy of Ernest Arthur Gardner's *A Handbook of Greek Sculpture*, 1902 (Rauner Special Collections Library. NB90. G28 1902).

21. Brooke to James Strachey, 10 July 1912. *Friends and Apostles* edited by Keith Hale (Yale University Press, 1998), p. 249.

22. Arthur Christopher Benson (1862–1925) was at this time Senior Fellow (and later Master) of Magdalene College, Cambridge, as well as being an essayist, poet and author.

23. A C Benson, *Memories and Friends* (London: John Murray, 1924), pp. 329–30.

24. Brooke to Frances Cornford, 3 August 1912, LRB, p. 390.

25. Brooke to Dudley Ward, 27 August 1912, LRB, p. 394.

26. In Phyllis Gardner's memoir she continues at this point with the section beginning: 'He had written to say he should be in town soon…' But as this appears to be out of chronological order (she mentions both Brooke's proposed meeting at the National Gallery and what was almost certainly the post-Impressionist exhibition at the Grafton Galleries, which opened on 5 October and ran to 31 December 1912), the editor has placed this further down the text to maintain the sequence of events.

27. Brooke did actually have two aunts who lived together beside the sea, at Bournemouth. In a letter written while he was staying with them in 1907, he commented to his friend St John Lucas: 'My Evangelical aunts always talk at meals like people in Ibsen. They make vast Symbolical remarks about Doors and Houses and Food' (LRB, p. 90).

28. David Garnett, *The Golden Echo* (Chatto and Windus, 1953), pp. 223–5. Garnett recounts Brooke telling him this same story, at a similar time. It was surely a parable that he created to express his feelings about religion.

29. In 2007, when the present owner of Farm Corner kindly showed me the house, he recalled seeing paintings upon the walls in the attic. However, these were destroyed when alterations were made a few years ago.

30. Brooke was a great admirer of Housman's work. He had written two poems to him in 1911, 'Letter to A SHROPSHIRE LAD' and 'Letter to a Live Poet'. The latter won a competition run by the *Saturday Westminster*.

31. On 10 July 1912 Denham Russell-Smith had died at the age of 23, after suffering a series of illnesses. It is believed that he finally succumbed to septicaemia from an abscessed tooth. Brooke had befriended both Hugh, who was in his year, and Denham, a year younger, at Rugby School; both were boys in his father's House, School Field. Denham Russell-Smith played a rather notable role in Brooke's life. In 1911, at Orchard House in Grantchester, Brooke decided 'to do away with the shame … of being a virgin' and had sex with Denham, the first and only known homosexual relationship Brooke was to experience. It would seem from all available evidence that he was not a homosexual, but was a classic product of the single-sex public-school environment – something he discusses with Phyllis (p. 165) – where having crushes on fellow schoolmates were part of the culture.

32. Phyllis's fears were to prove wrong as both Colley and Reigate Hill were bought by the National Trust following a public appeal. They remain unspoilt to this day and are enjoyed as part of an Area of Outstanding Natural Beauty.

TWO

1. Mrs Elgy, Edward Marsh's housekeeper.

2. The post-Impressionist exhibition that was held at the Grafton Galleries. Brooke wrote two articles about it in the *Cambridge Magazine*, 23 and 30 November 1912.

3. Wilfrid Wilson Gibson (1878–1962) was born in Hexham, Northumberland. He worked for a time as a social worker in London's East End. In 1902 he published his first book of poems, *Mountain Lovers*. Gibson became of one Brooke's close friends and found support and patronage under Edward Marsh. He was one of the Dymock Poets and had a number of his poems included in the five volumes of *Georgian Poetry* (1912–22) and four issues of *New Numbers* (1914). During the First World War Gibson served as a private in the infantry and spent a short time at the Front; the poetry he wrote during this time was from the perspective of an ordinary soldier. In his will Brooke named Gibson as one of his three heirs, the other two being Lascelles Abercrombie and Walter de la Mare. In 1916 he published a volume of poems entitled *Friends*, which he dedicated to Brooke. Gibson was a prolific writer, with much of his work dealing with the plight of the working class. His *Collected Poems: 1905–1925* was published by Macmillan in 1926.

4. Wilfrid Wilson Gibson.

5. Lady Mary Murray (née Howard) was wife to the eminent scholar of ancient Greek language and culture, Professor Gilbert Murray. It is probably through this link with Phyllis's father, and because the Murrays were close friends of Jane Harrison of Newnham College, where Aunt Alice taught, that she became known to Phyllis. It is interesting to note how anxious Brooke is for Phyllis not to mention his name to Lady Murray – with whom, along with her family, he had been staying with in Overstrand, Norfolk only a few weeks previously. Brooke had become very good friends with Lady Murray's daughter Rosalind, first introduced to him by Frances

Cornford during the rehearsals of *Comus*. Rosalind knew about his turbulent affair with Ka Cox and thought him still in the depths of despair over it; this is probably why he didn't want Phyllis unwittingly tipping off Lady Murray to his new romance, with the inevitable repercussion of word getting back to his friends.

6. Professor Reid, Classics tutor at Gonville and Caius College, Cambridge, and his wife Ruth, Phyllis's father's sister.

7. Only six months earlier Gibson had decided to seek his fortune in London. He was indeed very hard up, eking out a living by writing reviews for the *Glasgow Herald*. It was about this time that Edward Marsh arranged for him to be assistant editor of the literary magazine *Rhythm*, founded by John Middleton Murry and Katherine Mansfield. Unbeknown to Gibson, this publication was in financial difficulties, so Marsh, on the understanding that Gibson was not told, paid his weekly wage from his own pocket. He was later to become one of Brooke's beneficiaries.

8. Iolo Aneurin Williams (1890–1962), author, journalist and botanist. He wrote a bibliographical column for the *London Mercury* from 1920–39, and was museums correspondent for *The Times* from 1936–62. Williams's publications included works on literature, bibliography and art. Through his poetry anthologies and articles in publications such as the *London Mercury* and the *Observer*, he played an important role in reviving interest in eighteenth-century literature.

9. 'Rupert Brooke' by Wilfrid Wilson Gibson, *Friends* (London: Elkin Mathews, 1916), p. 13.

10. 'To a Fat Lady seen from the Train' by Frances Cornford, *Poems* (Hampstead: The Priory Press, Cambridge: Bowes and Bowes, 1910), p. 20.

11. *Poetical Works of Rupert Brooke*, ed. Geoffrey Keynes (London: Faber & Faber, 1946), p. 155.

12. From the song entitled 'A Little Girl's Fancies', the relevant line being: 'O little moss, Observed by few, / That round the tree is creeping'.

13. In fact Brooke won it for 'The Old Vicarage, Grantchester' – the competition was being run by the *Poetry Review*, No. 1, p. 7. Judges were: T E Hulme, Edward Thomas, Harold Monro, Henry Newbolt, Edward Marsh and Ernest Rhys. CH, p. 384.

14. The editor believes this is a reference to the period of Phyllis's childhood when she lived in Sandgate, Kent, which has a single beach.

15. Scopas (*c*.395 BC–350 BC) was a sculptor and architect from ancient Greece. He sculpted a wide range of subjects, mostly based on the more romantic mythological figures or subordinate deities. He is best known as being one of four sculptors who carved the beautiful marble friezes for the Mausoleum of Halicarnassus, considered one of the Seven Wonders of the Ancient World (sections from this frieze are held in the British Museum). Scopas's figures are known for their almost quadrate heads, with deeply sunken eyes and slightly opened mouths.

16. On her manuscript, Phyllis has added and then crossed out the following: 'And then I heard a sound like music, & I said "What's that? Someone playing on the piano?" and he laughed a little & said "No, that's the good old English Sunday morning sound of church bells!" and I listened again, & so it was. "I'd forgotten it was Sunday," I said.'

17. When the Brooke and Gardner letters and memoir were de-reserved by the British Library in 2000, this playfully erotic 'strangling' was taken out of context by a Library spokesman. It was in turn inevitably misconstrued by the press, who concluded that, based upon this episode, Brooke had been 'sadistic' and 'threatened [Phyllis] with physical violence' (*The Times*, 10 March 2000). No mention was made of Phyllis's responses, which don't appear to suggest fear, or to the flirtatious, sexually charged atmosphere in which the action took place. Taken in context, such behaviour may be often witnessed between lovers: the male assuming a dominant role, demonstrating his superior physical strength; the female playing up to an idea of mock-submissiveness and fragility. Although much can be said in general terms about such role-playing in relation to human psychology and Darwinism, such behaviour does not reveal anything in Brooke's personality that has not already been frequently expressed in his writing.

18. Better known as 'The Thinker'.

19. Brooke is probably using the male moth as an allegory for his own feelings, but there is also some truth in what he says. The majority of moths drawn to lights are males, who are active during the night hours looking for a mate; females, in contrast, expend their energy on seeking food plants. However, the females do not have a 'faint radiance'. Connecting moths and love seems in fact to have been an ongoing theme of Brooke's. In Christopher Hassall's biography he quotes a scrap of verse Brooke had jotted down towards the end of 1911 (p. 292):

> All night I went between a dream and a dream
> As one walking between two fires.
> …like the moths.
> But do not love as they do,

With a strange feathery soft inhuman love.
And there is sorrow in the leaf,
And in the flower forgetfulness
The soul, like a thin smoke, is spread
Crying upon the air.

THREE

1. Brian Rhys.
2. Vol.1, No. XI, November 1912. Contained five of Brooke's latest poems: 'Song', 'Mary and Gabriel', 'Beauty and Beauty', 'Unfortunate' and 'The Old Vicarage, Grantchester'.
3. Gibson to Marsh, 17 October 1912, Berg Collection.
4. Gibson to Marsh, undated letter but contents suggest October 1912, Berg Collection.
5. Although the following remains faithful to the order in which Phyllis wrote her memoir, it should be noted that the two subsequent meetings she recalls having with Brooke at Gray's Inn must have occurred at a later date as there is only the lapse of one day between their previous meeting, the first since Grantchester, and their correspondence regarding the *Poetry Review* just before Brooke left for Berlin.
6. The following is crossed through by Phyllis in her manuscript: 'and as he was in any case large and conspicuous, and in addition had a habit, unusual in peace time, of going about in a Colonel hat, it was not an altogether hopeless task. But, needless to say, I hardly ever saw him unless I had actually arranged to meet him, though that never deterred me [last few words indistinguishable due to heavy crossing out]' and has been used earlier in her text.
7. Christopher Hassall, *Edward Marsh: A Biography* (Longmans, 1959), p. 602.
8. Two articles written by Brooke on the post-Impressionist exhibition appeared over two editions of the *Cambridge Magazine*: Vol.2, No. 6, 23 November 1912, 'The Post-Impressionist Exhibition at the Grafton Galleries', pp. 125–6; Vol.2, No. 6, 30 November 1912, 'The Post-Impressionist Exhibition at the Grafton Galleries. II', pp. 158–9.
9. These notes by Brooke on Phyllis's poetry are reminiscent of Frances Cornford's account of how he worked with her. 'He was endlessly kind in helping me with my verses (except that kindness seems the wrong word, because he did it as a matter of course). He would sit for an hour or two at a time, generally on the ground, frowning and biting the end of his pencil and scribbling little notes on the margin before we talked. Of the better things he would only say "I like that," or "That's good." I can't imagine him using a word of that emotional jargon in which people usually talk or write poetry. He made it feel more like carpentering.' Quoted from Edward Marsh's *Memoir* (London: Sidgwick and Jackson, 1918), p. 38.
10. Brooke to Clive Carey, 23 November 1912, LRB, p. 408.
11. In a letter Brooke wrote to Clive Carey at this time he refers to Carey's work on 'the Greek play' (LRB, p. 408). According to Christopher Hassall in his biography on Edward Marsh, the Marlowe Society was performing *Oedipus* in Cambridge at this time (Christopher Hassall, *Edward Marsh: A Biography*, Longmans, 1959) p. 200.
12. 'Reuben Fell', as mentioned previously by Phyllis.

FOUR

1. Brooke's telegram from this time says King's Cross – Phyllis has perhaps misremembered?
2. Phyllis must be referring to the following letter quoted in Marsh's *Memoir*. It was first included in *The Collected Poems of Rupert Brooke*, (p. cxxx) published in July 1918, and then published separately in November 1918 (p. 129): 'It's queer to see the people who *do* break under the strain of danger and responsibility. It's always the rotten ones. Highly sensitive people don't, queerly enough. I was relieved to find I was incredibly brave! I don't know how I should behave if shrapnel were bursting over me and knocking the men round me to pieces. But for risks and nerves and fatigues I was all right. That's cheering.' Marsh did not disclose that Brooke had written this letter to Cathleen Nesbitt, in fear of upsetting Mrs Brooke, but in 1968 when Keynes reproduced the letter in LRB (p. 624) this fact was finally acknowledged.
3. Major John Wilson (1830–1923) was in the Scots Greys. He had been one of the courageous 'Scarlett's Three Hundred' to charge in the now legendary battle of Balaclava, where the British were outnumbered ten to one against the Russians but still gained victory. He received a sabre cut across his face during the battle and was nursed by one of Florence Nightingale's nurses.
4. The Poetry Bookshop did not open until January 1913, and this meeting between Phyllis and Brooke took place in December 1912. It is only in hindsight, when writing her memoir, that Phyllis must have connected her dislike of the readings held at the Bookshop and Brooke's comments at this time.

5. Brooke seemed to be suffering from a fear of threatening strangers lurking in the shadows at this time, demonstrated here and in a letter written to Noel Olivier on 28 January 1913: 'Please read this part, and don't pass it over in unconcern – and don't misjudge it. It'll relieve me so to impress it on you. It's this. So many people get kidnapped nowadays: and you're always drifting about alone. Please, I'm perfectly serious – be careful. When I lie awake at nights – Don't ever, on any pretext, go off with people you don't know, however well authenticated, or get into cabs – it's impossible to be too careful. I demand this' (SL, p. 231). This rather paranoid state of mind was probably caused by Brooke's having pushed himself too hard to complete his dissertation, bringing about a slight relapse of his recent breakdown.

6. *Oxford Book of Victorian Verse*, edited by Sir Arthur Quiller-Couch (Oxford University Press, 1912). Poems by Brooke included in this anthology were: 'Dust', 'The One Before the Last' and 'Second Best'. Not listed in Brooke bibliographies by Keynes or Schroder.

7. In English, 'Nor the father, nor the son, nor the pigeon!'.

8. Quote taken from an article written by Henry Nevinson, published in *Christian Science Monitor*, 26 May 1920. The war in the 'Near East' referred to the Balkan Wars of 1912–13.

9. Brooke had told Ka Cox in a letter that Nevinson had agreed to take him, no doubt thinking she would be relieved that he would be out of the country for a while. LRB, p. 427.

10. Daughter of Gilbert Murray, the Classical scholar, and Lady Murray.

11. Denis Murray, Rosalind's younger brother.

12. Brooke to Rosalind Murray, December 1912, LRB, p. 410.

13. Brooke to Gwen Raverat, January or February 1913, LRB, p. 421.

14. *Donne's Poetical Works* edited by H J C Grierson (Oxford University Press, 1912). These reviews appeared in the *Nation*, 15 February 1913, and *Poetry and Drama*, June 1913. Brooke was at the forefront of Donne's literary revival and admired his work greatly; this enthusiasm shone through in his reviews. 'He was the one English love poet,' he wrote, 'who was not afraid to acknowledge that he was composed of body, soul, and mind; and who faithfully recorded all the pitched battles, alarms, treaties, sieges, and fanfares of that extraordinary triangular warfare.' Was Brooke purely talking about Donne here – or did he perhaps feel he was trying to forge the same path and fight the same battles?

15. *The Felician*, July 1913, No. 37. The magazine of Phyllis's old school.

16. Written by Robert Louis Stevenson.

17. The official opening of The Poetry Bookshop was on 8 January 1913.

18. *Lithuania*, the only play written by Brooke to be posthumously performed and published by Maurice Browne and his Chicago Little Theatre company in 1915. Sidgwick and Jackson later published *Lithuania* with a note by John Drinkwater in 1935.

19. Printed originally in the *Westminster Gazette*, 30 January 1913, p. 2, signed simply 'Delphis', then in Mary Gardner's *Plain Themes* (London: J M Dent, 1913), illustrated with woodcuts by Phyllis, p. 7.

FIVE

1. Brooke to Ka Cox, January 1913, LRB, p. 417.

2. Quoted in Paul Delany, *The Neo-Pagans* (London: Macmillan, 1987), p. 122.

3. A reference by Phyllis to Frances and Francis Cornford. Frances Crofts Cornford, née Darwin (1886–1960), was an English poet. Born into the Darwin–Wedgwood family, she was a granddaughter of the British naturalist Charles Darwin, and daughter of the botanist Francis Darwin and Ellen Crofts. Frances was raised in Cambridge, among a dense social network of aunts, uncles and cousins, and was educated privately. In 1909 she married Francis Cornford; the couple had five children. Frances Cornford published several books of verse, including *Poems* (1910), *Spring Morning* (1915), *Autumn Midnight* (1923) and *Different Days* (1928). *Mountains and Molehills* (1935) was illustrated with woodcuts by Cornford's cousin, Gwen Raverat.

   Her husband Francis Macdonald Cornford (1874–1943) was an English Classical scholar and poet. He was a Fellow of Trinity College, Cambridge from 1899 and held a university teaching post from 1902. He became Laurence Professor of Ancient Philosophy in 1931 and was elected a fellow of the British Academy in 1937. Cornford wrote a number of books including *Thucydides Mythistoricus* (1907), *Microcosmographia Academica* (1908), *From Religion to Philosophy: A Study in the Origins of Western Speculation* (1912) and *Principium Sapientiae: The Origins of Greek Philosophical Thought* (posthumously published, 1952).

   It is not clear why Phyllis had such a bad opinion of the couple, especially as they seemed far less radical than many of Brooke's other friends. Their son Hugh Cornford, in his memoir on his mother, wrote: 'My parents had different but complementary characters. My father was introverted, reserved and practical ... Frances was an extrovert and got on easily with people.'

He touches upon his mother's relationship with Brooke: 'Rupert felt that he could trust Frances as she was happily married ... She listened and offered him sensible advice, such as, after the end of his affair with Ka Cox, that he should go abroad for at least a year and do hard physical work until he was so tired at night that he could only just crawl to bed and sleep ... She was very fond of him, but thought him neurotic and drifting.' *Frances Cornford: Selected Poems*, edited by Jane Dowson with a memoir by Hugh Cornford (London: Enitharmon Press, 1996), pp. xxx–xxxi.

4. The first Balkan War was declared on 8 October 1912.

5. The New English Art Club was founded in London in 1885 by a group of artists who had studied and worked in Paris, and were tired with the Royal Academy's preference for the academic style when selecting work for its exhibitions. Artists including John Singer Sargent and Philip Wilson Steer were represented in the club's first exhibition in April 1886. During the late nineteenth and early twentieth centuries the New English grew greatly in influence, and the time of Sickert, Augustus John, Tonks, Steer and William Rothenstein was a golden period.

6. This sequence of events given by Phyllis as an explanation for Brooke's 'pleasure-seeking' attitude is incorrect. It had been six years since Brooke's brother Richard had died – in 1907, while Brooke was in Rugby, having just recovered from influenza; but illness was a routine event for him. A few months later, after he had fully recovered, Brooke holidayed in Italy, and it was in 1910 that Mr Brooke died. Did Brooke tell Phyllis this 'story'? The only published biographical account of his life available to Phyllis at the time she wrote this was Marsh's *Memoir*, but he had not linked these events or made any reference to a trip to Italy.

7. With Brooke being both an agnostic and in a depressed state of mind, he was in no mood to be presented with religious scripts of optimism. During his stay with the Raverats Brooke had already been annoyed by their pangs of guilt over not fully believing in God, something he related to Ka in a letter: 'One discussion on God, in which I with difficulty controlled myself' (LRB, 13 February 1913, p. 422).

8. Brooke to Jacques Raverat, August 1912, LRB, p. 396.

9. The Heretics Society, co-founded in Cambridge by Charles. K Ogden in 1909, questioned traditional authorities in general and religious dogma in particular. The Heretics began as a group of 12 undergraduates interested in the agnostic views of William Chawner (Master of Emmanuel College and a past Vice-Chancellor). The Society was nonconformist and open to women. Other speakers included Jane Harrison, G K Chesterton and Bertrand Russell.

10. Quoted in CH, p. 378. Rupert later wrote an article on Strindberg which was published in the 11 October 1913 issue of the *Cambridge Magazine*.

11. Ibid.

12. Brooke had originally written 'what I meant', but then crossed it out and replaced it with 'what we thought'.

13. Brooke to Noel Olivier, 12–14 February 1913, SL, p. 233.

14. Brooke to Ka Cox, March 1913, LRB, p. 427.

15. Notice of this award appeared in *Poetry and Drama*, No. 1, p. 7. The competition was judged by T E Hulme, Edward Thomas, Harold Monro, Henry Newbolt, Edward Marsh and Ernest Rhys. Prize money of £30 was awarded.

16. Article by Sherril Schell entitled: 'The Story of a Photograph', *The Bookman*, August 1926, p. 688.

17. Brooke to Cathleen Nesbitt, quoted in CH, p. 390.

18. Brooke to Ka Cox, 25 March 1913, LRB, p. 439.

19. Violet Asquith (1887–1969) was the only daughter of Liberal Prime Minister, Henry Asquith and his first wife Helen Melland. She was privately educated and in 1915 married Maurice Bonham-Carter, a scientist. An active member of the Liberal Party, Violet Bonham-Carter served as president of the Women's Liberal Federation (1923–5). In 1941 she was appointed governor of the BBC, and in 1944 was elected as the first woman president of the Liberal Party. She failed in her attempt to win election to the House of Commons in the 1945 General Election. In 1965 she wrote *Winston Churchill As I Knew Him*.

20. Brooke to Edward Marsh, 19 May 1913, LRB, p. 459.

21. Brooke to Frances Cornford, May 1913, LRB, p. 458.

SIX

1. Brooke to W Denis Browne, 22 May 1913, LRB, p. 461.

2. Brooke to Cathleen Nesbitt, 24 May 1913, LRB, p. 464.

3. Brooke to Cathleen Nesbitt, 31 May 1913, p. 468.

4. Mary Gardner (translator), *A Short and Easy Modern Greek Grammar... after the German of C. Wied*, with a preface by Ernest Gardner (London: David Nutt, 1892).

5. Elinor M Frost to Margaret Bartlett, 3 July 1913, *Selected Letters of Robert Frost* edited by Lawrance Thompson (Holt, USA: Rinehart and Winston, 1964), pp. 78–9.
6. The 'Erise' blessing is, in modern spelling: *'Dia agus Muire dhuit'* – literally: 'God and Mary to you'. The traditional greeting in Irish is: *'Dia dhuit'* ('God to you') – to which the response is *'Dia agus Muire dhuit'* ('God and Mary to you').
7. The archaic term 'Erise' (from 'Erische'). It is originally a Scots form of the word 'Irish' applied in Scotland (by Lowlanders) to all of the Goidelic languages.
8. It is interesting to note that this sentiment is echoed by Violet Bonham-Carter in her letter to Brooke, March(?) 1915: 'You rarely give one warmth – but more light than anyone in the world'. *Champion Redoubtable* edited by Mark Pottle (London: Weidenfeld and Nicolson, 1998), p. 34.
9. *Poetry and Drama*, Vol.1, No. 4, December 1913.
10. Greek for 'Farewell'.
11. A reference to Brooke's poem 'Clouds', also published in the December 1913 edition of *Poetry and Drama*, Vol.1, No. 4. Beneath this poem is printed 'THE PACIFIC, October 1913'.
12. Greek for 'I wrote'.
13. A reference to the Latin proverb *'De mortuis nihil nisi bonum'*. Translated into English, it reads 'Of the dead, (say) nothing but good'. Probably a translation from a Greek sentence by Chilon.
14. Brooke to Edward Marsh, 7 March 1914, LRB, p. 564.
15. Ibid.
16. Brooke spells her name in several different ways, for example 'Taata-mata', 'Tuatamata', 'Taate Mata', and 'Taatamata').
17. Brooke to Edward Marsh, 7 March 1914, LRB, p. 565.
18. Brooke to Dudley Ward, 15? November 1914, LRB, p. 529.
19. A number of his poems written at this time show this, including 'Waikiki', 'A Memory' and 'He Wonders Whether to Praise or to Blame Her'.
20. This poem, considered by many to be one of Brooke's finest, is an enduring tribute to Taatamata, or 'Mamua' as he refers to her in the poem.
21. Brooke to Edward Marsh, March 1914, LRB, p. 568.
22. Brooke borrowed money twice from Chauncey Wells, a professor from Berkeley whom he met on his travels – £50 while in New Zealand, followed by another loan towards the end of his stay in Tahiti, which more than paid for his passage home.
23. In Chicago Brooke spent time with a past acquaintance, Maurice Browne, director of the Little Chicago Theatre, and his wife Ellen Von Volkenburg, an actress. Between them they made plans to perform his one and only play, *Lithuania*.
24. Brooke to Marchesa Capponi, 25 April 1914, LRB, p. 583.
25. Cathleen Nesbitt, *A Little Love and Good Company* (London: Faber & Faber, 1975), p. 89.

SEVEN

1. Brooke to Jacques Raverat, 9 June 1914, LRB, p. 591.
2. Brooke to Mrs Chauncey Wells, 18 June 1914, LRB, pp. 593–4.
3. Ibid.
4. Brooke to Jacques Raverat, July 1914, King's College Archive L/3. Edited version of this letter in LRB, p. 595.
5. Almost certainly a reference to Phyllis Gardner.
6. Brooke to Jacques Raverat, 2 July 1914, King's College Archive L/3. Edited version of this letter in LRB, p. 596.
7. Brooke to Cathleen Nesbitt, April 1913, LRB, p. 451.
8. Brooke's 27th, and final, birthday.
9. Brooke to Edward Marsh, 2 August 1914, LRB, p. 605.
10. CH, p. 457.
11. Edward Thomas (1878–1917) was educated at St Paul's School and Lincoln College, Oxford. He worked for the *Daily Chronicle*, but was encouraged to write poetry by Robert Frost, who had become a close friend. Thomas became a member of both the Georgian and the Dymock poets. Most of his poems are about nature and the countryside, although he wrote a handful of war poems before his death in the trenches at Arras.
12. Edward Thomas to Robert Frost, 19 September 1914, Dartmouth College, Rauner Special Collections Library, reference no. Frost-Thomas 914519.
13. Rupert Brooke, 'An Unusual Young Man', *New Statesman*, 29 August 1914, pp. 638–40.
14. Brooke to Lady Eileen Wellesley, 15–17 August 1914, LRB, pp. 608.
15. Brooke to Jacques Raverat, quoted in CH, p. 458.
16. Maitland Radford had been working as Assistant Medical Officer at the North Eastern Hospital,

but at the outbreak of war joined the Royal Army Medical Corps. He was in France by August 1914, in charge of the Medical Division of No. 3 General Hospital.

17. Reference to Brooke's article 'An Unusual Young Man', published 29 August 1914.

18. Phyllis to Maitland Radford, 1914. Radford Archive, British Library, Add MS 89029/1/49.

19. Edward Marsh to W Denis Browne, quoted in Christopher Hassall, *Edward Marsh* (Longmans, 1959), p. 295.

20. Edward Marsh to W Denis Browne: although written to Browne, in this instance Marsh is referring to both Browne and Brooke. Quoted in Christopher Hassall, *Edward Marsh* (Longmans, 1959), p. 295.

21. The whereabouts of this poem is unknown.

22. Phyllis to Maitland Radford, 30 September 1914. Radford Archive, British Library, Add MS 89029/1/49.

EIGHT

1. Leonard Sellers, *The Hood Battalion* (London: Leo Cooper, 1995), p. 9.

2. The Second Boer War, 1899–1902.

3. Phyllis to Maitland Radford, 4 October 1914. Radford Archive, British Library, Add MS 89029/1/49.

4. Brooke to Leonard Bacon, 11 November 1914, LRB, pp. 632–3.

5. *The Cambridge Magazine*, 10 October 1914.

6. Phyllis to Maitland Radford, 16 November 1914. Radford Archive, British Library, Add MS 89029/1/49.

7. Brooke to Rosalind Arnold Toynbee, 20 November 1914, LRB, p. 633.

8. In the *Felician*, No. 41, December 1914, p. 7, the following entry is published under the title 'Old Felicians and the War': 'P. Gardner has designed a Holy Family for the window of the Toy Shop, 21 Old Bond Street, which gives its profits to Belgian Relief. Her design is copied in miniature by their fretwork factory at Fulham and sold in the shop. Other designs of hers are carried out by wounded Belgians in hospital at Tadworth, who receive half the profits.'

9. Phyllis to Maitland Radford, 6 December 1914. Radford Archive, British Library, Add MS 89029/1/49. This letter has been badly affected by water and insect damage, therefore some of the writing is hard or impossible to make out; where this is the case square brackets are used.

10. Brigadier-General Arthur Melland Asquith (1883–1939) was educated at Winchester College with his brothers and later attended New College, Oxford. He was the third son of Prime Minister Asquith. A senior officer of the Royal Naval Division, Arthur Asquith was wounded four times in the war and three times awarded the Distinguished Service Order for his bravery under fire. In December 1917 Asquith was seriously wounded during fighting near Beaucamp; he was evacuated to Britain where one of his legs was amputated. Asquith retired from the military following his wound and worked for the Ministry of Munitions.

11. Frederick Septimus Kelly, nickname 'Cleg' (1881–1916), composer and sportsman, was born in Australia. He was educated at Eton and Balliol College, Oxford (BA, 1903; MA, 1912), as a Lewis Nettleship musical scholar; he graduated with fourth-class honours in history. He won the Diamond Sculls at Henley in 1902, 1903 and 1905, and was also a member of the gold medal winning team at the London Olympic Games in 1908.

    In 1903–8 Kelly studied piano under Ernst Engesser and composition and counterpoint with Ivan Knorr at the Dr Hoch Konservatorium, Frankfurt am Main, Germany. He dedicated himself to fulfilling his dual ambition to become 'a great player and a great composer'. Kelly's comparatively few compositions include some effectively written and charming piano pieces, followed by more substantial works such as *Theme, Variations and Fugue* for two pianos and a *Violin Sonata*. At the outbreak of war in 1914 Kelly joined the Royal Naval Division and served at Gallipoli, where he was awarded the Distinguished Service Cross and reached the rank of lieutenant-commander.

    Fellow officers in the Hood Battalion were composer William Denis Browne and other scholar–soldiers such as Arthur Asquith, Patrick Shaw-Stewart, Charles Lister and Rupert Brooke; they were known upon their ship, the *Grantully Castle*, as the 'Latin Club'. His *Elegy* for string orchestra was written in memory of Rupert. Kelly was killed in action at Beaucourt-sur-Ancre, while serving in the last battle of the Somme.

12. Charles Lister (1887–1915), the only surviving son of Lord Ribblesdale, was educated at St Aubyn's School in Rottingdean, Eton, and Balliol College, Oxford. He served in the diplomatic services in Rome and Constantinople, and became second lieutenant in the Middlesex Hussars in 1914. Lister joined the Royal Naval Division in 1915, and died from wounds sustained in the Dardanelles.

13. Lieutenant-General Bernard Cyril Freyberg, 1st Baron Freyberg VC, GCMG, KCB, KBE, DSO & Three Bars (1889–1963), was a British-born New Zealander; he later served as the seventh Governor-General of New Zealand. At the outbreak of the First World War Freyberg went to England and volunteered for service, gaining a commission in the Hood Battalion. He was the youngest general in the British Army during the First World War and later served on the Western Front, where he was awarded the Victoria Cross. During the Second World War Freyberg commanded the New Zealand Expeditionary Force in the Battle of Crete, the North African Campaign and the Italian Campaign.

14. Antediluvian – of or relating to the period before the biblical flood.

NINE

1. Brooke to Mrs Brooke, 22(?) February 1915, LRB, p. 661.
2. Brooke to Violet Asquith, 22 February 1915, *Champion Redoubtable*, edited by Mark Pottle (London: Weidenfeld and Nicolson, 1998), p. 26.
3. Violet Asquith diary entry written 22–23 May 1915, *Champion Redoubtable*, edited by Mark Pottle (London: Weidenfeld and Nicolson, 1998), p. 30.
4. This letter from Lascelles Abercrombie was not present among the Brooke/Gardner letters.
5. Letter from the John Schroder Collection.
6. Letter from the John Schroder Collection.
7. Poem from the John Schroder Collection. Mary Gardner's name added in pencil within brackets, probably by Marsh.
8. W Denis Browne to Edward Marsh, 25 April 1915, LRB, p. 684.
9. *Rupert Brooke's Death and Burial: Based on the Log of the French Hospital Ship DUGUAY-TROUIN*. Translated from the French of J Perdriel-Vaissèires by Vincent O'Sullivan (Yale University Press, 1917), pp. 5–6.
10. *The Times*, 26 April 1915.
11. Dr Edwin Freshfield (1832–1918) was educated at Winchester and Trinity College, Cambridge. He was Solicitor to the Bank of England and a trustee of the British School of Archaeology in Athens. His father-in-law, J F Hanson, was the Levant Company's representative in Smyrna. Dr Freshfield lived at Lower Kingswood in Surrey, and had been a member of the committee which commissioned the Greek Orthodox church of Saint Sophia (later the Orthodox Cathedral) in Moscow Road, London in 1882. In 1891 he joined with Mr H C Bonsor to build The Wisdom of God church in Byzantine style at Lower Kingswood – the main place of worship for Phyllis and her family.
12. Phyllis to Maitland Radford, 8 May 1915, Radford Archive, British Library, Add MS 89029/1/49.
13. Walt Whitman, quote from 'When Lilacs Last in the Dooryard Bloom'd' (1881): 'Come lovely and soothing death, / Undulate round the world, serenely arriving, arriving, / In the day, in the night, to all, to each, / Sooner or later, delicate death'.
14. Mary Gardner to Maitland Radford, 7 July 1915, Radford Archive, British Library, Add MS 89029/1/49.
15. Brooke to Edward Marsh, 9 March 1915, LRB, p. 669.
16. Evidently it would seem that either Phyllis or Delphis later gave Geoffrey Keynes permission to reproduce one of Brooke's letters to Phyllis in his *The Letters of Rupert Brooke* (London: Faber & Faber, 1968), pp. 565–6.
17. Letter from the John Schroder Collection. It is not known whether the carved figure was ever found and returned to Phyllis.

EPILOGUE

1. Second Lieutenant William Alfred Cotterill Brooke, who was serving with the 8th Battalion London Regiment (Post Office Rifles), was killed in action near Le Rutoire Farm on the historic Loos battlefield on 14 June 1915, aged 24. He is buried in Fosse 7 Military Cemetery (Quality Street), Mazingarbe.
2. Geoffrey Keynes later noted that by 1941 *1914 and other Poems* had sold 159,836 copies. Up to May 1932, 98,855 copies of *Poems* had been sold, and up to 1953 120,812 copies of *Collected Poems*. Geoffrey Keynes, *A Bibliography of the Works of Rupert Brooke: Third Edition, Revised* (The Soho Bibliographies, 1964).
3. Lascelles Abercrombie, *Morning Post*, 27 April 1915.
4. Gilbert Murray, *The Cambridge Magazine*, I May 1915, Vol.IV. No. 19, p. 371.
5. Harold Monro, *The Cambridge Magazine*, 22 May 1915, Vol.IV. No. 22, p. 424.
6. Phyllis's articles do not bear her name, but appear under the title 'Women at the Wheel'. To the editor's knowledge she wrote three: 'Some Experiences of a Lady Driver on War Service'

(*The Motor*, 22 August 1916, pp. 77–9); 'More Exciting Experiences of a Lady Driver of a War Lorry' (*The Motor*, 10 October 1916, pp. 247–9); 'Some Experiences of a Lady Driving a Private Hire Car' (*The Motor*, 16 January 1917, pp. 612–3).

7. List of contributors to the Rugby School Memorial Appeal, Rupert Brooke Collection at King's College, Cambridge, Modern Archive, Ref. No. Xe/9.

8. Letter from Phyllis to Delphis, 22 February 1918. Gardner Family Archive Papers, British Library, Add MS 89076/1/4.

9. Given to the editor by Katharine Beal: it was a gift from Phyllis to her mother.

10. *The London Mercury*, Vol.1, No. 12, p. 711.

11. Stanley Casson, *Rupert Brooke and Skyros* (London: Elkin Mathews, 1921).

12. This image bears a remarkable resemblance to Vincent van Gogh's 'Sorrow', 1882. However, research suggests it is very unlikely that Phyllis would have seen either the drawing or lithograph of this image as, to the editor's knowledge, it was only reproduced once prior to 1921 in *Lettres de Vincent van Gogh à Emile Bernard*, Paris 1911, and had not been exhibited in the UK.

13. This copy of *Rupert Brooke and Skyros*, given by Phyllis to a friend, has the woodcut pasted in to its front pages; along the bottom of the woodcut Phyllis has written the following inscription: 'You can paste this into one of the fly-leaves of a little book called "Rupert Brooke & Scyros" which I will send you – only my own copy has one on: this has been shown separately'. Also tucked into this book is a folded piece of paper with '2 poems' written on its outer page. Within its centre pages are two manuscript poems by Phyllis, entitled 'Rondeau' (July 1907) and 'Sonnet' (February 1926). In the editor's possession.

14. Phyllis Gardner, *The Irish Wolfhound: A Short Historical Sketch* (Ireland: Dundalgan Press, 1931).

15. Ernest Rhys, *Letters from Limbo* (London: J M Dent, 1936), pp. 272–4. On page 272 Rhys mentions that 'Mrs Gardner has written a remarkably interesting book of her own which contains many live glimpses of people she has known', but the editor has been unable to locate this book and can only assume that it was never published.

16. Letter from Katharine Beal (née Bovenschen) to the editor, 5 January 2001.

17. The manuscript of this poem, written in Phyllis's hand, was found inserted into a copy of *Rupert Brooke and Skyros* that she had given to a friend. In the editor's possession.

18. In a column Phyllis wrote during this time for the *Dog World* in her typical style, she told her readers: 'I am said to be making quite remarkable progress considering the serious nature of the operation … I am quite sure my recovery has been hastened by the enlightened attitude of the authorities here, who do not refuse to admit patients' friends simply because they happen to be on four legs. Other hospitals please copy!' *Dog World*, 15 July 1938, p. 150.

19. In her will Phyllis appointed Delphis and Christopher as her joint executors and trustees, and left everything to them. Her probate reads as follows: 'Phyllis Gardner of Recess, Boyn Hill, Maidenhead, Berkshire, spinster died 16 February 1939. Probate London 3 April to Delphis Gardner spinster and Christopher Stewart Gardner dog breeder. Effects £3383 13s. 6d'. (Approx. equivalent in 2010: £167,221.)

20. Ernest Arthur Gardner left £11,443 14s. 8d (approx. equivalent in 2010: £565,549) in his will: probate, 18 March 1940, *Calendars of the Grants of Probate and Letters of Administration England and Wales* (Oxford Dictionary of National Biography).

21. Article entitled 'Caused Suffering to Eleven Dogs' in the *Maidenhead Advertiser*, 10 October 1947, p. 1.

22. Kennel Affix: Molys. Delphis's Welsh springer spaniels were unusual for that time as she refused to dock their tails; her aim was to regain the old look seen in seventeenth-century English paintings.

23. Nicolas Furlong, 'Gardners, Bently, Curracloe', *Wexford Echo*, Wednesday 22 August 2007, p. 37.

24. Christopher Gardner's will, 27 May 1959.

25. On 13 May 1959, aged 58. Delphis's death certificate records her occupation as 'Wolfhound Breeder' and gives her cause of death as: 'Myocardial Degeneration/Cholangitis/3 months'. In layman's terms she had a weak heart, but then also developed an infected gallbladder. She was ill for three months and then died from heart failure, probably brought about by the infection.

26. On 24 February 1968, aged 75, at Wexford County Hospital. Christopher's death certificate describes him as an 'Annuitant', no doubt referring to an annuity inherited through his family estate which was put in place to ensure him lifetime security. His cause of death is given as 'Bronchopneumonia/Fractured Humerus'.

INDEX

Illustrations are indicated in *italic* after main entries